Microsoft®

POWERPOINT® 4

For Windows™

Step by Step

Perspection

MicrosoftPress®

PUBLISHED BY
Microsoft Press
A Division of Microsoft Corporation
One Microsoft Way
Redmond, Washington 98052-6399

Library of Congress Cataloging-in-Publication Data
Microsoft PowerPoint 4 for Windows step by step / Perspection, Inc.
     p.   cm.
   Includes index.
   ISBN 1-55615-622-7
   1. Computer graphics.   2. Microsoft PowerPoint for Windows.
I. Perspection, Inc.
T385.M52 1994
001.4'226'028566869--dc20   93-47601
                                          CIP

Printed and bound in the United States of America.

2 3 4 5 6 7 8 9 MLML 9 8 7 6 5 4

Distributed to the book trade in Canada by Macmillan of Canada, a division of Canada Publishing
Corporation.

A CIP catalogue record for this book is available from the British Library.

Microsoft Press books are available through booksellers and distributors worldwide. For further
information about international editions, contact your local Microsoft Corporation office. Or
contact Microsoft Press International directly at fax (206) 936-7329.

For Perspection, Inc.
Managing Editor: David W. Beskeen
Author: Steven M. Johnson
Editor: Darvin Wilson

For Microsoft Press
Acquisitions Editor: Casey D. Doyle
Project Editor: Laura Sackerman
Graphics Specialist: Bill Teel

Perspection
Information Media

Perspection, Inc. is a multimedia development company dedicated to providing information and training to help you make decisions, solve problems, and communicate the results. Perspection designs and develops interactive multimedia applications and produces software training books for Windows-based and Macintosh personal computers.

Our publication and technical team combine performance-based training principles with an in-depth knowledge of Microsoft PowerPoint to create simplified lessons and exercises that help you develop confidence, increase productivity, and utilize the full power of your Microsoft application. Our technical team worked along with Microsoft software developers, quality assurance engineers, and customer support trainers to give you inside information about PowerPoint. You'll learn tips and techniques not documented in any other publication.

This book and others in the Microsoft *Step by Step* series will help you develop the confidence necessary to achieve increased productivity with your Microsoft products.

Perspection's corporate headquarters are in Castro Valley, California.

Acknowledgments

Perspection, Inc. would like to thank our families for their patience and understanding during the long days and nights it took to complete this book. We'd also like to thank Mark Keener for reviewing the lessons.

Thank you to the Microsoft Graphics Business Unit for the opportunity to work together on a great product. Thanks especially to Glenn Hobin for providing PowerPoint product information and for encouraging us along the way, to Pierre Aoun for tracking down answers to technical questions and sending software on a moments notice, and to Ellen Fetty for her marketing input.

At Microsoft Press, we'd like to thank Laura Sackerman for her editorial expertise and help working out technical difficulties, Bill Teel for his graphical expertise and constant availability, and Casey Doyle for his insight and experience working on Microsoft *Step by Step* books and encouraging words.

WE'VE CHOSEN THIS SPECIAL LAY-FLAT BINDING

to make it easier for you to work through the step-by-step lessons while you're at your computer.

With little effort, you can make this book lie flat when you open it to any page. Simply press down on the inside (where the paper meets the binding) of any left-hand page, and the book will stay open to that page. You can open the book this way every time. The lay-flat binding will not weaken or crack over time.

It's tough, flexible, sturdy—and designed to last.

Contents

Part 1 Learning Microsoft PowerPoint Basics

Part 3 Making Your Ideas Communicate

Part 4 Adding Graphs and Organizational Charts

Part 5 Inserting and Linking Information

Part 6 Printing and Producing a Presentation

Appendixes

About This Book

Whether they're delivering a company's fiscal results to a shareholders' meeting or analyzing sales figures at a hastily scheduled meeting, presentations play a major role in how business people communicate. Microsoft PowerPoint 4 for Windows, the leader in presentation graphics software, has all the tools presenters need every day to put together professional, compelling presentations quickly and easily.

Microsoft PowerPoint 4 for Windows Step by Step is a comprehensive tutorial that shows you how to take advantage of PowerPoint's features—text handling, outlining, drawing, graphing, and presentation management tools—to create professional looking presentations. You can use this book in a classroom setting, or you can use it as a tutorial to learn PowerPoint at your own pace and convenience. Each lesson includes a sample presentation to help you learn and practice new skills. The sample presentations contain information about PowerPoint features to help simplify your work and increase your productivity.

Finding the Best Starting Point for You

This book is designed for both new users learning PowerPoint for the first time and experienced users who want to learn to use the new features in PowerPoint version 4. If you are familiar with PowerPoint version 3 for Windows or for the Apple Macintosh, you'll have a head start on the basics of PowerPoint 4 for Windows. Among the features you'll want to learn about are the new toolbars and buttons, which you can use to carry out common commands with a click of the mouse; AutoContent Wizard and Pick a Look Wizard, which make it easier than ever to create presentations that look great and get your point across; Outline view, which enables you to organize and arrange your ideas to create a presentation; OfficeLinks, which makes it possible to easily share text, data, and graphics—either between programs or with other people in your workgroup; and the PowerPoint Viewer, which is a separate program that allows you to share your presentations with others without installing PowerPoint on their computers.

The modular design of this book offers you considerable flexibility in customizing your learning. Lessons 1 and 2 teach basic skills; Lessons 3 through 15 teach advanced skills. To decide if you need to work through a lesson, look at the summary at the end of the lesson. If you are unsure about any of the summary topics, work through the appropriate section of the lesson. You can go through the lessons in any order, skip lessons, and repeat lessons later to brush up on certain skills. Each lesson builds on concepts presented in previous lessons, so if you don't understand the concepts or terminology presented in a particular lesson, you might want to review an earlier lesson.

You begin most lessons by opening a practice file from the accompanying Practice Files disk. You then rename the practice file so that the original file remains unchanged while you work on your own version. If you make a mistake in your presentation, you can simply start that lesson over using a new copy of the original presentation. You don't need to complete a lesson in order to go on to the next one.

The following table lists recommended starting points based on your presentation graphics software experience.

If you are	Follow these steps
New to Microsoft Windows	Read "Getting Ready" later in this book. Next, work through Lessons 1 and 2. Work through the other lessons in any order.
New to the mouse	Read "Using the Mouse" in the "Getting Ready" section. Next, work through Lessons 1 and 2. Work through the other lessons in any order.
New to presentation graphics	Read "Creating Effective Presentations" and "Getting to Know PowerPoint" in the "Getting Ready" section. Next, work through Lessons 1 and 2. Work through the other lessons in any order.
New to Microsoft PowerPoint	Read "Getting Ready" later in this book. Next, work through Lessons 1 and 2. Work through the other lessons in any order.
Familiar with PowerPoint version 3.0 for Windows	Read the summaries at the ends of Lessons 1 and 2. Next, read Appendix C, "PowerPoint Features at a Glance." Complete the lessons that best meet your needs.

Note If you are new to Microsoft Windows, it would be a good idea to familiarize yourself with the basic elements of Windows before you start the lessons in this book. To review techniques such as how to use a mouse, open a menu, and select options from a menu or dialog box, see the "Getting Ready" section, consult your Microsoft Windows 3.1 documentation, or see *Microsoft Windows 3.1 Step by Step*, published by Microsoft Press.

Using This Book As a Classroom Aid

If you're an instructor, you can use *Microsoft PowerPoint 4 for Windows Step by Step* to teach novice users about PowerPoint or to teach experienced users about PowerPoint's new features. You can also choose from the lessons to customize courses for your students.

If you plan to teach the entire contents of this book, you should probably set aside three full days of classroom time to allow for discussion, questions, and any customized practice you might create.

Conventions Used in This Book

Before you start any of the lessons, it's important that you understand the conventions and features used in this book.

Procedural Conventions

■ Numbered lists (1, 2, 3, and so on) indicate a sequence of steps you are to follow. A triangular bullet (▶) indicates a procedure with only one step.

■ The word *choose* instructs you to carry out a command.

■ The word *select* instructs you to highlight objects or text and to select options in a dialog box.

■ Characters you are to type appear in **bold**.

■ Important terms, titles of books, and text that you supply in a lesson appear in *italic*.

Keyboard Conventions

■ Names of keys are in small capital letters (for example, TAB and SHIFT).

■ A plus sign (+) between two key names means that you must press those keys at the same time. For example, "Press SHIFT+SPACEBAR" means that you hold down the SHIFT key while you press the SPACEBAR.

Other Features of This Book

Spelling

■ Many commands can be carried out by clicking a button on one of the PowerPoint toolbars. If a procedure instructs you to click a button, a picture of the button appears in the left margin, as it does here for the Spelling button.

■ Text in the left margin summarizes main points or gives additional useful information.

■ From time to time you will find an icon in the left margin that looks like the one here. This icon signifies a PowerPoint tip for simplifying your work or a helpful hint for creating presentations.

■ You'll find optional "One Step Further" exercises at the end of each lesson. These exercises are less structured than the lessons, and they help you practice what you learned in each lesson.

TROUBLESHOOTING: **If you get unexpected results as you work**   If what happens on the screen is not what you expected, look for a Troubleshooting note below the step where the problem occurred. Troubleshooting notes are marked in the left margin, as shown here.

Cross-References to Microsoft PowerPoint Documentation

Throughout this book you'll find references to other documentation, including the *Microsoft PowerPoint User's Guide,* that you can read to learn more about PowerPoint version 4. At the end of each lesson is a listing of topics covered and where to find them in your *Microsoft PowerPoint User's Guide* and PowerPoint on-line Help. Using these cross-reference sources will help you to make greater use of PowerPoint's powerful features.

Microsoft PowerPoint User's Guide   The user's guide is the single book with the information you need to use PowerPoint. Each chapter describes a particular task and explains the procedures you follow to accomplish that task.

On-line Help   You can get Help on your screen by pressing F1 or by choosing a command from the Help menu. Within Help, you can set bookmarks, search for specific topics by keyword, and print Help text.

Quick Preview   This is an on-line tutorial you can access through the Help menu that presents PowerPoint's new features and capabilities. Quick Preview is a self-running application that provides you with steps to create a presentation.

Cue Cards   Cue Cards are an on-line tutorial you can access through the Help menu that help you accomplish a specific PowerPoint task. Cue Cards look similar to the Help dialog box, but stay on the screen while you perform your task.

Tip of the Day   These are quick tips that suggest how to fully use PowerPoint features. The Tip of the Day feature can be accessed through the Help menu.

ToolTips and the Status Bar   When you position the pointer over one of the toolbar buttons, a yellow box appears telling you the name of the button. These boxes are called *ToolTips.* The status bar shows a longer description of the command while a ToolTip is displayed.

Technical Support   You can get technical support information by choosing a command from the Help menu so that you can get the most from PowerPoint and your other Microsoft products.

Building a Quick-Reference Notebook

As you complete each lesson in this book using the accompanying practice files, you'll compile useful information about PowerPoint. If you print the PowerPoint presentation at the end of each lesson, you can build a quick-reference notebook of helpful hints and techniques you can use later to help you create other presentations.

Getting Ready

This section helps you to start, get to know, and work with Microsoft PowerPoint so that you can use it to quickly and easily create presentations. Before you begin the lessons in this book, there are a few things you need to do. You will learn how to install the practice files on your computer's hard disk and how to start Microsoft Windows and PowerPoint.

If you have not yet installed Windows or Microsoft PowerPoint version 4, you'll need to do that before you continue with the lessons. For instructions on installing Windows, see your Windows documentation. If you need instructions for installing PowerPoint version 4, see Appendix A, "Installing PowerPoint," or your PowerPoint for Windows documentation.

You will learn how to:

- Install the practice files on your computer's hard disk.
- Start Microsoft Windows.
- Start Microsoft PowerPoint.
- Use basic Windows features such as windows, menus, and dialog boxes in the PowerPoint environment.
- Use Microsoft PowerPoint Help.

Installing the Step by Step Practice Files

Inside this book, you'll find a disk labeled "Practice Files for Microsoft PowerPoint 4 for Windows Step by Step." The disk includes a special program to copy the practice files for each lesson into a directory named PRACTICE on your hard disk.

1 Turn on your computer.

2 Insert the Practice Files disk into drive A or B of your computer.

3 If Windows is already running, open the Program Manager and choose Run from the File menu. If you have not started Windows yet, skip to step 5.

4 In the Command Line box, type **a:\install** (or **b:\install**) and click the OK button.

Do not type a space between the drive letter and the slash. Follow the instructions on the screen to complete the installation process, and skip steps 5 and 6.

5 At the MS-DOS command prompt (usually C:\>) type **a:\install** (or **b:\install**) and press ENTER.

Do not type a space between the drive letter and the slash.

6   Follow the instructions on the screen to complete the installation process.

The Step by Step setup program copies the practice files from the floppy disk onto your hard disk in a subdirectory (called PRACTICE) of the PowerPoint home directory (called POWERPNT). You'll need to remember the name of the drive and directory where the practice files are stored so that you can open a file for each lesson.

About the Practice Files

Each lesson has a corresponding practice file to help you learn useful PowerPoint concepts and techniques so that you can create compelling presentations. As you work through the lessons using the practice files, be sure to follow the instructions for saving the files and giving them new names. Renaming the practice files allows you to make changes, experiment, and observe results without affecting the original practice files. With the practice files intact, you can reuse the original files later if you want to repeat a lesson.

For a complete list of the practice files and the lessons in which they are used, see Appendix E, "List of Step by Step Practice Files."

Starting Microsoft PowerPoint

After you've installed PowerPoint and the practice files, you're ready to start PowerPoint. To start PowerPoint, you'll need to start Windows first.

Start Windows

1   At the MS-DOS prompt (usually C:\>), type **win**

2   Press ENTER.

After you press ENTER, the Windows Program Manager appears. From the Program Manager, you can start PowerPoint and all your other applications.

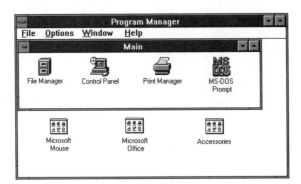

The appearance of your Program Manager window might be different depending on your screen setup. For more information about Windows, see your Microsoft Windows documentation.

Start Microsoft PowerPoint

In the Program Manager, you'll notice a program group named Microsoft Office. Double-clicking the Microsoft Office icon opens the program group window, which contains the icons for PowerPoint and its related applications.

Microsoft
Office

1   Double-click the Microsoft Office group icon.

The Microsoft Office program group opens.

Microsoft
PowerPoint

2   Double-click the Microsoft PowerPoint icon.

The first time you run PowerPoint after installing it, PowerPoint displays a dialog box asking whether you want to go through the Quick Preview. Quick Preview is a short introductory tour of PowerPoint features and abilities. If you want to view Quick Preview later, choose Quick Preview from the Help menu.

3   Click the OK button to go through the Quick Preview.

4   When you're done, click the Quit button.

The Tip Of The Day dialog box appears. The Tip of the Day feature is a collection of tricks and tips for learning how to use PowerPoint features more efficiently. The Tip Of The Day dialog box appears each time PowerPoint starts when the Show Tips At Startup check box is checked.

5   Click the OK button.

The Tip Of The Day dialog box closes and the PowerPoint Startup dialog box appears.

Creating Effective Presentations

Each time you start PowerPoint, you can either create a new presentation using the AutoContent Wizard, the Pick a Look Wizard, a template, or a blank slide, or you can open an existing presentation that you or someone else created. To quickly and easily create a presentation, follow the series of steps listed below.

Step 1   Enter your ideas

Concentrate on entering your ideas first and formatting them later. If you need help organizing the content of your presentation, PowerPoint assists you with the AutoContent Wizard. The AutoContent Wizard helps you formulate and organize your ideas by asking questions, and then creates a fully formatted presentation. If you know what you want to say, instead of using the AutoContent Wizard, open a blank presentation. Type in a title and some supporting information on a slide or in the outliner, incorporate slides from other presentations, or import outlines from other applications such as Microsoft Word for Windows.

Step 2   Edit and arrange your content

Refine your content by editing and rearranging text in Outline and Slide views. You can move slides around in the Slide Sorter view to achieve just the look you want.

Step 3   Format your presentation for a consistent look

As you refine your content, you can start formatting your presentation to give it a professional, consistent look. You can use the Pick a Look Wizard to help format your presentation or you can simply apply a template to your presentation. Applying a template formats your content to match the template format. You can also format text and graphical objects individually.

Step 4   Add clip art, drawings, graphs, and organizational charts

PowerPoint makes it easy to communicate your ideas with graphical images. More than 1100 clip art images come with PowerPoint. Between the Drawing Toolbar and the AutoShapes Toolbar, PowerPoint gives you 29 different shapes to choose from when adding graphical images. You can also create professional-looking graphs and organizational charts easily in PowerPoint.

Step 5   Enter notes and create handout pages

In addition to your presentation slides, you can create speaker's notes pages and audience handouts to support your PowerPoint presentation.

Step 6   Save and print your slides, notes, handouts, and outline pages

Save and print your presentation to complete the steps for creating an effective presentation. You'll save and print presentations during each lesson. If you're unable to print your presentation, read Appendix B, "Installing and Selecting a Printer."

Getting to Know PowerPoint

Before you begin to work on a presentation, PowerPoint allows you to choose how you want to create your presentation. The PowerPoint Startup dialog box appears.

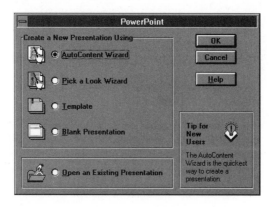

PowerPoint Startup Dialog Box

In order to access any other PowerPoint feature or function, you must first choose from one of five options in the PowerPoint Startup dialog box. The following table describes the available options:

Select	To	Toolbar button
AutoContent Wizard	Start the AutoContent Wizard, which prompts you for a presentation title and information about your topic. Select a common presentation type, and then PowerPoint provides a basic outline to guide you in organizing your content into a professional presentation.	
Pick a Look Wizard	Start the Pick a Look Wizard, which helps you choose a template, slide setup, and format that will best convey your content. The Wizard changes your presentation masters based on your selections.	
Template	Choose a presentation template. The Apply Template dialog box appears, allowing you to choose a template.	
Blank Presentation	Choose a blank slide layout. The New Slide dialog box appears with 21 pre-designed slide layouts to help you create a new slide.	
Open an Existing Presentation	Choose an existing PowerPoint presentation. The File Open dialog box appears. Select a presentation file.	

Create a blank presentation

1   Click the Blank Presentation option button.

2   Click the OK button.

The New Slide dialog box appears with the Title Slide layout chosen. The New Slide dialog box displays 21 ready-made slide layouts with placeholders for titles, text, and objects such as clip art, graphs, and charts.

3   Click the OK button.

A blank presentation appears with the Title Slide layout.

PowerPoint Presentation Window

Once you finish making your selection in the PowerPoint Startup dialog box, the PowerPoint *presentation window* appears. The presentation window is PowerPoint's equivalent of a presentation slide. It is the canvas on which you type text, draw shapes, create graphs, add color, and embed objects. The buttons you see at the top of the window on the *toolbars* are the commands you need to create a professional looking presentation. The buttons on the toolbar at the left side of the window are the text and drawing tools you need to communicate your ideas. At the bottom of the window are view buttons you use to switch to different PowerPoint views.

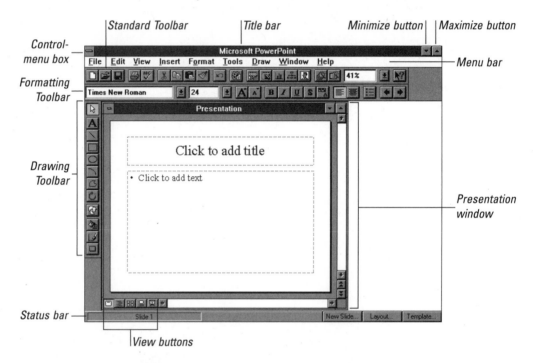

You can adjust the size of the PowerPoint window with the Minimize and Maximize buttons. You can also drag the Title bar to move the Microsoft PowerPoint and presentation windows. With the Control-menu box, you can close or restore the PowerPoint window or switch to another Windows-based application.

Status bar and ToolTips

Messages appear at the bottom of the window in an area called the status bar. These messages describe what you are seeing and doing in the PowerPoint window as you work. The status bar tells you which slide you are working on (Slide 1, Slide 2, and so on). When you choose a command, the status bar provides a short message telling you what that command will do.

ToolTip

When you place your pointer over a tool button, a yellow box appears telling you the name of the button, as shown in the margin. These yellow boxes are ToolTips, which can be turned on and off by choosing the Toolbars command in the View menu.

PowerPoint Views

PowerPoint has five views to help you create, organize, and show your presentation. *Slide view* allows you to work on individual slides. *Outline view* allows you to work on the title and body text of your presentation. *Slide Sorter view* allows you to organize each slide of your presentation. *Notes Pages view* allows you to create speaker's notes. *Slide Show view* allows you to see your slides as an electronic presentation on your computer. Slide Show view displays your slides as you would see them in Slide view using the entire screen. You can switch between views with the buttons at the bottom of the presentation window. An illustration of Slide view, Outline view, Notes Pages view, and Slide Sorter view is shown below.

Click this button for Slide view

Click this button for Outline view

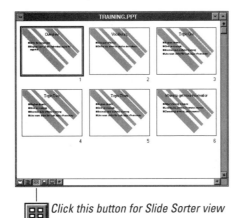

Click this button for Slide Sorter view

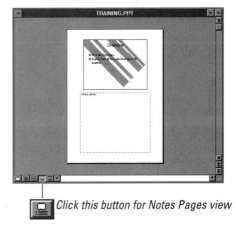

Click this button for Notes Pages view

PowerPoint Toolbars

PowerPoint has nine built-in toolbars. Each can be customized and moved within the presentation window depending on your layout needs. Across the top and down the left side of the presentation window, PowerPoint's toolbars offer shortcuts to commonly used menu commands. By default, each PowerPoint view is laid out with specific toolbars that help accomplish your presentation tasks in that view. The default toolbars that appear in each view are illustrated below.

Standard Toolbar

The Standard Toolbar appears below the PowerPoint menu bar in all views.

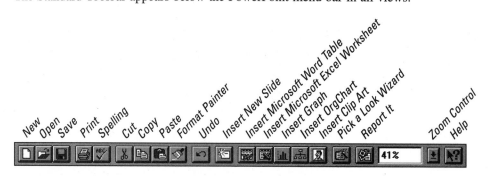

Formatting Toolbar

The Formatting Toolbar appears below the Standard Toolbar in Slide, Outline, and Notes Pages views.

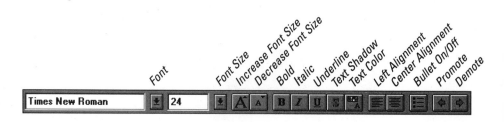

Drawing Toolbar

Sometimes vertical toolbars appear horizontally in this book

The Drawing Toolbar appears vertically along the left side of the window in Slide and Notes Pages views.

Outlining Toolbar

The Outlining Toolbar appears vertically along the left side of the window in Outline view.

Slide Sorter Toolbar

The Slide Sorter Toolbar appears below the Standard Toolbar in Slide Sorter view.

Using the Mouse

Toolbars, shortcut menus, and many other PowerPoint features were designed for working with the mouse. Though you can use the keyboard for some actions, many actions are easier to do with the mouse.

Mouse Pointers

In PowerPoint your mouse controls five different pointers that allow you to perform a variety of operations. When the pointer passes over certain parts of the presentation window, it changes shape to indicate what it does at that position. The following table describes PowerPoint's pointer shapes:

Pointer shape	Description
⍄	This pointer, known as the "pointer," appears after you select the Selection Tool button from the Drawing Toolbar. With the pointer you can select any object by clicking the object or by clicking on a blank area and dragging the pointer across the object, which creates a *selection box*.
⌶	This pointer, known as the "text cursor," appears after you select the Text Tool button from the Drawing Toolbar. Use this pointer to create text objects.

Pointer shape	Description
$+$	This pointer, known as the "cross hairs cursor," appears after you select a drawing tool from the Drawing Toolbar. Click on a blank area and drag to create a box or a line.
I	This pointer, known as the "I-beam cursor," appears after you select a text object or a shape that includes text. Use this pointer to indicate where you want to begin typing or to select and edit text.
$\displaystyle \leftrightarrow\!\updownarrow$	This pointer, known as the "four-headed arrow," appears when you move the pointer over a bullet or slide icon in Outline view or over a bullet in Slide view.

Using the Mouse

There are three basic mouse actions that you use throughout the lessons of this book. The actions are *clicking*, *double-clicking*, and *dragging*.

Clicking   Pointing to an item on your screen and then quickly pressing and releasing the mouse button is called *clicking*.

Double-clicking   Pointing to an item and quickly pressing and releasing the mouse button twice is called *double-clicking*.

Dragging   Holding down the mouse button as you move the pointer is called *dragging*. You can use this technique to move objects and perform other tasks.

Using PowerPoint Commands and Menus

A *command* is an instruction that tells PowerPoint to perform an action such as copying text, making text bold, or printing a presentation. PowerPoint commands are grouped together in *menus* and *submenus* on the *menu bar*. The buttons on the toolbars provide quick access to the most frequently used PowerPoint commands. All PowerPoint commands, including those on the toolbars, are available by opening menus on the menu bar.

Choosing Menu Commands

You can choose PowerPoint commands by using the mouse or the keyboard. In this book it is assumed that you are using the mouse to choose commands.

Choose a command with the mouse

To choose a command with the mouse, click the menu name and then choose the command. If a command leads to a submenu, an additional menu of more choices appears when you choose the command. If a submenu appears, click a command from the submenu. To cancel a menu without choosing a command, click outside the menu.

Shortcut menus

A Shortcut menu gives you quick access to relevant commands you might use with objects or the slide background. You access a Shortcut menu by moving your pointer over an object or a blank area of the slide and clicking the right mouse button or holding down the CTRL key and clicking the left mouse button. The following diagram illustrates an object Shortcut menu:

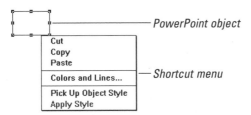

Menu Conventions

PowerPoint menus follow certain conventions. If you click a menu name, you'll see commands with keyboard shortcuts, arrows, and ellipses (...), as well as some dimmed commands.

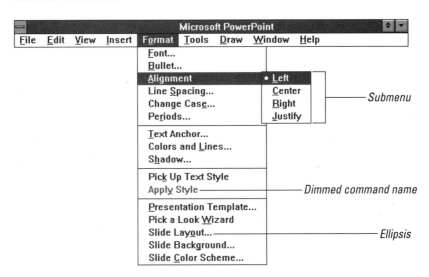

Keyboard shortcuts   Shortcut key combinations are listed to the right of some menu commands. For example, CTRL+U is the keyboard shortcut for the Underline command. As you become familiar with menus and commands, using these shortcut keys instead of choosing commands from the menus can save you time.

Submenus   When you choose a command with a black arrow to the right of the command name, a *submenu* opens with more command choices.

▶
Submenu

Ellipses   When you choose a command that is followed by an ellipsis (...), PowerPoint displays a dialog box so that you can provide more information. The dialog box prompts you to enter information or to choose from a list of options. For example, the Slide Layout command on the Format menu is followed by an ellipsis because you need to tell PowerPoint which layout you want to open.

Dimmed command names   When a command is dimmed, it doesn't apply to your current situation and is unavailable. For example, the Apply Style command appears dimmed in the previous illustration because no style has been picked up.

PowerPoint indicators

Some PowerPoint menus and dialog boxes contain command settings that indicate status. These settings appear with either a bullet or a check mark symbol.

●

Bullet

Bullet   A bullet indicates the existing choice for a selected object, a chosen view, or an option in a dialog box.

✔

Check mark

Check mark   A check mark indicates that a feature is turned on. For example, if a check mark appears next to the Snap to Grid command on the Draw menu, the Snap to Grid feature is turned on. If the check mark does not appear, the Snap to Grid feature is turned off.

Using the Practice Files

You begin most of the lessons in this book by opening one of the practice files on the Practice Files disk. The practice files should already be stored on your hard disk in a subdirectory called PRACTICE. If they aren't, refer to "Installing the Step by Step Practice Files," beginning on page xv. After the practice files are copied onto your hard disk, you can open them by doing the following:

Open

1   On the Standard Toolbar, click the Open button.

   PowerPoint displays the Open dialog box, from which you select the name of the presentation you want to open.

2   If the box under "Drives" does not display the drive on which the practice files are stored, click the down arrow next to the box and choose the correct drive from the drop-down list. For most users, this is drive C.

3   In the box under "Directories," find the name of the directory where the PRACTICE subdirectory is stored. The POWERPNT directory is a likely location for the PRACTICE subdirectory. You might need to click the up arrow or down arrow next to the box to see all the directories in the list. When you find the name of the directory, double-click it to open the directory and display the PRACTICE subdirectory.

4   Double-click the PRACTICE subdirectory. The box under "File Name" lists the names of the practice files. Click the up arrow or down arrow next to the box to see the names of all the practice files.

You are now ready to open a file. Return to the lesson to get the name of the file you need and then continue. Open the file by clicking the file name and then clicking the OK button or by double-clicking the file name.

Using Cue Cards

Microsoft PowerPoint comes with Cue Cards, an on-line step-by-step guide that provides instructions for performing specific PowerPoint tasks. Once Cue Cards are opened, they stay on the screen to assist you while you perform the operation on your presentation.

The following steps explain how to use Cue Cards:

1   From the Help menu, choose Cue Cards.

    PowerPoint displays the PowerPoint Cue Cards window, which asks you what you want to do first. Let's say you are interested in learning how to edit PowerPoint clip art.

2   Click the forward arrow button next to "Edit PowerPoint clip art."

    A five-step instruction appears, telling you how to edit clip art.

3   When you want to quit Cue Cards, double-click the Control-menu box on the PowerPoint Cue Cards window.

Getting Help

With PowerPoint Help you can quickly reference on-line Help topics for specific information. You can get help by clicking the Help button or by selecting an item from the Help menu. Within Help, you can view the contents list, search for a certain topic, move backward and forward through a Help topic, or display the history of Help topics you've viewed.

Use the Help button

Clicking the Help button and selecting an item on the screen with the Help button cursor jumps you to the help text for that item.

Help

1   On the Standard Toolbar, click the Help button.

    The pointer changes to a Help cursor, as shown in the left margin.

Help Cursor

2   Click any of the View buttons.

    The Help window appears with a definition of the view you selected and instructions on where to find related information.

3   From the Help File menu, choose Exit.

Search for a topic in Help

1   Press the F1 key.

    Pressing F1 displays the Help window. You can select any underlined topic and browse for information, or you can have PowerPoint search for what you need.

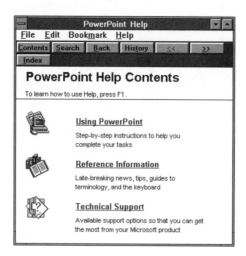

2 Click the Search button.

The Search dialog box appears. You'll begin your search at the top of the dialog box by typing a word or selecting one from the list of categories. In the future, to go directly to this dialog box from PowerPoint, choose Search For Help On from the Help menu.

3 Type **auto** but do not press the ENTER key.

As you type, PowerPoint searches for categories of information associated with the word "auto." The categories are displayed in the middle box, as shown below:

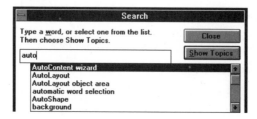

In the middle box, the category "AutoContent wizard" is selected.

4 Click the Show Topics button.

5 Select "PowerPoint Wizards" in the bottom box.

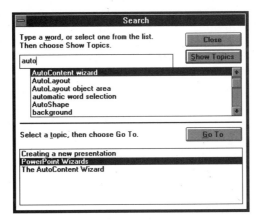

6   Click the Go To button.

PowerPoint displays information about "PowerPoint Wizards" as well as other related topics.

Jump to a related topic

If you do not see what you need in the selected Help topic, you can select any green underlined phrase, usually under "See also," to jump to related information.

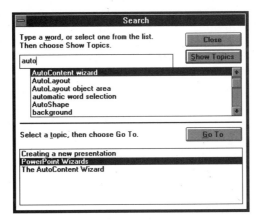

Hand Pointer

1   Position your pointer (which changes to a hand pointer) over the underlined phrase "AutoContent wizard."

2   Click the help phrase.

Help jumps to information on using the AutoContent Wizard. Take a moment to scroll through the topic, reading any definitions. At the bottom of the Help dialog box, under "See also," you can click the "Quick Steps for Creating a Presentation" topic to find out related information.

3   To quit Help, double-click the Control-menu box on the Help window.

Quitting Microsoft PowerPoint

Let's complete the "Getting Ready" section by quitting PowerPoint so that you can start with a new presentation in Lesson 1.

Quit PowerPoint

1   From the File menu, choose Exit (CTRL+Q).

2   If a dialog box appears asking if you want to save changes to the presentation, click the No button.

Learning Microsoft PowerPoint Basics

Creating a Presentation

With Microsoft PowerPoint you can create overhead slides, speaker's notes, audience handouts, and an outline, all in a single presentation file. PowerPoint uses powerful wizards to help you create and organize your presentation step by step. In this lesson, you'll learn to use the AutoContent Wizard to create a presentation and how to change, insert, and format text. You'll edit title and body text, create new slides, move around in your presentation, and look at your content in different views. At the end of the lesson, your presentation will consist of the following slides:

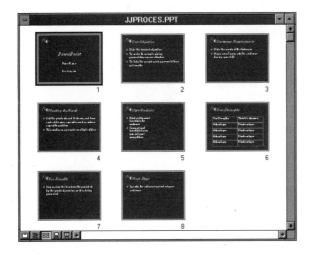

You will learn how to:

- Create a presentation using the AutoContent Wizard
- Change outline and slide text
- Change presentation views
- Move from slide to slide
- Preview slides
- Name and save your presentation for future use
- End your PowerPoint session

Estimated lesson time: 35 minutes

Start PowerPoint

For information about starting PowerPoint, see "Getting Ready," earlier in this book.

To start the first lesson, start PowerPoint, which is located in the Microsoft Office group in the Program Manager.

1   Double-click the Microsoft PowerPoint icon.

The Tip Of The Day dialog box appears each time PowerPoint starts if the Show Tips At Startup check box is checked. The Tip of the Day feature is a collection of tips and tricks that help you to use PowerPoint features more efficiently.

2   Click the Show Tips At Startup check box.

The next time you start PowerPoint, the Tip Of The Day dialog box will not appear. If you would like a tip for the day, choose the Tip Of The Day command from the Help menu.

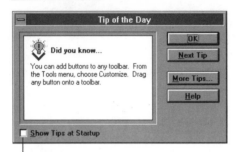

Click the Show Tips At Startup check box to turn the feature off

3   Click the OK button.

The PowerPoint Startup dialog box appears, giving you a choice of five presentation types.

Using the AutoContent Wizard

If you have trouble thinking of how to say what you want to say in your presentation, let PowerPoint help you get started with the AutoContent Wizard, the easiest way to make a presentation. In this lesson, you'll use the AutoContent Wizard to organize a presentation in minutes.

Select the AutoContent Wizard

The AutoContent Wizard gets you started with ideas and an organization for your presentation in an easy step-by-step process.

1   Click the AutoContent Wizard option button.

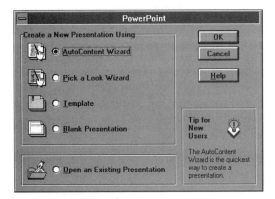

2   Click the OK button.

AutoContent Wizard Step 1

The AutoContent Wizard displays an introduction dialog box. The AutoContent Wizard leads you through creating a title slide and choosing a presentation category.

▶   After reading the introduction, click the Next button.

AutoContent Wizard Step 2

The AutoContent Wizard starts by creating a title slide. Type in the following title slide information. If you make a mistake as you type, press the BACKSPACE key to delete the mistake, and then type the correct text.

Throughout this book, bold indicates text you should type exactly as it appears; italic indicates text that you supply.

1   Type **PowerPoint 4.0** and press TAB.

The name in the next box is selected.

2   If your name appears correctly, press TAB. Otherwise type in your *name* and press TAB.

The information in the next box is selected.

3   If your company name appears correctly, continue to the next step. Otherwise, type in your *company name*.

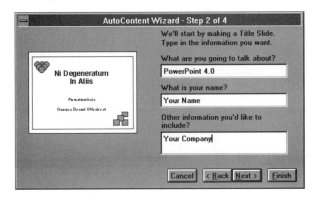

4   Click the Next button.

AutoContent Wizard Step 3

After creating the title slide, the AutoContent Wizard prompts you to select a presentation type with the suggested outline content provided for you. You'll use the selected type: Selling a Product, Service or Idea.

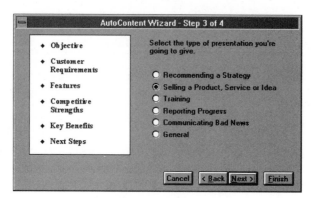

▶   Click the Next button.

AutoContent Wizard Step 4

If you want to make any changes to the information before the AutoContent Wizard creates your presentation, you can click the Back button.

1   Click the Finish button.

The AutoContent Wizard gives you an outline of suggested content for the Selling a Product, Service or Idea presentation type you've chosen and opens Cue Cards to give you tips for working in PowerPoint. Read the Cue Card tips to learn how to edit text in Outline view.

2   Double-click the Cue Cards Control-menu box to close the dialog box.

The title of the first slide is selected. To use the information provided by the AutoContent Wizard, simply type your own ideas over the sample text in the outline.

Tip   You can customize the content of an AutoContent presentation to meet your specific needs. Open the AutoContent presentation from the Wizards directory, make your changes, and save the presentation.

Understanding the Presentation Window

Along the top of the presentation window are the tools and features you'll use to do most of your text and object handling tasks. The toolbars make common tasks easy. Simply click a button on the appropriate toolbar for one-step access to tasks such as copying, pasting and formatting text, adding frames and shadows to objects, and saving your presentation. When you place your pointer over a toolbar button, a ToolTip appears, telling you the name of the button. Move your pointer over toolbar buttons to find out their names.

At the left of the presentation window are the tools you'll use to rearrange title and body text in Outline view, draw shapes, arc objects, and freeform objects, and create word-processing and label text in Slide view.

At the bottom of the presentation window are view buttons that allow you to look at your presentation in different ways—in Slide, Notes, Slide Sorter, and Outline views—as well as the New Slide button and the View Status box.

In Outline view, a slide icon appears to the left of each slide's title. The paragraph text underneath each title appears indented one level with bullets. The presentation content provided by the AutoContent Wizard appears in outline form. The title and name you entered appear on the first slide.

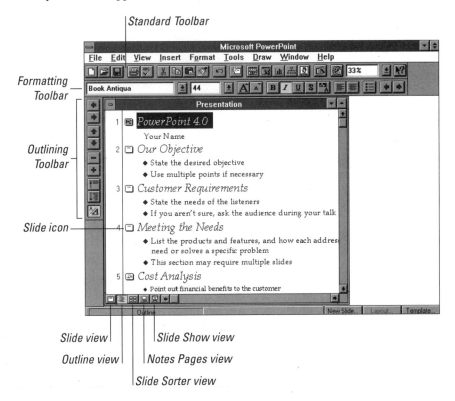

Scrolling Through a Presentation

The presentation outline you're working on contains more text than you can see on the screen at one time. To see the rest of the text, you need to *scroll* through the outline. Scrolling means moving text across or up and down the screen to bring text that's currently out of the window into view. You use the *scroll arrows* and the *elevator* located on the *vertical* and *horizontal scroll bars* to move the outline through the window.

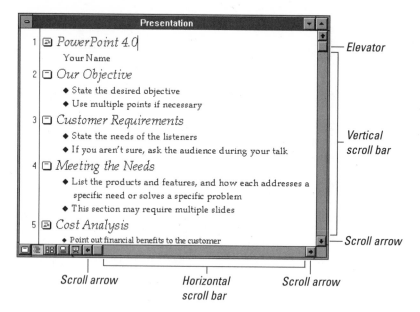

You can use one of three methods for scrolling, depending on how quickly you want to move through the outline. You can scroll line by line, jump immediately to the beginning, middle, or end of the outline, or scroll window by window.

Scroll line by line

Each time you click a scroll arrow, PowerPoint changes the screen to show you one more line.

1   Click the down scroll arrow a few times to see the text below the current window display.

2   Click the up scroll arrow a few times to see the text above the window display.

3   Position your pointer over the down scroll arrow and hold the mouse button down. To stop scrolling, release the mouse button.

The outline text "rolls" down the page. When you scroll to the end of the outline, PowerPoint displays the blank space beyond the end of the text. The next procedure shows you a fast way to get back to the top of the screen.

Jump to a different part of the outline

You can also quickly jump to the beginning, middle, or end of an outline, or anywhere in between.

1   Position your pointer over the elevator and drag it to the top of the scroll bar—you cannot drag it off the scroll bar.

The top of the outline appears.

2   Drag the elevator to the bottom of the scroll bar.

The bottom of the outline appears.

This method offers an advantage over scrolling line by line; the elevator always stops at the last line of text or slightly below the last line.

Tip   You can drag the elevator to any location on the scroll bar. For example, if you want to work on text that is in the middle of the outline, you can drag the elevator halfway down the scroll bar.

---

3   Drag the elevator back to the top of the outline.

Scroll window by window

Sometimes you need to move faster than line by line, but you don't need to scroll very far—the text you need to see is in the window area above or below the text currently displayed. The following procedure explains the best shortcut for this situation.

1   Click below the elevator in the scroll bar or press PAGE DOWN.

A new window of text appears.

2   Click above the elevator or press PAGE UP.

A new window of text appears.

Practice for a moment

You've learned three ways to scroll through an outline. If you frequently create outlines that are longer than one-half page, scrolling is a necessary skill to learn.

▶   Click the up or down scroll arrow to scroll line by line.

▶   Practice dragging the elevator to various positions on the scroll bar—first to the top, then to the middle, and then to the bottom.

▶   Click in the scroll bar above or below the elevator to move one window at a time toward the beginning or end of the outline.

▶   Practice dragging the horizontal elevator to see more of the outline.

▶   When you've finished practicing, scroll to the beginning of the outline.

Changing Text Attributes

Text can have attributes associated with it, such as font type, size, and style, as well as frame, fill, and shadow color. You can apply attributes to individual text or to an entire text object.

Change text attributes in Outline view

1   Position the I-beam cursor to the right of the text "PowerPoint 4.0" and double-click to select the entire line of text, if it is not selected already.

Bold

2   On the Formatting Toolbar, click the Bold button.

Click here to make text bold

The text format for the entire title changes to bold.

Increase Font Size

3   On the Formatting Toolbar, click the Increase Font Size button.

The font size increases from 44 to 48 points. The font size increases in increments of more than one point at a time. If you select more than one object with different font sizes, clicking the font size buttons on the toolbar increases or decreases font sizes in the selected objects relative to their original sizes.

4   Move your pointer to the blank area next to slide 1 and click to deselect the title.

Your presentation window should look similar to the following illustration:

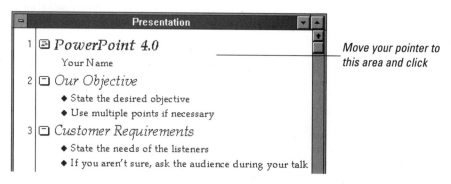

Move your pointer to this area and click

Changing Text in Outline View

The AutoContent Wizard helps you get started with a suggested presentation outline. Now, your job is to add and modify the outline text to meet your specific needs.

Change text attributes in Outline view

1   Position the I-beam cursor (which changes to a four-headed arrow) over the bullet next to the text "State the desired objective" in slide 2 and click.

PowerPoint selects the text (highlighted in black). Once you've selected text, the subsequent text you type—regardless of its length—replaces the selection.

2   Type **To make the process of creating presentations easier**

Your presentation window should look similar to the following illustration:

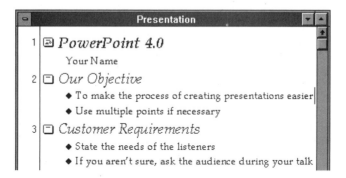

Change your mind

A handy feature in PowerPoint is the Undo command (CTRL+Z), which reverses your last action. For example, choosing the Undo command now will put back into your presentation outline the text that you just replaced. Whenever something happens that is confusing or is not what you intended, choose Undo as the *next* action.

Undo

1   On the Standard Toolbar, click the Undo button to reverse your last action.

Click here to undo your last action

TROUBLESHOOTING: **If the original sentence is not restored**   You might have pressed another key before you chose the Undo command. Undo reverses only the last action you took.

2   From the Edit menu, choose Redo.

Changing Views

The View buttons at the bottom of the presentation window let you view or work on your presentation in different ways—in Slide view, Outline view, Slide Sorter view, and Notes Pages view. These view commands are also available on the View menu.

Change to a different slide in Slide view

You can change to Slide view and look at the slide you just changed in your outline. In Slide view, you can see how the title and paragraph objects appear on the slide. PowerPoint changes the view of the current slide when you click one of the view buttons.

Slide View

▶ Click the Slide View button.

|Click here to change to Slide view

Tip   Double-clicking the slide number or slide icon in Outline view also takes you to the selected slide in Slide view.

Your presentation window should look similar to the following illustration:

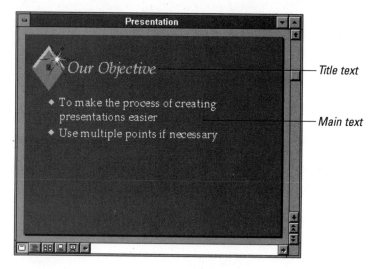

Changing and Adding Text in Slide View

Changes to the text that you make in Outline view appear in Slide view. You change text in Slide view the same way you change text in Outline view.

Change text in Slide view

1   Position your pointer (which changes to an I-beam) over the main text and click.

   The main text object is surrounded by a rectangle of gray slanted lines called a *selection box* with the I-beam cursor placed in the text.

2   Position the I-beam cursor (which changes to a four-headed arrow) over the bullet next to the text "Use multiple points if necessary" and click.

3   Type **To make the people giving presentations more effective**

Add text in Slide view

To add more bulleted text, place the insertion point at the end of a line of text and press ENTER.

1   Press ENTER to create a new bullet.

A new bullet automatically appears in the outline.

2   Type **To help the people giving presentations get results**

Your presentation window should look similar to the following illustration:

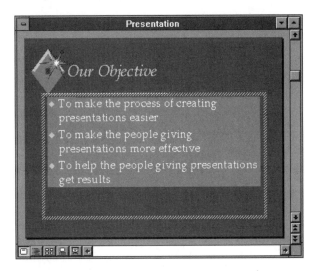

Moving from Slide to Slide

In Slide view or Notes Pages view, you use the scroll bar or the Next and Previous buttons to move from slide to slide. To move from one slide to another, click the Next Slide and Previous Slide buttons located in the lower-right corner of the presentation window. To move more than one slide at a time, drag the elevator in the vertical scroll bar. As you drag the elevator, a Slide Indicator box appears that tells you the number of the slide you're about to display.

Move from slide to slide

▶   Drag the elevator up the vertical scroll bar to view slide 1.

A Slide Indicator box appears telling you which slide is selected.

Slide Indicator

Your presentation window should look similar to the following illustration:

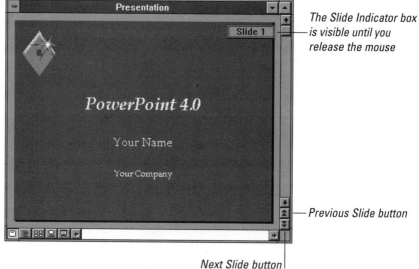

The Slide Indicator box is visible until you release the mouse

Previous Slide button

Next Slide button

The text in the status bar changes from "Slide 2" to "Slide 1," and the elevator changes position to the top. The elevator indicates the relative position of the slide in the presentation. You can also click the down arrow on the scroll bar to view the next slide or click the up arrow to view the previous slide. In Slide or Notes Pages view, the PAGE UP key changes the view to the previous slide and the PAGE DOWN key changes the view to the next slide.

Practice for a moment

You've learned three ways to move from slide to slide. If you frequently create large presentations with many slides, moving from slide to slide will be an action you perform often.

▶   Click the Next Slide and Previous Slide buttons to move from slide to slide.

▶   Practice dragging the elevator to various positions on the scroll bar—first to the top, then to the middle, and then to the bottom—to move from one slide to another.

▶   Click in the scroll bar above or below the elevator to move one slide at a time toward the beginning or end of the outline.

▶   Change to different views and practice the scrolling methods you've learned.

▶   When you've finished practicing, make sure you are in Slide view and move to the first slide of the presentation.

Previewing Slides in Slide Sorter View

Another way to view your presentation is to use Slide Sorter view. Slide Sorter view allows you to preview your entire presentation as if you were looking at slides on a light board. In this view—as well as in Outline view—you can easily rearrange the order of the slides in your presentation.

Change to Slide Sorter view

Slide Sorter View

▶ Click the Slide Sorter View button at the bottom of the window.

│*Click here to change to Slide Sorter view*

All the slides now appear in miniature on the screen, and the slide you were viewing in Slide view is selected. Your presentation window should look similar to the following illustration:

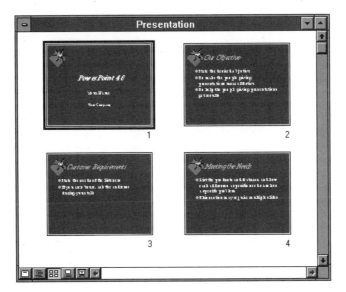

Change to a specific slide in Slide view

1   Position your pointer over slide 4.

2   Double-click slide 4.

The presentation view changes to Slide view showing slide 4.

Saving a Presentation

The work you've done is currently stored only in the computer's memory. To save the work for further use, you must give the presentation a name and store it on your hard drive.

Use the following procedure to save the presentation in the same directory as the Step by Step practice files. During the procedure, PowerPoint displays a *dialog box*. Dialog boxes supply PowerPoint with more information about what you want to do.

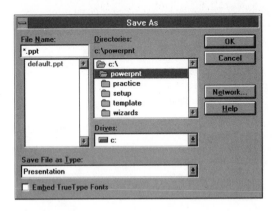

Save

1   On the Standard Toolbar, click the Save button.

PowerPoint displays the Save As dialog box. The insertion point is positioned in the box under the label "File Name," so that you can type a name for the presentation.

Document names can be no more than eight characters long. They cannot have any spaces in them.

2   Type your initials, with no periods or spaces, followed by **proces**

For example, if your initials are J. J., type the following without any spaces: **jjproces**

In later lessons, we'll write this instruction as "Type *your initials***proces**"

3   In the box under "Drives," ensure that drive C is selected (if that is where you stored your Step by Step practice files). If you need assistance, see the "Getting Ready" section earlier in this book.

4   In the list under "Directories," ensure that the PRACTICE directory is open. If it is not, open it by double-clicking it.

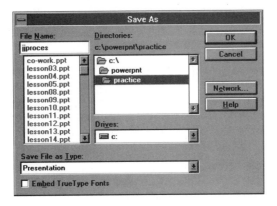

5 Click the OK button or press ENTER to save the presentation.

The Summary Information dialog box appears. If you would like, type in the summary information. Press TAB to move between fields.

6 Click the OK button.

The Title bar name changes from "Presentation" to "JJPROCES.PPT."

One Step Further

In this lesson, you have learned how to use the AutoContent Wizard to enter your ideas into your PowerPoint presentation. In addition, you have learned how to enter and arrange title and paragraph text in Slide and Outline views, how to switch between views, and how to move from slide to slide. If you would like to practice these and other basic skills in your practice presentation, try the following:

▶ Change to Outline view and change some text attributes. Use the Formatting Toolbar buttons and keyboard commands to change title and paragraph text.

▶ Change to Slide view and move from slide to slide.

▶ In Slide view, replace title and paragraph text provided by the AutoContent Wizard.

If You Want to Continue to the Next Lesson

1 From the File menu, choose Close (CTRL+W).

2 If a dialog box appears asking whether you want to save the changes to your presentation, click the No button.

Choosing this command closes the active presentation; it does not exit PowerPoint.

If You Want to Quit PowerPoint for Now

1 From the File menu, choose Exit (CTRL+Q).

2 If a dialog box appears asking whether you want to save changes to the presentation, click the No button.

Lesson Summary

To	Do this	Button
Create a presentation using the AutoContent Wizard	From the File menu, choose New and select AutoContent Wizard.	
Change text to bold or italic	Select the text object or text and click the corresponding toolbar button.	
Change text to underlined or shadowed	Select the text object or text and click the corresponding toolbar button.	
Change the font size	Select the text object or text and click the Increase Font Size or the Decrease Font Size button.	
Change presentation views	Click any of the view buttons: Slide, Outline, Slide Sorter, or Notes Pages.	
Reverse an action	From the Edit menu, choose Undo.	
Save a new presentation	From the File menu, choose Save.	
End a PowerPoint session	From the File menu, choose Exit.	

For on-line information about	From the PowerPoint Help menu, choose Contents, select "Using PowerPoint," and then
Understanding PowerPoint	Select the topic "An Overview of PowerPoint."
Creating a presentation	Select the topic "Creating Presentations and Slides" and click the title "Quick Steps for Creating a Presentation."

For more information on	See the *Microsoft PowerPoint User's Guide*
Understanding PowerPoint	Chapter 1, "An Overview of PowerPoint"
Creating a presentation	Chapter 2, "Creating Presentations and Slides"

Preview of the Next Lesson

In the next lesson, you'll create a presentation using the Pick a Look Wizard and learn how take advantage of work that's already done by opening an existing presentation, copying a slide, and changing it slightly. You'll also learn how to rearrange slides in Slide Sorter view and enhance the look of your presentation. Finally, you'll print a presentation to include in your quick-reference notebook.

Working with a Presentation

In order to work efficiently with PowerPoint, you'll need to become familiar with the important features of the product. In the previous lesson, you learned how to create a presentation using the AutoContent Wizard, change title and paragraph text, change text styles, change between Outline and Slide views, move from slide to slide, and preview slides in Slide Sorter view. In this lesson, you'll learn how to use the Pick a Look Wizard, enter new text, create new slides, open an existing presentation, incorporate slides from other presentations, rearrange slides in Slide Sorter view, enter text in Notes view, and print a presentation. At the end of the lesson, your presentation will consist of the following slides:

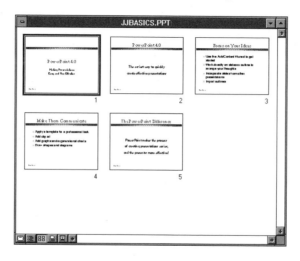

You will learn how to:

- Start a presentation using the Pick a Look Wizard
- Enter text in Slide and Outline views
- Create new slides
- Open an existing presentation
- Incorporate slides from other presentations
- Rearrange slides
- Create speaker's notes pages
- Print a presentation

Estimated lesson time: 40 minutes

Start a presentation

If you quit PowerPoint at the end of the last lesson, restart PowerPoint now. If you are continuing from the previous lesson, click the New button on the Standard Toolbar.

▶ Double-click the Microsoft PowerPoint icon.

The PowerPoint Startup dialog box appears.

or

New

▶ On the Standard Toolbar, click the New button.

Click here to open a new presentation

The New Presentation dialog box appears.

Using the Pick a Look Wizard

If you have trouble choosing a look for your presentation, let PowerPoint help you get started with the Pick a Look Wizard. The Pick a Look Wizard helps you select and format presentation slides, speaker's notes, and audience handouts that look professionally designed. You can use the Pick a Look Wizard at any time by clicking the Pick a Look Wizard button on the Standard Toolbar.

Select the Pick a Look Wizard

You'll use the Pick a Look Wizard to choose a presentation template and type general presentation information for each slide.

1   Click the Pick a Look Wizard option button.

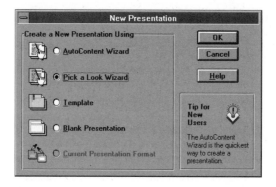

2   Click the OK button.

The Pick a Look Wizard opens to an introduction screen.

Pick a Look Wizard Step 1

▶   Read the introduction screen and click the Next button.

Pick a Look Wizard Step 2

The Pick a Look Wizard prompts you to select the type of output you want to use for your presentation.

1   Click the Color Overheads option button.

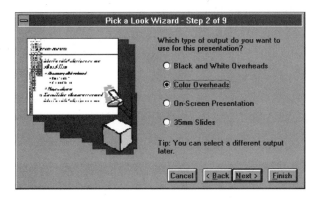

2   Click the Next button.

Pick a Look Wizard Step 3

The Pick a Look Wizard prompts you to select the template design you want to use for your presentation.

1   Click the Double Lines option button.

The Double Lines template design appears in the preview box.

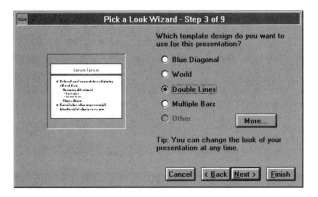

2   Click the Next button.

Pick a Look Wizard Step 4

The Pick a Look Wizard prompts you to select printing options. You can choose Full-Page Slides, Speaker's Notes, Audience Handout Pages, and Outline Pages in any combination. You'll use the default settings.

▶   Click the Next button.

Pick a Look Wizard options

For each of the Print options you chose in the previous step, you're prompted to choose the information you want to include on each page.

1   Click the Name, Company, or Other Text check box.

2   Position the I-beam cursor over the name in the text box and double-click.

The name in the box is selected.

Italic indicates text that you supply.

3   Type in your *name, company,* or *other text.*

4   Click the Date check box.

5   Click the Page Number check box.

The Date and Page Number boxes are checked, which indicates that the date and page numbers will be placed on every slide in the presentation.

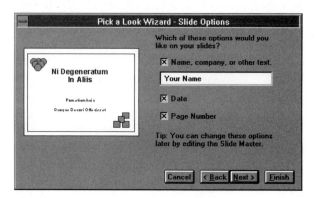

6   Click the Next button.

The Notes Options Wizard screen appears.

7   Complete the following screens, checking the same option buttons, until you reach the finish screen.

8   Click the Finish button.

PowerPoint creates a new presentation with the options you have chosen with the Pick a Look Wizard.

Entering Text in Slide View

The new presentation window includes an empty slide with two text boxes called *text objects*. The box at the top is a placeholder for the slide's title. The lower box is a placeholder for the slide's body or paragraph text.

Type title text in Slide view

To give your slide a title, click the title placeholder, and start typing.

1   Click the text "Click to add title" and type **PowerPoint 4.0**

The object is surrounded by a rectangle of gray slanted lines called a *selection box* to indicate the title object is selected.

2   Click the text "Click to add sub-title."

The title object is deselected.

3   Type **Making Presentations** and press ENTER.

4   Type **Easy and You Effective**

Your presentation window should look similar to the following illustration:

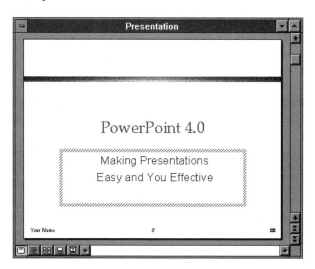

Creating a New Slide in Slide View

You can create a new slide in any view in your presentation using either the New Slide button or the New Slide command from the Slide menu.

New Slide

1   Click the New Slide button in the lower-right corner of the window.

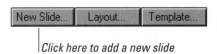

_|*Click here to add a new slide*

The New Slide dialog box appears. You can choose a different layout for each slide to create a look or make a specific point. Choose a layout by selecting it from the AutoLayout gallery list. The layout title for the selected slide type appears to the right of the gallery list.

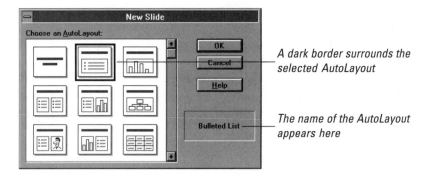

A dark border surrounds the selected AutoLayout

The name of the AutoLayout appears here

2   Click the OK button to use the default Bulleted List.

A new empty slide is added after the current slide in Slide view. The Status bar displays slide 2.

Tip   You can also hold down the SHIFT key and click the New Slide button to add a new slide with the same layout as the current slide without having to select the layout from the New Slide dialog box.

Enter text in a new slide

If you start typing on an empty slide with nothing selected, PowerPoint enters the text into the title object.

▶   Type **Focus on Your Ideas**

PowerPoint lets you work directly in Slide view or Outline view to enter your ideas. Let's change views and complete this slide in Outline view.

Change to Outline view

Outline view shows your presentation text in outline form just as if you had typed the text in Microsoft Word. From Slide view, switch to Outline view.

Outline View

▶   Click the Outline View button.

Outline view

Slide Icon

A slide icon appears to the left of each slide's title. Text underneath each title appears indented one level. The title from slide 2 is selected, as shown in the following illustration:

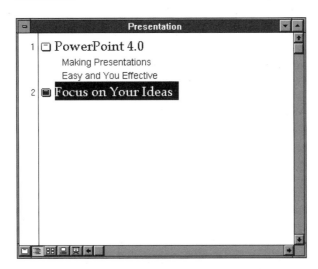

Entering Text in Outline View

To enter text in Outline view, position the insertion point where you want the text to start or choose New Slide from the Slide menu, and begin typing. Adding a new slide in Outline view creates a new slide icon.

Create a new slide and enter text

In this section, you'll create a new slide, change a paragraph text indent level, and type in paragraph text to complete slide 2. If you make a mistake as you type, press the BACKSPACE key to delete the mistake, and then type the correct text.

New Slide

1   Click the New Slide button.

The slide icon for slide 3 appears with the insertion point flashing.

Demote

2   On the Outlining Toolbar, click the Demote button.

Click here to demote text

The Demote button indents your text to the right one level. The slide icon changes to a small bullet. The new text for this bullet point becomes the paragraph text for slide 2.

3   Type **Use the AutoContent Wizard to get started** and press ENTER.

A new bullet point is added at the same indent level.

4   Type **Work directly on the outline to arrange your thoughts** and press ENTER.

5   Type **Incorporate slides from other presentations** and press ENTER.

6   Type **Import outlines**

Create a new slide using the keyboard

With the insertion point after the word "outlines," create a new slide from an indented outline level using a keyboard command.

1   Hold down the CTRL key and press ENTER.

A new slide is created with the insertion point to the left of the slide icon. Type in title and paragraph text.

2   Type **Make Them Communicate** and press ENTER.

3   Press TAB.

The current slide title is indented a level to become paragraph text for the previous slide.

4   Type **Add clip art** and press ENTER.

5   Type **Apply a template** and press ENTER.

6   Type **Add graphs and organizational charts** and press ENTER.

7   Type **Draw shapes and diagrams**

Insert new text

You can easily insert new text anywhere in Outline view and in Slide view.

1   Position the I-beam cursor just after the word "template" and click.

This places the blinking insertion point where you are to begin typing, as shown in the following illustration:

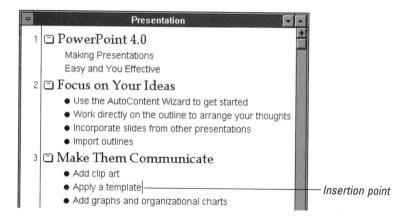

Insertion point

TROUBLESHOOTING: **If the insertion point is not where you want it**   Reposition the I-beam cursor and click again to place the insertion point in the desired location.

2   Press the SPACEBAR and type **for a consistent look**

PowerPoint makes room in the outline for the new text.

Select and replace text

You can select individual characters, sentences, paragraph text, or title text in either Outline or Slide view.

Note   Selecting text in PowerPoint works just as it does in Microsoft Word for Windows.

---

1   Position the I-beam cursor over any part of the word "consistent" in the second bullet point of slide 3.

2   Double-click to select the word.

Your presentation window should look similar to the following illustration:

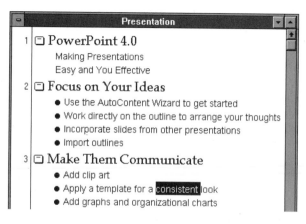

The text is now highlighted, indicating it has been selected. When you double-click a word, PowerPoint also selects the space that follows. This maintains correct spacing if you delete a word. Once you've selected text, the next text you type—regardless of its length—replaces the selection.

3   Type **professional**

The text in the outline is replaced with the new word.

Select and rearrange text

You can easily select and rearrange title and paragraph text in Outline and Slide views. In Outline view, you can select and rearrange a text object, a group of text objects, an individual slide, or a group of slides.

1   Move your pointer over the second bullet in slide 3.

The pointer changes to a four-headed arrow.

2   Click the bullet to select the entire line.

Note   You can select an entire slide by moving the pointer over the slide icon and clicking once.

Move Up

3   On the Outlining Toolbar, click the Move Up button.

The entire line moves up one level.

TROUBLESHOOTING: **If you move the text past the top of the outline**   Moving text above the top of the outline creates new slides. Select and delete the new slides.

Tip   A line of text doesn't need to be selected to be moved. Placing the insertion point anywhere in a line of text and clicking any of the Outlining buttons will move the line of text one level.

Change to Slide Sorter view

Slide Sorter View

▶   Click the Slide Sorter View button at the bottom of the window.

All the slides appear in miniature on the screen, and the third slide is selected.

Opening an Existing Presentation

You can open an existing presentation—one that you or a co-worker has already created—and work on it in the same way you would a new presentation. To open an existing presentation, you must first tell PowerPoint the name of the presentation and where it's located. You do this by using the Open command from the File menu.

PowerPoint makes it easy to open recently used files by adding the presentation names to the File menu. You can open a presentation by choosing the file name from the File menu. The number of files displayed in the File menu can be changed using the Options command.

Open a presentation

Open

1   On the Standard Toolbar, click the Open button or choose Open (CTRL+O) from the File menu to display a list of presentations.

PowerPoint displays the Open dialog box, in which you can select the name of the presentation you want. The dialog box you see might look different from the following, depending on where the practice files are located:

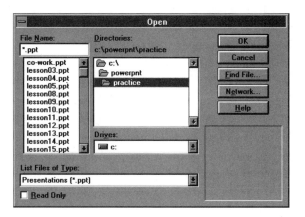

Tip   If you can't find a file, click the Find File button in the Open dialog box. In the Find File dialog box, click the Search button and type in your file name.

2   In the box under "Drives," ensure that drive C is selected (if that's where you stored your Step by Step practice files). Click the drop-down arrow next to the box to see and select from other listed drives.

If you do not see PRACTICE in the list of directories, see "Getting Ready," earlier in this book.

3   In the list under "Directories," ensure that the PRACTICE directory is open. If it isn't, select it by double-clicking it.

4   In the list of file names, select CO-WORK.PPT.

A miniature picture of the first slide appears in the Preview box. If you can't remember the name of your presentation, you can select any of the available presentations for a preview.

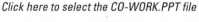
Click here to select the CO-WORK.PPT file

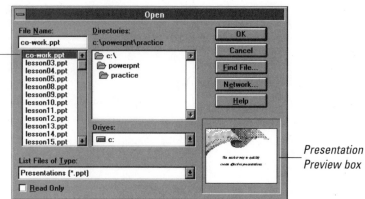

Presentation Preview box

5   Click the OK button.

PowerPoint closes the dialog box and displays the presentation CO-WORK.PPT.

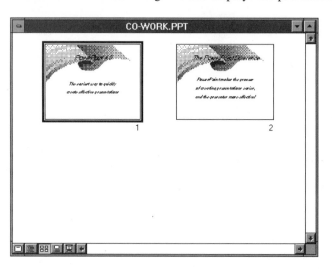

Tip   If you double-click the file name (CO-WORK.PPT) from the Open dialog box, PowerPoint will open the file directly and you will not see the first slide in the Presentation Preview box or need to click the OK button.

Incorporating Slides from Other Presentations

You can save time creating a presentation by using work that has already been done by a co-worker. Let's copy slides from the co-worker's open presentation into your own. The incorporated slides conform to the characteristics of your presentation, so you don't have to make many changes.

Copy slides from one presentation to another in Slide Sorter view

1   From the Edit menu, choose Select All (CTRL+A).

A black rectangle appears around both slides, indicating they are selected.

Copy

2   On the Standard Toolbar, click the Copy button or choose Copy (CTRL+C) from the Edit menu.

The slides are copied to the Windows Clipboard for temporary storage.

3   From the File menu, choose Close (CTRL+W).

The co-worker's presentation window closes and your presentation window becomes active.

4   Click after the last slide in the presentation.

An insertion point appears after the slide. The slides copied from the other presentation will be inserted at this point.

Note   If you select a slide in the Slide Sorter view, the slides copied from the other presentation appear after the selected slide.

Paste

5   On the Standard Toolbar, click the Paste button or choose Paste (CTRL+V) from the Edit menu.

The slides are pasted into your presentation. The pasted slides take on the characteristics of your presentation. PowerPoint makes it easy to incorporate slides from other presentations to efficiently create a new presentation.

Tip   You can also move slides between two or more open presentations. Open each presentation, switch to Slide Sorter view, and drag the slides from one presentation window to the other.

Zoom Control

6   On the Standard Toolbar, click the Zoom Control drop-down arrow and select 50%.

7   Click a blank area to the right of slide 5 to deselect the pasted slides.

When you paste slides in Slide Sorter view, they remain selected until you deselect them.

Rearranging Slides in Slide Sorter View

After copying slides from your co-worker's presentation into your own, you'll want to rearrange the slides into the order that most effectively communicates your message. In Slide Sorter view, you can drag slides from one location to another.

Move a slide in Slide Sorter view

▶   Drag slide 4, titled "PowerPoint 4.0," to the left side of slide 2, titled "Focus on Your Ideas."

You'll notice the pointer changes to a slide icon when you begin to drag. When you release the mouse, slide 4 moves to its new position as slide 2 and the other slides are repositioned.

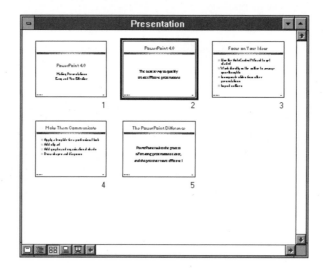

Change to Slide view

1   From the View menu, choose Slides.

PowerPoint changes to Slide view for slide 2.

Previous Slide

2   Click the Previous Slide button to move to slide 1.

Entering Text in Notes Pages View

In Notes Pages view, you can create speaker's notes for your presentation. Each slide in your presentation has a corresponding notes page. At the top of each notes page is a reduced image of the slide. To enter speaker's notes on a notes page, change to Notes Pages view, select the Notes placeholder, and begin typing. Entering and changing text in Notes Pages view works the same as it does in Slide view.

Notes Pages View

1   Click the Notes Pages View button at the bottom of the presentation window.

Click here to change to Notes Pages view

Notes Pages view appears at 33% view for most screens to display the entire page. Your view scale might be different depending on the size of your monitor. At the top of the page a reduced image of the slide appears, and at the bottom is a placeholder for paragraph text.

Your presentation window should look similar to the following illustration:

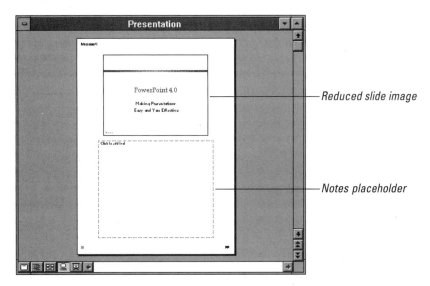

Reduced slide image

Notes placeholder

2   Click the Notes placeholder to select it.

Zoom Control

3   On the Standard Toolbar, click the Zoom Control drop-down arrow and select 66%.

The view scale size increases from 33% to 66%, and displays the selected Notes object for the notes page.

4   Type the paragraph below without pressing the ENTER key. If you make a mistake as you type, press the BACKSPACE key to delete the mistake, and type the correct text.

PowerPoint 4.0 makes presentations easy and you effective by delivering new features—such as AutoContent Wizard, Pick a Look Wizard, AutoLayouts, customizable toolbars, OfficeLinks with other applications, and branching in a slide show—that focus on the entire process of creating presentations.

Move from notes page to notes page

In Notes Pages view, you can move from notes page to notes page in the same way as in Slide view.

Next Slide

1   Click the Next Slide button to view the other notes pages in the presentation until you reach notes page 5.

2   Drag the elevator back to slide 1.

Slide View

3   Click the Slide View button.

Printing a Presentation

For more information on printing, see Lesson 13.

PowerPoint is able to print your presentation in four formats—as slides, notes pages, handouts (2, 3, or 6 slides per page), and outlines—to help you effectively present your message with the highest quality output.

If you have not yet printed a document using a Windows-based application, you might not yet have installed or selected a printer. If this is the case, take a moment to work through Appendix B, "Installing and Selecting a Printer." For complete instructions about installing and setting up a printer, see your Windows documentation.

Print presentation slides

1   From the File menu, choose Print (CTRL+P).

The Print dialog box appears.

2   Click the drop-down arrow next to Print What.

A drop-down list appears with these options: Slides, Notes Pages, Handout (2, 3, 6 slides per page) and Outline View.

3   Select Slides from the drop-down list.

4   Click the OK button.

A dialog box appears, giving your printing status. If you want to print the first part of the quick-reference notebook, choose Print and select Handouts (2 slides per page) from the drop-down list next to Print What.

Save the presentation

Save

1   On the Standard Toolbar, click the Save button or choose Save (CTRL+S) from the File menu.

PowerPoint displays the Save As dialog box, in which you can type a new name for your presentation. For more information about using this dialog box, see "Saving a Presentation" in Lesson 1.

2   In the File Name box, type *your initials***basics**

Remember, this means that you type your initials with no space between them, followed by the word "basics." For example, if your initials are J. J., you would type **jjbasics**

3   Click the OK button.

The Summary Info dialog box appears. If you would like, type in the summary information. Press TAB to move between fields.

4   Click the OK button.

PowerPoint closes the dialog box and saves the presentation with the new name "JJBASICS.PPT," which appears in the Title bar.

Review the lesson

The presentation for this lesson contains reference information about working with an existing presentation. To review the lesson, click the Slide Show button on the Toolbar and view the on-screen presentation.

Slide Show

1   Click the Slide Show button.

PowerPoint displays the first slide in the presentation.

2   Click to advance to the next slide.

3   Click once for each slide to advance through the rest of the presentation.

After the last slide in the presentation, PowerPoint returns to the current view.

One Step Further

You have learned to open a presentation, change text attributes, copy and paste slides between presentations, rearrange slides in Slide Sorter view, and print a presentation. If you'd like to practice these and other basic skills in your practice presentation, try the following:

▶   In Notes view, use the Text menu to change text styles and sizes.

▶   Move slides around in Slide Sorter view. Use the SHIFT key to select multiple slides.

▶   Enter and rearrange text in Outline view.

If You Want to Continue to the Next Lesson

1   From the File menu, choose Close (CTRL+W).

2   If a dialog box appears asking whether you want to save the changes to your presentation, click the No button. You do not need to save the changes you made to the presentation after you printed it.

Choosing this command closes the active presentation; it does not exit PowerPoint.

If You Want to Quit PowerPoint for Now

1   From the File menu, choose Exit (CTRL+Q).

2   If a dialog box appears asking whether you want to save changes to the presentation, click the No button.

Lesson Summary

To	Do this	Button
Create a presentation using the Pick a Look Wizard	From the File menu, choose New and select Pick a Look Wizard.	
Type title or main text on a slide	Select the title object or main text object and begin typing.	
Create a new slide	Click the New Slide button or from the Slide menu, choose New Slide.	New Slide...
Open a presentation	Choose Open from the File menu. When the Open dialog box appears, select the file you want opened and click the OK button.	
Copy slides between presentations	Select slides in Slide Sorter view or Outline view. From the Edit menu, choose Copy. Open the file where you want to paste the slides. Click the Slide Sorter View button and choose Paste from the File menu.	
Rearrange slides in Slide Sorter view	Select slides in Slide Sorter view. Drag the slides to the desired locations.	
Enter text in Notes Pages view	Click the Notes Pages View button. Select the Notes placeholder and type.	
Print a presentation	From the File menu, choose Print. Select print options and click the OK button.	

For on-line information about	From the PowerPoint Help menu, choose Contents, select "Using PowerPoint," and then
Working with a presentation	Select the topic "Creating Presentations and Slides" and click a desired title.

For more information on	See the *Microsoft PowerPoint User's Guide*
Working with a presentation	Chapter 2, "Creating Presentations and Slides"

Preview of the Next Lesson

In the next lesson, you'll import an existing outline, edit outline text and slides, and print an outline. You'll also learn how to rearrange text and slides in Outline view and view your outline with only titles and unformatted text. By the end of the lesson, you'll have produced another presentation for your quick-reference notebook.

2 Organizing Your Ideas

Outlining Your Ideas

In PowerPoint you can outline your thoughts and ideas to help you clearly organize the overall content of your presentation. Outline view shows you the slide title text and paragraph text for each slide in your presentation. The alternating sequence of titles and paragraphs forms an outline, with each title appearing at the first level and each paragraph appearing indented below. You can edit and rearrange both title and paragraph text in Outline view. Your changes also appear in Slide view. You can also import outlines created in other applications and place them in your outline.

In this lesson, you'll create an outline, insert a Microsoft Word document, change the way you view your outline, rearrange text, format text, and save your outline. At the end of the lesson, your presentation will consist of the following slides:

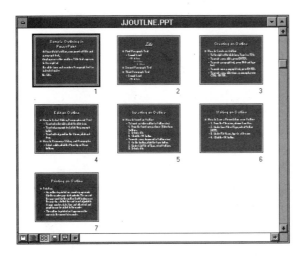

You will learn how to:

- Work with an outline

- Insert an outline

- Change views of text in an outline

- Edit and rearrange outline text

- Format text and change fonts

- Save an outline

Estimated lesson time: 40 minutes

Open a presentation

If you haven't already started PowerPoint, do so now. For instructions about starting PowerPoint, see "Getting Ready," earlier in this book.

Open

1   On the Standard Toolbar, click the Open button or select Open an Existing Presentation from the Startup dialog box and click OK.

2   In the Directories box, ensure that the PRACTICE directory is open. If it is not, select the drive where the Step by Step practice files are stored and open the appropriate directories to find the PRACTICE directory.

For information about opening a sample presentation, see Lesson 2.

3   In the list of file names, select LESSON03.PPT.

If you do not see LESSON03.PPT in the list of file names, check to be sure the correct drive and directory are selected. If you need help, see "Getting Ready."

4   Click the OK button.

Your presentation opens to the following slide:

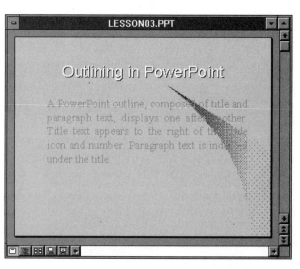

Save the presentation with a new name

Give the presentation a new name so that the changes you make in this lesson do not overwrite the original presentation.

1   From the File menu, choose Save As.

2   In the File Name box, type *your initials***outlne**

For example, if your initials are J. J., type **jjoutlne**

3   Click the OK button.

A Summary Info dialog box appears. If you would like, type in the summary information. Press TAB to move between fields.

4   Click the OK button.

Preview the lesson

The presentation for this lesson contains reference information about outlining your ideas. To preview the information in this lesson, click the Slide Show button and view the on-screen presentation.

Slide Show

1   Click the Slide Show button.

PowerPoint displays the first slide in the presentation.

2   Click to advance to the next slide.

3   Click once for each slide to advance through the rest of the presentation.

After the last slide in the presentation, PowerPoint returns to the first slide.

Viewing Your Presentation in Outline View

Slide Icon

In Outline view, each title appears on the left side of the window with a slide icon and slide number. Paragraph text is indented under its title on the outline. If there are graphic objects on your slides, the slide icon appears with shapes inside.

Change to Outline view

Outline View

▶   Click the Outline View button.

The slide icon and title for slide 1 are selected. The paragraph text is not selected when you change from Slide view to Outline view.

Your presentation window should look similar to the following illustration:

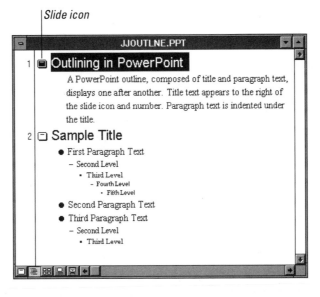

Inserting an Outline

PowerPoint can insert outlines created in other applications, such as Microsoft Word. When you insert a Microsoft Word document with outline heading styles, PowerPoint creates slide titles and paragraphs based on the heading and paragraph levels.

1   Position the I-beam cursor below the text of the last slide in the outline and click.

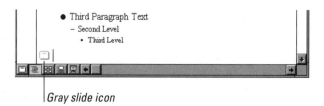

Gray slide icon

A gray slide icon appears. The gray slide icon is a placeholder for the next slide in the presentation. When you insert an outline or enter title or paragraph text, PowerPoint creates a new slide.

TROUBLESHOOTING: **If the gray slide icon doesn't appear**   Reposition the I-beam cursor below the text in the last slide and click.

2   From the Insert menu, choose Slides from Outline.

3   In the Directories box, ensure the PRACTICE directory is open. If it is not, select the drive where the Step by Step practice files are stored and open the appropriate directories to find the PRACTICE directory.

4   Select OUTLINE.DOC from the list of file names.

If you do not see OUTLINE.DOC in the list of file names, ensure the correct drive and directory are selected. If you need help, see "Getting Ready."

5   Click the OK button.

A bar meter shows you the progress of reading the outline. After you insert an outline, the insertion point is displayed at the bottom of the outline.

Note   You can also open a Microsoft Word document to create a presentation by choosing the Open command from the File menu and then selecting Outline (RTF) from the List Files of Type drop-down list.

Scrolling Through an Outline

The sample outline you're working on contains more text than you can see on the screen at one time. In Lesson 1, you learned three methods for scrolling. The method you use depends on how quickly you want to move through the outline. You can scroll line by line, you can jump immediately to the beginning, middle, or end of the outline, or you can scroll window by window. If you need to review, see "Scrolling Through a Presentation" in Lesson 1.

▶   Scroll to the top of the outline.

Viewing Your Outline

There are different ways of viewing your presentation in Outline view. You can collapse or expand your outline, use plain or formatted text, or change the view scale.

1 Position the I-beam cursor over the slide 1 title and click to place the insertion point in the line.

Show Titles

2 On the Outlining Toolbar, click the Show Titles button.

Click here to show titles

The view switches from titles and paragraphs to titles only. The Show Titles button allows you to work with the main points of your outline.

Your presentation window should look similar to the following illustration:

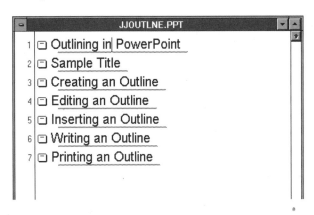

Show All

3 On the Outlining Toolbar, click the Show All button.

Outline view expands to include title and paragraph text for the entire presentation.

Collapse Selection

4 On the Outlining Toolbar, click the Collapse Selection button.

Slide 1 collapses down to show the title only.

Expand Selection

5 On the Outlining Toolbar, click the Expand Selection button.

Slide 1 expands back to include the paragraph text.

Show Formatting

6 On the Outlining Toolbar, click the Show Formatting button.

The view switches from formatted text to plain text. The Show Formatting button allows you to work with your content without formatting, so you can see your content easier. The formatting information is not deleted or cleared; it's just turned off. When you print an outline, it will print with formatting on or off, depending on how you set the Show Formatting button. Slide view always includes formatting when printing.

Your presentation window should look similar to the following illustration:

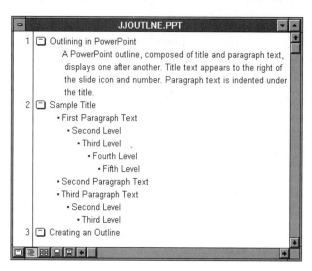

Show Formatting

7   On the Outlining Toolbar, click the Show Formatting button again.

The text in Outline view changes from unformatted to formatted text.

Changing the View Scale

You can change the scale of your view by changing the Zoom Control on the Standard Toolbar or the View menu. The view scales available in Outline view are 25%, 33%, 50%, 66%, 75%, and 100%. In other views, 150%, 200%, 300%, and 400% are also available for working on detailed items—such as graphics or objects.

Zoom Control

1   On the Standard Toolbar, click the Zoom Control drop-down list button and select 25%.

Click here to change the view scale

The view scale decreases from 33% to 25%. The Zoom Control command allows you to increase the view scale to see smaller text or decrease the view scale to see more of the presentation.

Zoom Control

2   On the Standard Toolbar, click the Zoom Control box to select the percentage size.

3   Type **33** and press ENTER.

The view scale changes to 33%. You can type in any view size.

Editing and Rearranging in Outline View

In Outline view, you can edit and rearrange slides, paragraphs, and text by using Outlining Toolbar buttons or by dragging the slides, paragraphs, or text.

Selecting Slides, Paragraphs, and Text

To edit or rearrange slides and paragraphs, you'll need to select the text first. To select a slide or paragraph, click the corresponding slide icon or paragraph bullet. To select a word, double-click the word, and to select text, drag a selection across the text.

Select an entire slide

▶ Position the I-beam cursor (which changes to a four-headed arrow) over the icon for slide 1 and click to select the slide.

PowerPoint selects both the title and paragraph text. The entire slide, including all text and graphic objects (even those that are not visible in Outline view), is selected. You can also select a slide by clicking the slide number.

Your presentation window should look similar to the following illustration:

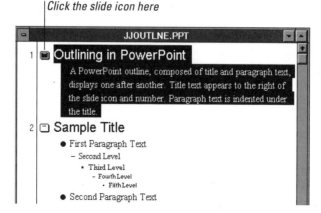

Click the slide icon here

Note Slide commands from the Edit menu (*Cut* or *Copy*) affect the entire slide, while text commands from the Format menu (*Font*) affect only the Title and Paragraph objects.

Select a paragraph

Selecting paragraphs works the same way as selecting slides. Pressing the ENTER key ends one paragraph and begins the next paragraph.

▶ Position the I-beam cursor (which changes to a four-headed arrow) over the bullet next to the paragraph titled "First Paragraph Text" in slide 2 and click.

PowerPoint selects the paragraph, including all related indented paragraphs, as shown in the following illustration:

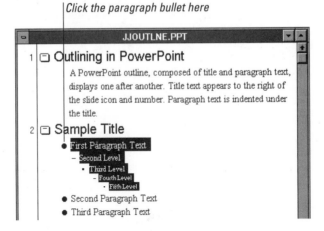

Click the paragraph bullet here

Select multiple paragraphs

▶   Hold down the SHIFT key and click the bullet for the paragraph titled "Third Paragraph Text." Notice that the second bullet point is also selected.

Your presentation window should look similar to the following illustration:

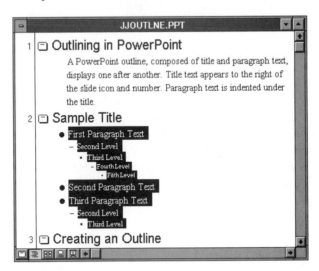

Tip You can also select multiple paragraphs with the I-beam cursor. Click the I-beam cursor where you want the selection to begin, then while holding down the SHIFT key, click the I-beam cursor where you want the selection to end. PowerPoint selects everything between the first click and the second click.

Select text

Selecting text in Outline view is the same as selecting text in Slide view.

1   Position the I-beam cursor in the middle of the word "Creating" in the title of slide 3.

2   Drag through the title "Creating an Outline" to select the title.

With the Automatic Word Selection feature turned on, even though you started the selection in the middle of the word "Creating," PowerPoint automatically selects the entire word.

Note The Automatic Word Selection command can be turned off by choosing Options from the Tools menu.

Rearranging Slides, Paragraphs, and Text

You can rearrange slides and paragraphs in Outline view by using the Move Up button and the Move Down button on the Outlining Toolbar or by dragging the slides and paragraphs to where you want them to appear.

Rearrange a slide

In Lesson 1, you learned how to move text in Outline view by using the Demote, Promote, Move Up, and Move Down buttons on the Outlining Toolbar. In this part of the lesson, you'll learn how to rearrange slides and text by dragging.

1   Position the four-headed arrow over the slide icon of slide 2 titled "Sample Title" and then drag vertically to the top of the outline.

You'll notice the four-headed arrow changes into a two-headed placement arrow that indicates which direction you are moving the text. A placement line appears showing you where the text can be placed.

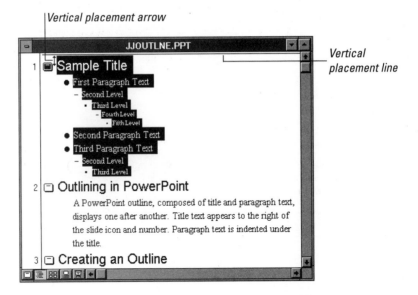

Vertical placement arrow

Vertical placement line

2   Drag the slide icon titled "Sample Title" back to its original position.

Tip   You can also click the Undo button on the Standard Toolbar to return the slide to its original position.

Rearrange paragraphs

You can rearrange paragraphs by dragging them just like you do entire slides. Instead of moving the paragraph up or down, you want to rearrange a paragraph so it becomes a part of another paragraph.

1   In slide 2, position the four-headed arrow over the bullet of the text line titled "Second Paragraph Text."

2   Drag the text line horizontally to the right one level.

The text moves one indent level to the right. The "Second Paragraph Text" is now an indent level under "First Paragraph Text."

Your presentation window should look similar to the following illustration:

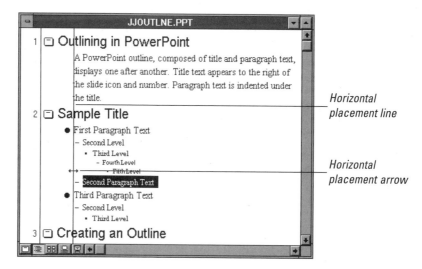

Horizontal placement line

Horizontal placement arrow

3   On the Standard Toolbar, click the Undo button.

Undo

Rearrange words

Selected words can be moved by simply dragging the selection to a new position.

1   Position the I-beam cursor over the word "Sample" in slide 2.

2   Double-click to select the word.

3   Position the I-beam cursor (which changes to the pointer) over the selection.

4   Drag the selection to the left of the word "Outlining" in slide 1.

After you click the mouse, the cursor changes to the Insert pointer. When you release the mouse, the word is moved to its new position.

Insert Pointer

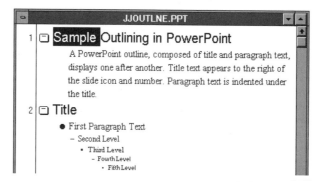

Formatting Text

In Outline view, you can modify the style of text by changing fonts, sizes, and styles, just as you can in Slide view.

Format title and paragraph text

1   Position the I-beam cursor to the right of the word "Title" in slide 2.

2   Double-click to select the slide title.

3   On the Formatting Toolbar, click the Italic and Underline buttons.

Italic   Underline

Click here for italic text   Click here for underlined text

The selected text is now italicized and underlined.

Change the font

1   In slide 2, position the I-beam cursor to the left of the word "First" in the first bullet point under the title.

If you move the cursor too far to the left, the cursor changes to the four-headed arrow.

2   Drag the I-beam cursor until it's positioned at the end of the bullet point titled "Third Level" under "Third Paragraph Text."

All of the paragraph text for slide 2 is selected, as shown in the following illustration:

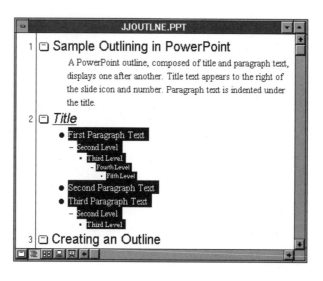

TROUBLESHOOTING: **If you drag past the end of the paragraph or select too much text**   Drag the I-beam cursor back up beyond the text you want to select. To ensure the selection of a specific text line when dragging, position the cursor over the text in that last line you want to select. If you select too much text, reposition the cursor to the left of the word "First," and then drag again.

Font

3   On the Standard Toolbar, click the Font drop-down arrow and select Book Antiqua.

The selected text changes from Times New Roman to Book Antiqua.

4   On the Standard Toolbar, click the Font drop-down arrow again.

Notice the Book Antiqua font is at the top of the list. PowerPoint places the fonts you use the most at the top of the list, separated by a double line, so you don't have to scroll down the list of fonts.

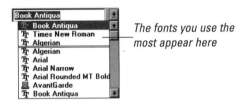

The fonts you use the most appear here

5   Select Times New Roman.

6   Click a blank space to the right of slide 2.

The slide 2 paragraph text is deselected.

Saving an Outline

For information on reporting slides to Word, see Lesson 12.

To save the outline for use in other applications, you must give the outline a name and store it on a disk. PowerPoint saves the outline in a format called *Rich Text Format* (RTF), which saves your text format. Other applications can import outlines saved in RTF. With OfficeLinks, you can send your outline directly to Word with the Report It feature in PowerPoint.

Save as an outline

Use the following procedure to save the outline in the same directory as the Step by Step practice files. During the procedure, PowerPoint displays a *dialog box*. You use dialog boxes to give PowerPoint information about what you want to do.

1   From the File menu, choose Save As.

PowerPoint displays the Save As dialog box. In the File Name box, JJOUTLNE is selected.

Document names can be no more than eight characters long. They cannot have spaces in them.

2   Type your initials, with no periods or spaces, followed by the word **outrtf**

For example, if your initials are J. J., type **jjoutrtf**

3   In the Save File as Type box, click the drop-down arrow and select Outline (RTF).

4 In the Drives box, ensure that drive C is selected, if that is where you stored your Step by Step practice files. If you need assistance, see "Getting Ready," earlier in this book.

5 In the Directories box, ensure that the PRACTICE directory is selected. If it is not, select it by double-clicking it.

6 Click the OK button.

The outline is saved as JJOUTRTF.RTF.

Note The RTF outline, JJOUTRTF.RTF, is saved to the PRACTICE directory and does not appear on your screen as a presentation title.

Print the presentation in Outline view

For information on printing a presentation, see Lesson 13.

1 From the File menu, choose Print (CTRL+P).

The Print dialog box appears.

2 Click the drop-down arrow next to Print What.

3 Select Outline View from the drop-down list.

4 Click the OK button.

A dialog box appears, giving your printing status.

Save the presentation in Outline view

PowerPoint saves your presentation in the current view and view scale. Choosing the Save command in Outline view saves your presentation in Outline view with the current view scale setting.

Save

▶ On the Standard Toolbar, click the Save button.

When you open this presentation the next time, PowerPoint will open it in Outline view at the view scale it was last saved.

One Step Further

You have learned to insert an outline into PowerPoint to add text to slides, change the views of your outline, select and rearrange slides and paragraphs, save an outline in Rich Text Format, and print an outline. If you'd like to practice these and other basic skills in your practice presentation, try the following:

▶ Insert the outline you saved as *your initials***outrtf.rtf** into your presentation *initials***outlne.ppt**

▶ Increase the view scale and scroll up and down using the three different methods you learned in this lesson.

▶ Select and move slides and paragraphs with Show Titles turned on by dragging or by using the toolbar buttons.

▶ Select and change paragraph formats with the Show Titles option turned on by using the toolbar buttons.

▶ Save your presentation as an outline in RTF.

▶ Print an outline with unformatted text using different view scales.

If You Want to Continue to the Next Lesson

1 From the File menu, choose Close (CTRL+W).

2 If a dialog box appears asking whether you want to save the changes to your presentation, click the No button. You do not need to save the changes you made to the presentation since you printed it.

Choosing this command closes the active presentation; it does not exit PowerPoint.

If You Want to Quit PowerPoint for Now

1 From the File menu, choose Exit (CTRL+Q).

2 If a dialog box appears asking whether you want to save changes to the presentation, click the No button.

Lesson Summary

To	Do this	Button
Open an outline	From the File menu, choose Open. Click the List Files Of Type drop-down arrow and select Outlines. Select the file you want opened.	
View your slides in Outline view	Click the Outline View button.	
Insert an outline	From the Insert menu, choose Slides from Outline.	
Scroll through an outline	Click the scroll arrows, or drag the elevator, or click above or below the scroll box.	
View an outline with titles only	On the Outlining Toolbar, click the Show Titles button.	
View an outline with formatted text	On the Outlining Toolbar, click the Show Formatting button.	

To	Do this	Button
Increase or decrease the Outline view size	On the Standard Toolbar, click the Zoom Control drop-down arrow and select a view size, or select the view size percentage and type a new percentage.	41%
Select a slide or paragraph	Position the four-headed arrow to the left of the text and click.	
Move a slide or paragraph	Select the slide or paragraph. On the Outlining Toolbar, click one of the outlining buttons or drag the selection.	
Move text	Select the text. Drag it to a new position.	
Save an outline	From the File menu, choose Save As. Click the Save File as Type drop-down arrow and select Outline (RTF).	
Print an outline	From the File menu, choose Print. Click the Print What drop-down arrow and select Outline View.	

For on-line information about	From the PowerPoint Help menu, choose Contents, select "Using PowerPoint," and then
Outlining in PowerPoint	Select the topic "Putting Text on Slides" and click a title under "How to Work with Text in Outline View."

For more information on	See the *Microsoft PowerPoint User's Guide*
Outlining in PowerPoint	Chapter 4, "Putting Text on Slides"
Printing an outline	Chapter 6, "Notes, Handouts, Slide Shows, and Printing"

Preview of the Next Lesson

In the next lesson, you'll create text objects, change bullets, work with the ruler and tabs, change line spacing, and change text attributes. By the end of the lesson, you'll have produced another presentation for your quick-reference notebook.

Adding and Modifying Text

In PowerPoint, adding and modifying text is simple. Whether you're typing or editing text on a slide, an outline, or a speaker's notes page, you work with text in the same way. In addition to working with text in a text placeholder, PowerPoint allows you create, edit, and adjust text in a text label, a word processing box, or a drawing.

In this lesson, you'll learn how to create a text object, edit text, change the appearance of text, capitalize sentences, remove sentence periods, find and replace text, replace fonts, and check spelling. At the end of the lesson, your presentation will consist of the following slides:

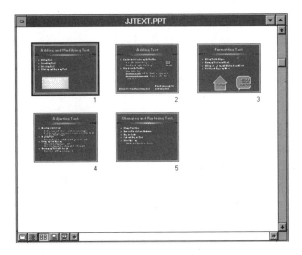

You will learn how to:

- Add text to slides
- Format text objects
- Align and arrange text
- Change line spacing
- Change sentence case and periods
- Find and replace text
- Check spelling

Estimated lesson time: 35 minutes

Open a presentation

If you haven't already started PowerPoint, do so now. For instructions about starting PowerPoint, see "Getting Ready," earlier in this book.

Open

1   On the Standard Toolbar, click the Open button or select Open an Existing Presentation from the Startup dialog box and click OK.

2   In the Directories box, ensure that the PRACTICE directory is open. If it is not, select the drive where the Step by Step practice files are stored and open the appropriate directories to find the PRACTICE directory.

For information about opening a sample presentation, see Lesson 2.

3   In the list of file names, select LESSON04.PPT.

If you do not see LESSON04.PPT in the list of file names, check to be sure the correct drive and directory are selected. If you need help, see "Getting Ready."

4   Click the OK button.

Your presentation opens to the following slide:

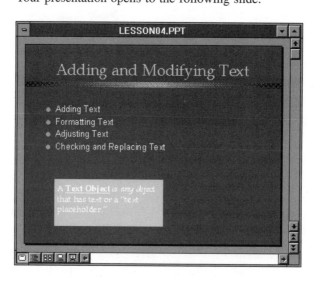

Save the presentation with a new name

Give the presentation a new name so that the changes you make in this lesson do not overwrite the original presentation.

1   From the File menu, choose Save As.

2   In the File Name box, type *your initials***text**

For example, if your initials are J. J., type **jjtext**

3   Click the OK button.

The Summary Info dialog box appears. If you would like, type in the summary information. Press TAB to move between fields.

4   Click the OK button.

Preview the lesson

The presentation for this lesson contains reference information about working with PowerPoint text. To preview the information in this lesson, click the Slide Show button and view the on-screen presentation.

Slide Show

1   Click the Slide Show button.

PowerPoint displays the first slide in the presentation.

2   Click to advance to the next slide.

3   Click once for each slide to advance through the rest of the presentation.

After the last slide in the presentation, PowerPoint returns to the first slide.

Next Slide

Change to the next slide

▶   Click the Next Slide button to advance to slide 2.

Adding Text

Usually, slides contain a title placeholder and a main text placeholder in which to enter your main ideas. With PowerPoint, you can also create other text on your slide or speaker's notes page by using the Text tool. With the Text tool, you can create a text label for short notes and phrases where text doesn't wrap, or a word processing box for sentences where text wraps inside the boundaries of the box.

Creating a Text Object

To create a text label, use the Text tool to select a place on the slide for your text, and start typing. To create a word processing box, use the Text tool to select a place on the slide for the text, draw a box, and start typing.

Create a text label

A "text label" refers to text that does not word-wrap within a defined box. For example, a text object with the word-wrap option turned off is a "text label."

Text Tool

1   On the Drawing Toolbar, click the Text Tool button.

Click here to type text

↓

Text Cursor

2   Position your pointer (which changes to the text cursor) below the bulleted text on the bottom left corner of the slide.

3 Click to place to the insertion point.

A blinking insertion point surrounded by a slanted-line selection box appears. The slanted-line selection box lets you know you're ready to enter or edit individual text within a text object.

4 Type **A text label doesn't word-wrap text**

Tip A text label can be converted to a word processing box by choosing Text Anchor from the Format menu and turning on the Word-wrap Text in Object option.

Your presentation window should look similar to the following illustration:

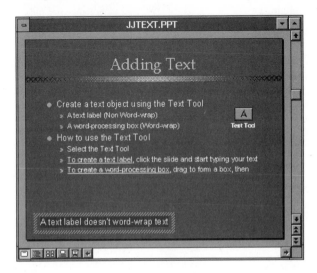

5 Click outside the slanted-line selection box to deselect the text label.

The text label is deselected.

Create a word processing box

A "word processing box" refers to text that word-wraps inside the boundaries of an object.

1 On the Drawing Toolbar, click the Text Tool button.

Text Tool

2   Position the text cursor to the right of the text label on the slide.

3   Drag to create a box approximately 2 inches long.

Cross Hairs Cursor

As you drag, the pointer changes to the cross hairs cursor shown to the left. When you release the mouse button, a slanted-line selection box appears. PowerPoint is ready for you to enter your text.

4   Type **A word processing box word-wraps text**

Tip   A word processing box can be converted to a text label by choosing Text Anchor from the Format menu and turning off the Word-wrap Text in Object option.

Your presentation window should look similar to the following illustration:

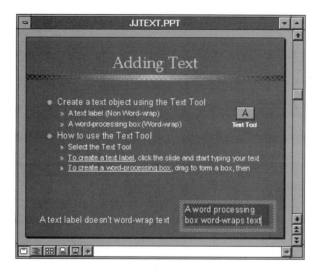

5   Click outside the selection box to deselect the text box.

Note   Text created on a slide with the Text tool doesn't appear in Outline view. Only text entered in a title placeholder and a main text placeholder appears in Outline view.

Adding Text in a Text Object

You can add text in any PowerPoint text object by placing the insertion point where you want the new text and typing your text.

1   Position the I-beam cursor to the right of the word "then" in the bottom of the main text and click to place the insertion point.

Your presentation window should look similar to the following illustration:

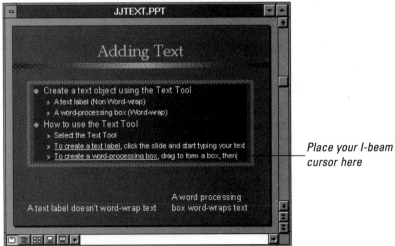

Place your I-beam
cursor here

A blinking insertion point appears where you clicked the I-beam cursor.

2   Press the SPACEBAR and type **start typing your text**

The text word-wraps to the next line. The size of the text object adjusts to contain the new text.

Change to the next slide

Next Slide

▶   Click the Next Slide button to advance to slide 3.

Formatting Text

In PowerPoint, you can add and arrange text in a drawing shape or text object. After you have finished adjusting your text, you can change text formatting, such as italic, bold, underline, shadow, or size, by selecting the text object and clicking one or more formatting buttons on the PowerPoint Formatting Toolbar.

Add text to a shape

You can add text to a shape by selecting the shape and typing your text. You can add text to all shapes in PowerPoint except for lines, freeforms, and arcs.

1   Click the arrow object to select it.

2   Type **Great!**

3   Position the pointer over the border of the voice bubble object and click to select the object.

Note   You must click the border (or the text) of an object that has no fill to select the object.

---

4   Type **Arranging text in a shape is easy**

Text in the bubble object extends beyond the edges of the shape because the word-wrap option is initially turned off. Your voice bubble should look similar to the following illustration:

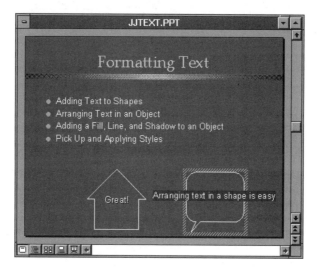

Arrange text in an object

You can arrange text in an object by setting the word-wrap option and fit text option in the Text Anchor dialog box. Turning on the word-wrap setting changes a text attribute from a text label to a word processing box, while turning on the fit text setting adjusts a text object to the size of the text.

1   The voice bubble object appears selected.

2   From the Format menu, choose Text Anchor.

The Text Anchor dialog box appears. If you can't see the voice bubble object because the Text Anchor dialog box is covering it, drag the dialog box title bar up until you can completely see the voice bubble object.

3   In the Anchor Point box, click the drop-down arrow and select Top.

4   Click the Preview button.

The text in the object moves to the top of the object.

5   Click the Word-Wrap Text In Object check box and click the Preview button.

The text wraps inside the boundaries of the object.

6   Click the Adjust Object Size To Fit Text check box and click the Preview button.

The object changes shape to fit the text.

7   Click the Adjust Object Size To Fit Text check box again and click the Preview button.

The object changes back to its original shape. The Text Anchor dialog box should look similar to the following illustration:

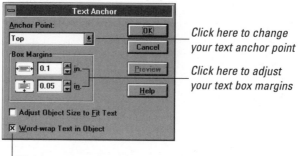

Click here to change
your text anchor point

Click here to adjust
your text box margins

Click here to word-wrap your text object

8   Click the OK button.

Format text in a shape

1   The voice bubble object appears selected.

2   On the Formatting Toolbar, click the Italic button.

Italic

Click here for italic text

The text in the object changes to italic.

Fill On/Off

3   On the Drawing Toolbar, click the Fill On/Off button.

The text object is filled with the default color scheme fill color.

Text Shadow

4   On the Formatting Toolbar, click the Text Shadow button.

The text in your voice bubble is now shadowed.

Text Color

5   On the Formatting Toolbar, click the Text Color button.

A text color menu of the current color scheme appears.

6   Click the yellow color as indicated in the following illustration:

Click the yellow color here

Your presentation window should look similar to the following illustration:

Format text with the Format Painter command

Using the Format Painter command, you can copy a set of styles from selected text and objects and apply them to other selected text and objects.

1   On the Standard Toolbar, click the Format Painter button.

Format Painter

| Click here to copy and apply object styles

PowerPoint copies and stores the specific text and object styles of the selected text object. The Format Painter button on the Standard Toolbar remains depressed when styles have been copied. The pointer changes to a painter cursor, as shown in the left margin.

Painter Cursor

2   Click inside the arrow object to copy the format to the object.

PowerPoint changes the text style and fill color of the arrow object by applying the style you picked up from the voice bubble object.

TROUBLESHOOTING: **If the arrow object does not look like the voice bubble**   The Format Painter tool works only when you select an object. You may have clicked the Format Painter button while no object was selected, or while a different object was selected. Repeat steps 1 and 2 after selecting the voice bubble object.

Your presentation window should look similar to the following illustration:

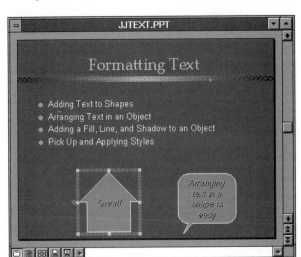

Next Slide

Change to the next slide

▶ Click the Next Slide button to advance to slide 4.

Adjusting Text

You have complete control over the placement and position of your text in PowerPoint. You can adjust the alignment, line spacing, and arrangement of text in an object to achieve the best look. To change all of the text in a text object, you need to select the text object.

Select a text object

1 Position the I-beam cursor over the title text and click.

The insertion point appears in the text with the slanted-line selection box around it indicating that only the text is ready for editing. The text object cannot be edited when the slanted-line selection box is visible.

2 Position the I-beam cursor (which changes to the pointer) over the edge of the slanted-line selection box and click.

The text object is selected and is ready to be edited.

Tip For a quick way to select a text object, hold down the SHIFT key and position the I-beam cursor (which changes to the pointer) over the text and click.

Change text alignment

▶   From the Format menu, choose Alignment and then choose Center.

The text alignment in the text object changes to the center.

Rearrange text in Slide view

Rearranging text in Slide view works in the same manner as it does in Outline view.

1   Position the I-beam cursor over the main text object and click.

The insertion point appears in the text, indicating the text is ready for editing.

2   Position the I-beam cursor (which changes to the four-headed arrow) over the bullet next to the text titled "Rearranging Text in Slide view."

3   Drag the selected text to the bottom of the text object.

The third bullet point moves into the fourth position.

Your presentation window should look similar to the following illustration:

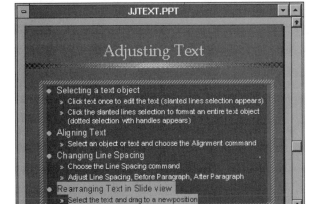

Change line spacing

1   Position the I-beam cursor (which changes to the pointer) over the edge of the slanted-line selection box and click.

The selection box changes to a dotted selection box with handles around the edges. When the dotted selection box is visible, text changes are applied to all the text in the selected object.

2   From the Format menu, choose Line Spacing.

The Line Spacing dialog box appears, showing the current spacing settings for lines and paragraphs.

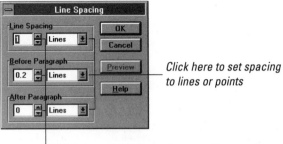

Click here to set spacing to lines or points

Click here to increase or decrease line spacing

3   Click the down arrow in the Line Spacing box until the line spacing is set to 0.8.

If you hold down the mouse when you click the up arrow or down arrow, the line spacing number will continue to change until you release the mouse.

4   Click the Preview button.

The text on the slide changes each time you make changes and click the Preview button in the dialog box.

5   Click the OK button.

Next Slide

Change to the next slide

▶   Click the Next Slide button to advance to slide 5.

Changing and Replacing Text

After entering and arranging your presentation text, you can change text case and add or remove periods from sentences with commands from the Format menu. In addition to changing text, you can also find and replace text and check spelling throughout your entire presentation with the Replace and Spelling commands.

Change the case of text

1   Hold down the SHIFT key and position the I-beam cursor (which changes to the pointer) over the bulleted text and click.

The text object is selected when handles appear around the edges of the object.

2   From the Format menu, choose Change Case.

3   Click the Title Case option button.

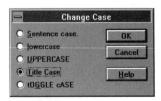

4   Click the OK button.

The paragraph text changes from lowercase to title case.

Remove periods

If you enter periods at the end of your sentences and then decide you don't want them, PowerPoint permits you to remove (or add) periods with the Periods command.

1   From the Format menu, choose Periods.

2   Click the Remove Periods option button.

3   Click the OK button.

Periods are removed from the selected text.

Replacing Fonts

With the Replace Fonts command, you can replace a current font style you have been using with another style throughout your entire presentation.

1   From the Tools menu, choose Replace Fonts.

2   In the With box, click the drop-down arrow.

3   Scroll down and select Times New Roman.

Click here to select Times New Roman

4   Click the Replace button.

Throughout your presentation, the text formatted with the Arial font changes to the Times New Roman font.

5   Click the Close button.

Your presentation window should look similar to the following illustration:

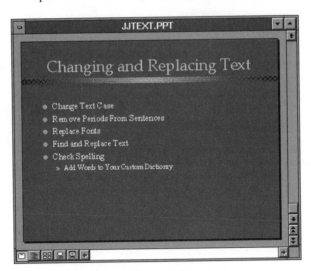

Finding and Replacing Text

The Find and Replace commands allow you to locate specific text in your presentation and change it to something different.

1   From the Edit menu, choose Replace (CTRL+H).

2   In the Find What box, type **Great**

3   Press TAB or click the I-beam cursor in the Replace With box.

4   Type **Fantastic**

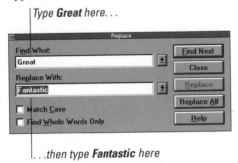

5   Click the Find Next button.

A dialog box appears, indicating PowerPoint has reached the end of the presentation.

6   Click the Continue button.

PowerPoint finds the word "Great" on slide 3. If you can't see the selected text in the arrow object, drag the Replace dialog box title bar up so you can see the arrow object.

7   Click the Replace button.

8   Click the Close button.

The Replace dialog box closes.

Checking Spelling

The spelling checker checks the spelling of the entire presentation, including all slides, outlines, notes pages, and handout pages views. PowerPoint uses a built-in dictionary to check your presentation. You can also use custom dictionaries from other Microsoft applications.

Check spelling in your entire presentation

Spelling

1   On the Standard Toolbar, click the Spelling button.

PowerPoint begins checking the spelling on the current slide.

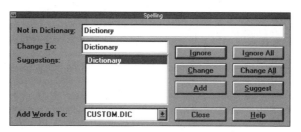

2   The spelling checker stops and highlights the misspelled word "Dictionry."

A list appears, showing possible correct spellings of the misspelled word "Dictionry."

3   Click the Change button to correct the spelling.

The spelling checker continues to check your presentation for misspelled words or words not found in the dictionary.

Use the custom dictionary

The custom dictionary allows you to add words that the PowerPoint dictionary doesn't recognize. Click the Add button in the Spelling dialog box to add a word to your custom dictionary. The spelling checker stops when it fails to recognize the word "PowerPoint" on the Notes Master.

1   Click the Add button.

The custom dictionary adds the word "PowerPoint" and continues to check your presentation. The spelling checker stops when it fails to recognize the word "placeholder."

2   Click the Ignore button.

The spelling checker continues to check your presentation. A dialog box appears, indicating the spelling checker has finished spell checking the entire presentation.

3   Click the Close button.

Print the quick-reference notebook presentation

*For information
on printing a
presentation, see
Lesson 13.*

1   From the File menu, choose Print (CTRL+P).

The Print dialog box appears.

2   Click the drop-down arrow next to Print What.

3   Select Handouts (2 slides per page) from the drop-down list.

4   Click the OK button.

A dialog box appears, giving your printing status.

Save the presentation

Save

▶   On the Standard Toolbar, click the Save button.

No dialog box appears because the presentation already has a name. The current information in your presentation is saved with the same name.

One Step Further

You have learned to create and edit a text object, format text using the toolbar, adjust text alignment and line spacing, check spelling, and find and replace text. If you would like to practice these and other basic skills in your practice presentation, try the following:

▶   Create text labels and word processing boxes. Convert a text label to a word processing box and vice versa. (Hint: Use the Text Anchor command.)

▶   Select a text object and rearrange its text by using the Outline buttons on the Outling Toolbar or Formatting Toolbar and by dragging.

▶   Create text objects and use the Fill On/Off command to change the fill.

▶   Select a text object, adjust the Fit Text margins, and change the word-wrap settings.

▶   Select a text object and adjust the Before Paragraph and After Paragraph line spacing.

If You Want to Continue to the Next Lesson

1   From the File menu, choose Close (CTRL+W).

2   If a dialog box appears asking whether you want to save the changes to your presentation, click the No button. You do not need to save the changes you made to the presentation since you printed it.

Choosing this command closes the active presentation; it does not exit PowerPoint.

If You Want to Quit PowerPoint for Now

1 From the File menu, choose Exit (CTRL+Q).

2 If a dialog box appears asking whether you want to save changes to the presentation, click the No button.

Lesson Summary

To	Do this	Button
Create a text label	Click the Text Tool button. Click the slide and type your text.	A
Create a word processing box	Click the Text Tool button. On the slide, drag to create a text box, and then type your text.	A
Select text to edit	Click the text to place the insertion point.	
Rearrange text in Slide view	Select text and then drag paragraphs.	
Add text to a shape	Select the shape and type your text.	
Arrange text in an object	Select an object with text. From the Format menu, choose Text Anchor.	
Format text in a shape	Select the shape and choose styles from the Formatting Toolbar or the Format menu.	
Format text with Format Painter	Select the object with the format you want to use. On the Standard Toolbar, click Format Painter. Select the object you want to format.	
Change text alignment	Select a text object. From the Format menu, choose Alignment.	
Change line spacing	Select a text object. From the Format menu, choose Line Spacing.	
Change text case	Select a text object. From the Format menu, choose Change Case.	
Add or remove periods	Select a text object. From the Format menu, choose Periods.	

To	Do this	Button
Replace fonts	From the Tools menu, choose Replace Fonts.	
Find or replace text	From the Edit menu, choose Find or Replace.	
Check spelling	From the Tools menu, choose Spelling.	

For on-line information about	From the PowerPoint Help menu, choose Contents, select "Using PowerPoint," and then
Working with the Text tool	Select the topic "Putting Text on Slides" and click a title under "How to Use the Text Tool."
Selecting and editing text	Select the topic "Putting Text on Slides" and click a title under "How to Select and Edit Text."
Formatting text	Select the topic "Putting Text on Slides" and click a title under "How to Format Paragraphs."
Finding and replacing text	Select the topic "Putting Text on Slides" and click a title under "How to Find and Replace Text."
Checking your spelling	Select the topic "Putting Text on Slides" and click a title under "How to Check Spelling."

For more information on	See the *Microsoft PowerPoint User's Guide*
Working with text	Chapter 4, "Putting Text on Slides"

Preview of the Next Lesson

In the next lesson, you'll draw shapes, arcs, and freeforms; edit and modify objects; and group and align objects. At the end of the lesson, you'll have another presentation for your quick-reference notebook.

3 Making Your Ideas Communicate

Drawing and Modifying Objects

With PowerPoint's drawing features, you can draw and modify shapes, lines, text, and pictures to create professional-looking images. Objects are the building blocks you use to create slides in PowerPoint. The shapes you draw, the pictures you import from other applications, the text you type—these are all objects.

In this lesson, you'll draw and edit objects, change object attributes, group and ungroup objects, draw and edit arcs and freeforms, and rotate and flip objects. At the end of the lesson, your presentation will consist of the following slides:

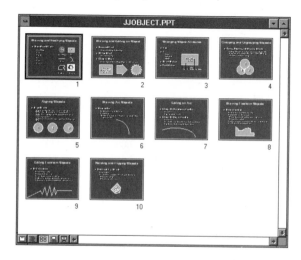

You will learn how to:

- Draw and edit objects
- Modify object attributes
- Group and ungroup objects
- Align objects
- Draw and edit an arc object
- Draw and edit a freeform object
- Rotate and flip objects

Estimated lesson time: 50 minutes

Open a presentation

If you haven't already started PowerPoint, do so now. For instructions about starting PowerPoint, see "Getting Ready," earlier in this book.

Open

1   On the Standard Toolbar, click the Open button or select Open an Existing Presentation from the Startup dialog box and click OK.

2   In the Directories box, ensure that the PRACTICE directory is open. If it is not, select the drive where the Step by Step practice files are stored and open the appropriate directories to find the PRACTICE directory.

For information about opening a sample presentation, see Lesson 2.

3   In the list of file names, select LESSON05.PPT.

If you do not see LESSON05.PPT in the list of file names, check to be sure the correct drive and directory are selected. If you need help, see "Getting Ready."

4   Click the OK button.

Your presentation opens to the following slide:

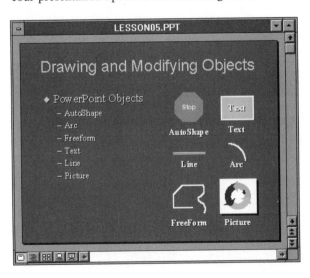

Save the presentation with a new name

Give the presentation a new name so that the changes you make in this lesson do not overwrite the original presentation.

1   From the File menu, choose Save As.

2   In the File Name box, type *your initials***object**

For example, if your initials are J. J., type **jjobject**

3   Click the OK button.

The Summary Info dialog box appears. If you would like, type in the summary information. Press TAB to move between fields.

4   Click the OK button.

Preview the lesson

The presentation for this lesson contains reference information about drawing and modifying objects in PowerPoint. To preview the information in this lesson, click the Slide Show button and view the on-screen presentation.

Slide Show

1   Click the Slide Show button.

PowerPoint displays the first slide in the presentation.

2   Click to advance to the next slide.

3   Click once for each slide to advance through the rest of the presentation.

After the last slide in the presentation, PowerPoint returns to the first slide.

Working with Objects

Objects are shapes, lines, text, and pictures that you create or insert into your PowerPoint presentation. You can create objects using the text tool or drawing tools on the Drawing Toolbar. An object can have graphic attributes (fill, line, shape, and shadow) and text attributes (style, font, color, emboss, and shadow).

Selecting and Deselecting Objects

To select an object, click a visible part of the object using the Selection tool or "pointer." To deselect an object, click the Selection Tool button or move your pointer off the object into a blank area of the slide and click. You can apply attributes only to objects you've selected.

Select and deselect an object

Selection Tool

1   On the Drawing Toolbar, click the Selection Tool button. (It should already be selected unless you've clicked another tool from the Drawing Toolbar.)

Click here for the Selection tool

2   Hold down the SHIFT key, position your pointer on any part of the text object titled "PowerPoint Objects," and click.

The text object is surrounded by a fuzzy outline called a *dotted selection box* that indicates the object is selected. The black squares at each corner of the object are resize handles, which are used to resize objects.

3   Click outside the selection box in a blank area of the slide.

The object is deselected.

Select and deselect multiple objects

You can select and deselect more than one object in different ways. One method uses the SHIFT key and the mouse.

1   Position your pointer on the frame of the "Text" object and click to select it.

2   Hold down the SHIFT key, and click the "Stop" object.

The "Text" object remains selected, and the "Stop" object is added to the selection. As long as you hold down the SHIFT key while clicking unselected objects, you continually add objects to the selection.

3   Hold down the SHIFT key, and then click the "Stop" object again.

The "Stop" object is removed from the selection.

Tip   You can select multiple objects by dragging a selection box around them.

Change to the next slide

Next Slide

▶   Click the Next Slide button to advance to slide 2.

Drawing an Object

You create all drawing objects in PowerPoint, except freeforms, using the same technique. Select a tool from the Drawing Toolbar and then drag with your mouse to create the object. Holding down the SHIFT key as you drag allows you to draw objects constrained vertically and horizontally. Holding down the CTRL key as you drag allows you to draw from the center outward.

AutoShapes

1   On the Drawing Toolbar, click the AutoShapes button.

The AutoShapes Toolbar appears.

Tip   The AutoShapes Toolbar will stay in view until you click its Control-menu box. You can move the AutoShapes Toolbar by dragging the "AutoShapes" title bar to a new location.

2   Click the Thick Right Arrow Tool button in the second from the bottom row.

Your AutoShapes Toolbar should look similar to the following illustration:

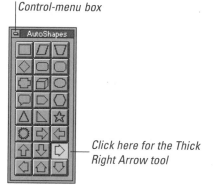

Control-menu box

Click here for the Thick Right Arrow tool

3   Click the AutoShapes Control-menu box to close the AutoShapes Toolbar.

4   Position the cross hairs cursor to the right of the text rectangle and drag to draw a thick right arrow shape.

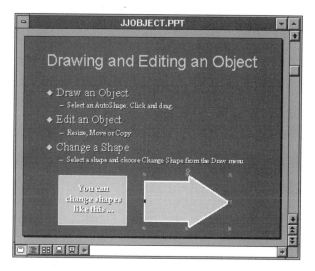

5   Click outside the selection box in a blank area to deselect the arrow object.

Note   When you draw an object, PowerPoint uses the default settings for the object, such as line style or fill color. For more information about changing default settings, see "Customizing PowerPoint Defaults" in Lesson 6.

Editing an Object

Resizing, copying, pasting, moving, cutting, and deleting are editing commands you can use on objects. To edit a PowerPoint object, select the object, and then choose a command from a menu or the toolbar.

Resize an object

Often you'll draw an object or import a picture that won't be the right size for your presentation. You can change the size of an object by dragging its resize handles.

1   Select the right arrow object.

     Resize handles appear around the edges of the selection box.

2   Drag the arrow's right middle resize handle to the left to match the following illustration:

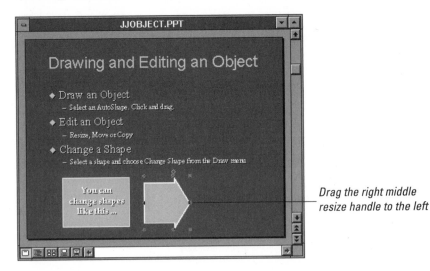

Drag the right middle resize handle to the left

Tip   Holding down the CTRL and SHIFT keys while drawing an object resizes the object proportionally from the center outward.

Adjust an object

Some PowerPoint objects, such as triangles, parallelograms, rounded rectangles, and arrows, are adjustable. Adjustable objects have an adjustable resize handle (which looks like a small diamond) positioned on one side of the object next to a resize handle. The cube in the margin illustrates an object with an adjustable resize handle.

1   Position your pointer (which changes to a small white arrow) on the arrow object's adjustable resize handle.

2   Drag the adjustable resize handle to the left.

Your presentation window should look similar to the following illustration:

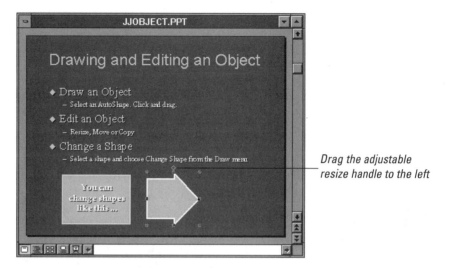

Drag the adjustable
resize handle to the left

Copy an object

You can copy the currently selected object or multiple objects to the Windows Clipboard and then paste the objects in other parts of your presentation.

Copy

1   On the Standard Toolbar, click the Copy button.

Click here to copy objects

The arrow is copied to the Windows Clipboard.

Paste

2   On the Standard Toolbar, click the Paste button.

A copy of the arrow is pasted to the slide from the Windows Clipboard. The pasted arrow is selected and overlaps the original arrow.

Your presentation window should look similar to the following illustration:

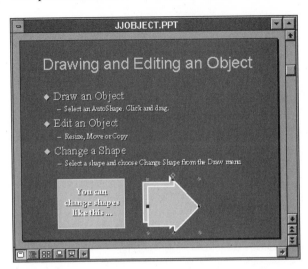

Move an object

1 Position your pointer over the new arrow object.

2 Drag the new arrow to the right of the original arrow as shown in the following illustration:

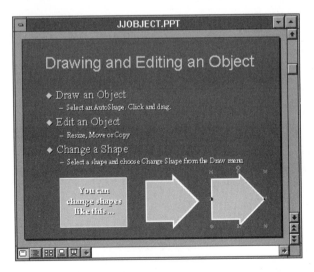

 Tip You can copy an object and move it in one step. Hold down the CTRL key and drag the object. The object copies itself. Choose Duplicate Again from the Edit menu to easily create another copy of the object with the same drag distance as the first.

Change the shape of an object

PowerPoint allows you to change an existing shape to another shape with one easy command.

1   From the Draw menu, choose Change AutoShape.

The AutoShape submenu appears.

2   Select the starburst shape from the submenu.

The arrow shape changes to the starburst shape. The new starburst shape fits in the same area and keeps the same attributes as the original arrow shape.

Your presentation window should look similar to the following illustration:

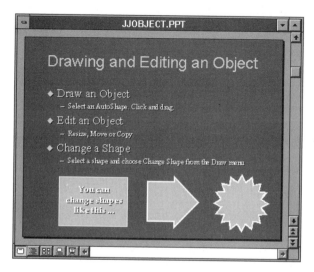

Add text to an object

When you add text to an object, PowerPoint automatically centers the text as you type. When you want to start a new line, you can press ENTER.

1   Type **... to this**

2   Click outside the object to deselect the object.

Next Slide

Change to the next slide

▶   Click the Next Slide button to advance to slide 3.

Modifying Object Attributes

Objects have attributes that define how they appear on the slide. An object has graphic attributes such as fill, line, shape, and shadow, and text attributes such as style, font, color, emboss, and shadow.

Viewing Another Toolbar

For more information on PowerPoint toolbars, see "Getting Ready" earlier in this book.

PowerPoint has nine different toolbars that can be customized at any time. In Slide view three toolbars appear by default when you start PowerPoint: the Standard Toolbar, the Formatting Toolbar, and the Drawing Toolbar. To view or add one or more toolbars, choose the Toolbars command from the View menu and select the ones you want to use. In this section, you'll learn how to add the Drawing+ Toolbar, which gives you one-step access to more drawing commands.

View the Drawing+ Toolbar

The Drawing+ Toolbar provides easy access to drawing commands such as Rotate/Flip, Group and Ungroup, Send Forward, Bring Backward, Colors and Lines, and Shadow.

1   From the View menu, choose Toolbars.

The Toolbars dialog box appears with a list of toolbars that you can view in Slide view.

2   Click the Drawing+ check box.

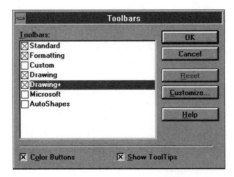

3   Click the OK button.

The Drawing+ Toolbar appears vertically next to the Drawing Toolbar.

Tip   You can turn a toolbar on and off in a single step by using a shortcut menu. Position your pointer over any toolbar, click the right mouse button, and then choose a toolbar name.

TROUBLESHOOTING: **If the Drawing+ Toolbar does not appear**   You probably selected the Drawing+ Toolbar name instead of the check box. The check box must be checked in order for the toolbar to be added.

Add and modify an object's frame

1 Hold down the SHIFT key, position your pointer over the text titled "PowerPoint Object" and click to select the text object.

2 On the Drawing Toolbar, click the Line On/Off button.

A frame with the default line color and style appears around the object.

3 On the Drawing+ Toolbar, click the Line Style button.

Click here to change line styles

A drop-down menu appears with a selection of line styles.

4 From the Line Style menu, choose the fourth line down from the top.

The new line style is applied to the object.

Add and modify an object's fill

1 On the Drawing+ Toolbar, click the Fill Color button.

A drop-down menu appears with a number of fill options.

2 From the menu, choose Pattern.

The Pattern Fill dialog box appears.

3 Select the diagonal line pattern in the third row.

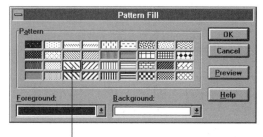

Click the diagonal line pattern here

4 Click the Preview button.

The diagonal line pattern is applied to the object.

5 Click the OK button.

The Pattern Fill dialog box closes.

Line On/Off

Line Style

Fill Color

Add and modify an object's shadow

Shadow On/Off

1   On the Drawing Toolbar, click the Shadow On/Off button.

The default shadow color appears around the object titled "PowerPoint Object."

2   From the Format menu, choose Shadow.

The Shadow dialog box appears.

3   Click the drop-down arrow under Color and select dark blue (below Other Color).

4   In the Offset area, click the Left option button.

5   In the Offset area, click the up arrow in the lower Points box until the number reaches 15.

6   In the Offset area, click the up arrow in the upper Points box until the number reaches 15.

The Shadow dialog box should look similar to the following illustration:

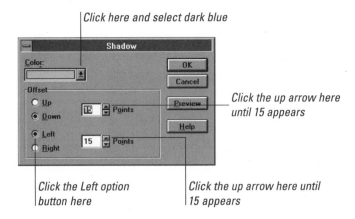

7   Click the Preview button.

The shadow offset is applied to the object so that you can see the shadow change before you leave the dialog box.

8   Click the OK button.

Add a shadow to text

Text Shadow

1   On the Formatting Toolbar, click the Text Shadow button.

A dark shadow appears behind the text.

2   Click outside the selection to deselect the object.

Your presentation should look similar to the following illustration:

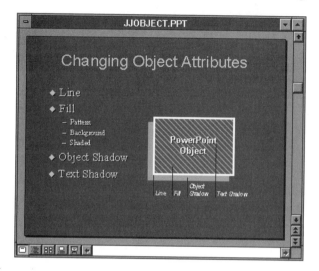

Next Slide

Change to the next slide

▶   Click the Next Slide button to advance to slide 4.

Grouping and Ungrouping Objects

Objects can be grouped together, ungrouped, and regrouped in PowerPoint to make editing and moving information easier. Grouped objects appear as one object, but each object in the group maintains its individual attributes. You can change an individual object within a group by ungrouping the objects, making the change, and then grouping the objects together again using the Regroup command.

Group objects

1   Drag a selection box around the three circles on slide 4.

Each circle has its own selection box, as shown in the following illustration:

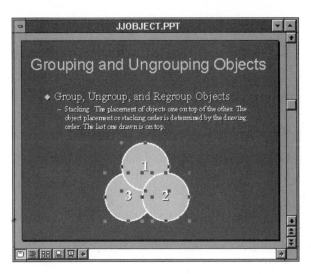

Group

2   On the Drawing+ Toolbar, click the Group button.

The three circle objects group together as one object.

Ungroup objects

Ungroup

1   On the Drawing+ Toolbar, click the Ungroup button.

2   Click outside the selection box to deselect the grouped object.

Object stacking order

Stacking is the placement of objects one on top of another. The drawing order determines the object stacking order. The first object you draw is on the bottom, and the last object you draw is on the top. You can change the placement of the objects by using the Bring to Front, Send to Back, Bring Forward, and Send Backward commands on the Draw menu.

1   Click circle 1 to select it.

Send Backward

2   On the Drawing+ Toolbar, click the Send Backward button.

Circle 1 moves down one level on the stack of objects.

3   From the Draw menu, choose Bring to Front.

Circle 1 moves to the top of the stack of circle objects.

Regroup objects

Objects previously grouped can be regrouped in one easy step. After you ungroup a set of objects, PowerPoint remembers each object in the group and automatically regroups the objects with the Regroup command.

▶   From the Draw menu, choose Regroup.

The three circles regroup as shown in the following illustration:

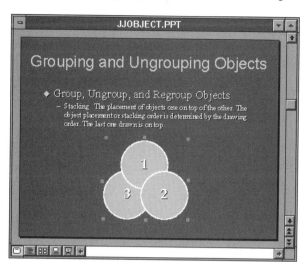

Note   When regrouping objects, PowerPoint remembers the objects of a specific group if you have at least one of the objects selected before you regroup them.

Next Slide

Change to the next slide

▶   Click the Next Slide button to advance to slide 5.

Aligning Objects

Objects can be aligned vertically or horizontally using the Align command or the PowerPoint guides. The Align command aligns two or more objects relative to each other vertically to the left, to the center, or to the right. You can also align objects horizontally to the top, to the middle, or to the bottom. The PowerPoint guides align an individual object or a group of objects to a vertical or horizontal straightedge. For exact alignment, turn on the Snap to Grid feature. Objects snap to an invisible grid of evenly spaced lines that helps you align objects.

Align objects with guides

1   Position your pointer in a blank area of the slide and click the right mouse button.

A Shortcut menu appears, which provides access to commonly used commands.

2   From the Shortcut menu, choose Guides.

Vertical and horizontal dotted lines appear in the middle of the slide, indicating that the guides are turned on.

3   Position your pointer on the vertical guide.

1.00

Guide Indicator

4 Drag the guide left until the Guide indicator reaches 1.00.

As you drag the pointer (which changes to a Guide indicator), a number indicating inches appears. When the Guides feature is turned on, the guides are placed in the middle of the slide at 0.00 inches. As you move a guide left, right, up, or down, the inches number indicates how far you are from the slide center.

Tip If your Guide indicator skips numbers as you drag the guides across the slide, turn off the Snap to Grid command in the Draw menu.

5 Drag circle 2 left to the vertical guide.

As the circle approaches the guide, the left edge of object snaps to the guide.

6 From the View menu, choose Guides.

The dotted guide lines turn off.

Align an object

1 Hold down the SHIFT key and click the other circle objects to select all three circles.

2 From the Draw menu, choose Align and then choose Middles.

The circle objects align horizontally to each other in the middle, as shown in the following illustration:

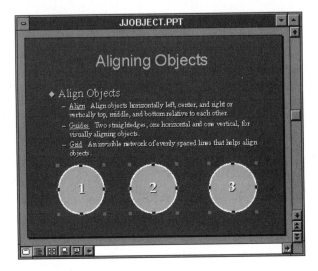

Change to the next slide

▶ Click the Next Slide button to advance to slide 6.

Next Slide

Drawing and Editing an Arc Object

With PowerPoint, you can draw and edit arcs of all sizes and shapes. You can change the shape of any arc by resizing it or moving its control handles. The direction in which you drag the arc determines whether the arc opens up or down, and the distance you drag the arc determines its size.

Draw an arc

Arc Tool

1 On the Drawing Toolbar, click the Arc Tool button.

   The pointer changes to a cross hairs cursor.

2 Position the cross hairs cursor under the center of the bulleted text.

3 Drag the cross hairs cursor down to the right.

   Your presentation window should look similar to the following illustration:

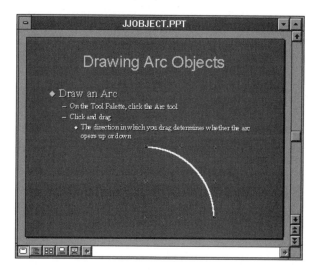

Next Slide

Change to the next slide

▶ Click the Next Slide button to advance to slide 7.

Edit the roundness of an arc

1 Position your pointer on the arc line and click to select it.

2 Drag the middle left resize handle to the left.

   As the arc changes, a dotted outline of the arc appears, indicating what the arc will look like when you release the mouse button.

Note Lines, arcs, and freeforms can't be changed using the Change AutoShape command.

Edit the angle of an arc

1 From the Edit menu, choose Edit Arc Object or double-click the arc line.

A control handle appears on each end of the arc.

2 Drag the left control handle to the left.

Your presentation window should look similar to the following illustration:

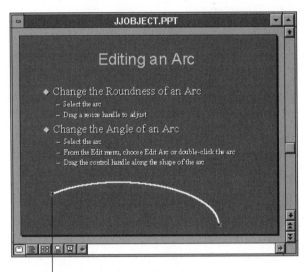

Drag this control handle

Next Slide

Change to the next slide

▶ Click the Next Slide button to advance to slide 8.

Drawing and Editing a Freeform Object

A freeform object can consist of straight lines, freehand lines, or a combination of the two. Freeform objects can be closed or open. A closed freeform has the end of its last line connected to the beginning of its first line, and an open freeform is not connected.   ´

Drawing a Freeform Object

Freeform Tool

1 On the Drawing Toolbar, click the Freeform Tool button.

2 Position your cursor just below the main text in the center.

The pointer changes to a cross hairs cursor.

You can draw freehand lines and straight lines with the Freeform Tool. You can switch back and forth between the pencil (freehand) and the cross hairs (straight line) cursors by dragging and releasing the mouse button.

3 Click once.

This sets the freeform starting point. *Don't hold down the mouse button while you move the mouse.*

4 Move the cross hairs cursor in a straight line down the slide about 1.5 inches to a new position, and click once.

5 Move your cross hairs cursor in a straight line to the right about 2 inches.

Tip To delete the last line of a freeform object while you're drawing, press the BACKSPACE key. You can delete all but the first point this way.

6 Hold down the mouse button and draw a line with the pencil to the freeform object's starting point and click once. (The pencil cursor follows your mouse movements.)

All of the space inside your freeform object is filled with the default fill color.

Your presentation window should look similar to the following illustration:

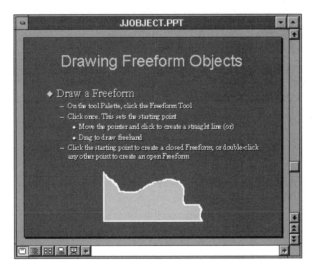

Note To create an open freeform object, double-click the last point of your freeform without connecting the object's ends.

Next Slide

Change to the next slide

▶ Click the Next Slide button to advance to slide 9.

Editing a Freeform Object

You can edit a freeform object by moving, adding, or deleting any of its points. A freeform object appears to include curved lines; however, these lines are only a series of short straight lines connected to one another.

Adjust a vertex

1 Double-click the freeform line.

Your presentation window should look similar to the following illustration:

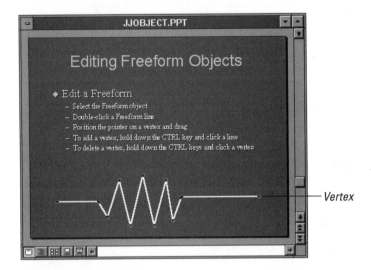

You're now in edit mode. In edit mode all the freeform points, called *vertices*, appear. Now you can edit the freeform object by moving vertices, adding vertices, or deleting vertices.

2 Position the pointer (which changes to a cross cursor) over the left vertex and drag to a new position on the slide.

As you drag the vertex, a dotted outline appears to show you how the vertex will look when you release the mouse button.

Add a vertex

▶ Hold down the CTRL key and click between the first two vertices on the line.

When you hold down the CTRL key with the pointer over a freeform line, the pointer changes to a cross with a box in the middle.

Subtract a vertex

▶ Hold down the CTRL key and click the vertex you just added to the freeform.

When you hold down the CTRL key with the pointer over a vertex, the cross changes to an "X." The vertex you added in the last step is deleted.

Next Slide

Change to the next slide

▶   Click the Next Slide button to advance to slide 10.

Rotating and Flipping Objects

Rotate Right

1   Click the edge of the "Text Rotates" object to select it.

2   On the Drawing+ Toolbar, click the Rotate Right button.

The object rotates to the right.

Note   Patterns, shadows, and bitmaps don't rotate or flip.

Your presentation window should look similar to the following illustration:

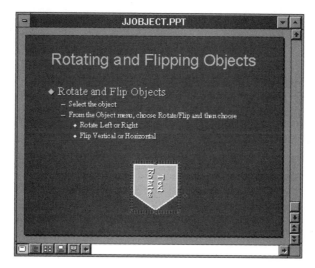

Free Rotate Tool

3   On the Drawing Toolbar, click the Free Rotate Tool button.

The cursor changes to a circular arrow.

4   Move the cursor (which changes to four diagonal arrows) over one of the object handles.

5   Drag to rotate the object.

The object rotates freely to any angle.

6   Click a blank area of the slide to turn off the Free Rotate tool.

Print the quick-reference notebook presentation

*For information
on printing a
presentation, see
Lesson 13.*

1   From the File menu, choose Print (CTRL+P).

The Print dialog box appears.

2   Click the drop-down arrow next to Print What.

3   Select Handouts (2 slides per page) from the drop-down list.

4   Click the OK button.

A dialog box appears, giving your printing status.

Save the presentation

Save

▶   On the Standard Toolbar, click the Save button.

No dialog box appears because the presentation already has a name. The current information in your presentation is saved with the same name.

One Step Further

You have learned to select and deselect objects; draw and modify objects; draw arcs and freeforms; and align, group, upgroup, rotate, and flip objects. If you would like to practice these and other basic skills in your practice presentation, try the following:

▶   Change the fill of an object to shaded.

▶   Draw lines, change line styles, and add arrowheads.

▶   Copy and move an object using the CTRL key and Duplicate command.

▶   Group, ungroup, and regroup different types of objects.

▶   Align objects with the different vertical and horizontal alignment types.

▶   Draw and edit arcs and freeform objects.

If You Want to Continue to the Next Lesson

1   From the File menu, choose Close (CTRL+W).

2   If a dialog box appears asking whether you want to save the changes made to the presentation, click the No button. You do not need to save the changes you made to the presentation after you printed it.

Choosing this command closes the active presentation; it does not exit PowerPoint.

If You Want to Quit PowerPoint for Now

1   From the File menu, choose Exit (CTRL+Q).

2   If a dialog box appears asking whether you want to save changes to the presentation, click the No button.

Lesson Summary

To	Do this	Button
Select an object	Click the Selection Tool button. Position the cursor on the object and click.	
Deselect an object	Click the Selection Tool button.	
Draw an object	On the Drawing Toolbar or the AutoShapes Toolbar, click a drawing tool and drag to create an object.	
Resize an object	Select the object. Drag a resize handle.	
View another toolbar	From the View menu, choose Toolbars. Click the toolbar's check box.	
Change an object's shape	Select the object. From the Object menu, choose AutoShape and select a shape.	
Change a line style	On the Drawing+ Toolbar, click the Line Style button. Choose a line style.	
Group or ungroup objects	Select the objects. On the Drawing+ Toolbar, click the Group or Ungroup button.	
Align objects	Select the objects. From the Format menu, choose Alignment, and then choose an alignment, or choose the Guides command and drag the objects to a guide.	
Draw an arc	On the Drawing Toolbar, click the Arc Tool button and drag.	
Edit an arc	Double-click the arc line. Drag a control handle.	
Draw a freeform	On the Drawing Toolbar, click the Freeform Tool button. Click to draw straight lines, or drag to draw freehand.	
Edit a freeform	Double-click a freeform line. Drag vertices.	
Rotate and flip an object	Select the object. On the Drawing+ Toolbar, click one of the Rotate and Flip buttons.	

For on-line information about	From the PowerPoint Help menu, choose Contents, select "Using PowerPoint," and then
Selecting objects	Select the topic "Working with PowerPoint Objects" and click a title under "How to Select and Group Objects."
Drawing in PowerPoint	Select the topic "Adding Visuals to Slides" and click a title under "Drawing Objects in PowerPoint," "How to Draw AutoShapes," or "Drawing Lines, Arcs, and Freeforms."
Formatting objects	Select the topic "Working with PowerPoint Objects" and click a title under "How to Enhance Objects."
Modifying objects	Select the topic "Working with PowerPoint Objects" and click a title under "How to Move and Align Objects," "How to Stack Objects," or "How to Rotate and Flip Objects."

For more information on	See the *Microsoft PowerPoint User's Guide*
Working with objects	Chapter 3, "Working with PowerPoint Objects"

Preview of the Next Lesson

In the next lesson, you'll change the Slide Master, change bullets, work with the ruler and tabs, apply a template, and change PowerPoint defaults. By the end of the lesson, you'll have produced another presentation for your quick-reference notebook.

Changing Masters and Applying Templates

PowerPoint uses masters to help create professional looking slides, audience handouts, and speaker's notes pages. A master is a set of formatting characteristics, graphics, and text placement information that is consistent throughout the entire presentation. Items from a master can be set individually to apply to any or all slides, handout pages, or speaker's notes pages. A template is a presentation that has a set of color and text characteristics that can be "applied" to your presentation. PowerPoint comes with more than 160 templates that are professionally designed to work well in different output formats: black and white overheads, color overheads, or color 35mm slides and on-screen presentations.

In this lesson, you'll learn how to format the master title and master text, add background objects to masters, add page number objects to masters, apply a PowerPoint template, and change default settings. At the end of the lesson, your presentation will consist of the following slides:

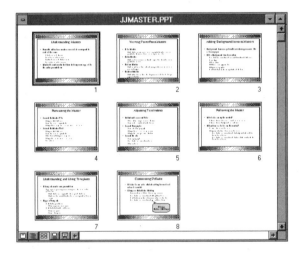

You will learn how to:

- Understand and view a master
- Add background items to a master
- Format a master title and master text
- Adjust master text indents
- Apply a template
- Customize the default settings

Estimated lesson time: 25 minutes

Open a presentation

If you haven't already started PowerPoint, do so now. For instructions about starting PowerPoint, see "Getting Ready," earlier in this book.

Open

1   On the Standard Toolbar, click the Open button or select Open an Existing Presentation from the Startup dialog box and click OK.

2   In the Directories box, ensure that the PRACTICE directory is open. If it is not, select the drive where the Step by Step practice files are stored and open the appropriate directories to find the PRACTICE directory.

For information about opening a sample presentation, see Lesson 2.

3   In the list of file names, click LESSON06.PPT.

If you do not see LESSON06.PPT in the list of file names, check to be sure the correct drive and directory are selected. If you need help, see "Getting Ready."

4   Click the OK button.

Your presentation opens to the following slide:

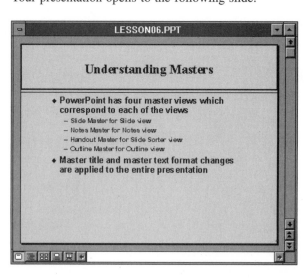

Save the presentation with a new name

Give the presentation a new name so that the changes you make in this lesson do not overwrite the original presentation.

1   From the File menu, choose Save As.

2   In the File Name box, type y*our initials***master**

For example, if your initials are J. J., type **jjmaster**

3   Click the OK button.

The Summary Info dialog box appears. If you would like, type in the summary information. Press TAB to move between fields.

4   Click the OK button.

Preview the lesson

The presentation for this lesson contains reference information about PowerPoint masters and templates. To preview the information in this lesson, click the Slide Show button and view the on-screen presentation.

Slide Show

1   Click the Slide Show button.

PowerPoint displays the first slide in the presentation.

2   Click to advance to the next slide.

3   Click once for each slide to advance through the rest of the presentation.

After the last slide in the presentation, PowerPoint returns to the first slide.

Understanding PowerPoint Masters

Each PowerPoint view has a corresponding master—Slide Master for Slide view, Notes Master for Notes Pages view, Handout Master for Slide Sorter view, and Outline Master for Outline view. When you add an object or change the format of text on a master, the changes are made in that corresponding view. The Slide Master, for example, controls the format of the title and main text objects for each slide in your presentation. Adding graphics and label text to a Slide Master places them on every slide.

View the Slide Master

1   From the View menu, choose Master and then choose Slide Master.

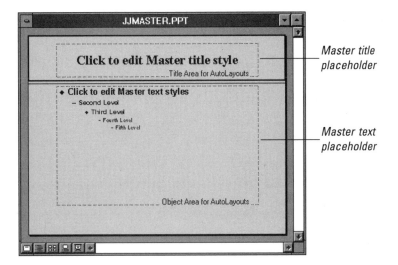

The Slide Master contains a master title placeholder called the *Title Area for AutoLayouts* and a master text placeholder called the *Object Area for AutoLayouts*. The master title and master text control the text format for your slide presentation. For example, when you change the master title text format to italic, the title on each slide changes to italic to follow the master. In PowerPoint, you're always in control; if you don't want to follow the Slide Master for any reason, you have the choice to turn it off.

Slide View

2   Click the Slide View button.

PowerPoint returns you to the first slide.

Change to the next slide

Next Slide

1   Click the Next Slide button to advance to slide 2.

Take a moment to read about the PowerPoint masters.

2   Click the Next Slide button to advance to slide 3.

Adding Background Items to Masters

You can add background items such as shapes, text headings, the date and time, page numbers, pictures, and graphics to all of the master views. Master background items appear in the corresponding views.

Add a text label to the Slide Master

Slide View

1   Hold down the SHIFT key and click the Slide View button.

The Slide Master view appears. Holding down the SHIFT key and clicking a view button switches you to the corresponding master view. The Slide View button becomes the Slide Master button.

Text Tool

2   On the Drawing Toolbar, click the Text Tool button.

Click here to type text

3   Position the text cursor in a blank below the master text and click.

4   Type **PowerPoint 4.0**

5   Position your pointer over the slanted-line selection box and click.

6   Drag the text object to the lower left corner of the Slide Master.

Add a page number

1   Click in a blank area to deselect the text object.

2   From the Insert menu, choose Page Number.

A small text object displaying two pound symbols (##) appears in the middle of your screen.

Note   If a text object is selected when you insert the page number, the page number will be positioned at the end of the text in that object.

PowerPoint replaces this text object with the page number when your presentation is printed or displayed in a slide show. You can also add the time or date to your presentation by choosing the Time or Date command from the Insert menu. The date, page numbers, and time do not show up on individual slides, but they do appear on the printed slide.

3   Drag the page number object to the lower right corner of the Slide Master.

Your presentation window should look similar to the following illustration:

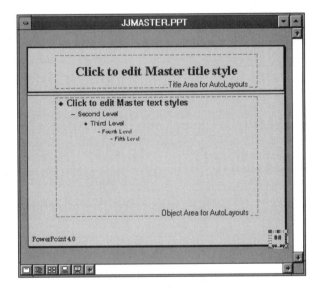

Add a header to the Outline Master

1   From the View menu, choose Master and then choose Outline Master.

The Outline Master appears with a placeholder (a dotted rectangle) in the middle of the presentation window. This placeholder lets you know where your outline text will be placed on the page when you print the outline. You can add background items outside the Outline Master placeholder without interfering with the outline text.

Text Tool

2   On the Drawing Toolbar, click the Text Tool button.

3   Place your text cursor just above the left corner of the Outline Master placeholder and click to place the insertion point.

4   Type **PowerPoint 4.0 Master and Template Outline**

5   Click outside the selection to deselect the text object.

Your presentation window should look similar to the following illustration:

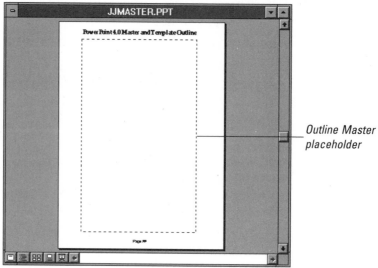

Outline Master placeholder

Note   Both the Outline Master and the Handout Master display placeholders (dotted lines) that indicate the text borders for those views. **Do not** place background items over or within the placeholder lines because the background items will interfere with the printed outline or handout.

Slide View

6   Click the Slide View button.

PowerPoint switches to Slide view.

Next Slide

Change to the next slide

▶   Click the Next Slide button to advance to slide 4.

Notice that the changes to text and background items you made to the Slide Master appear on this slide.

Formatting the Master Title and Master Text

Every PowerPoint presentation has a Slide Master that contains a master title placeholder and a master text placeholder. Formatting these placeholders in the Slide Master view provides consistency to your presentation. The master title placeholder and master text placeholder determine the style and placement of your slides' title and main text objects.

Format master text

Slide View

1   Hold down the SHIFT key and click the Slide View button.

PowerPoint switches to the Slide Master.

2   Hold down the SHIFT key and click the master title placeholder.

The master title placeholder is selected, showing the font size as 36 point.

Font Size

3   On the Formatting Toolbar, double-click the Font Size field, type **40**, and press ENTER.

Double-click here to change the font size

4   In the master text placeholder, position the I-beam cursor to the right of the word "styles" and drag left to select the line.

Font

5   On the Formatting Toolbar, click the Font drop-down arrow, and select Book Antiqua.

Italic

6   On the Formatting Toolbar, click the Italic button.

7   Click outside the master text placeholder in a blank area to deselect it.

Your Slide Master should look similar to the following illustration:

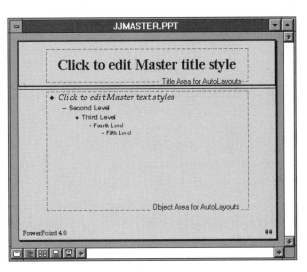

Slide View

8   Click the Slide View button.

The main text at the first level changes to Book Antiqua throughout the presentation.

Your presentation window should look similar to the following illustration:

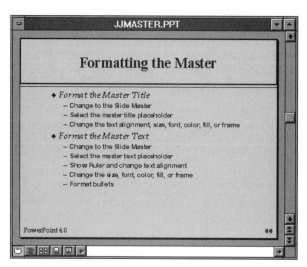

Format master bullets

PowerPoint allows you to customize the bullets in your presentation for individual paragraphs or entire objects.

Slide View

1 Hold down the SHIFT key and click the Slide View button.

The Slide Master appears.

2 Position the pointer anywhere on the first line of text titled "Click to edit Master text styles" in the master text placeholder.

3 Click to place the insertion point on the line.

4 From the Format menu, chose Bullet.

The Bullet dialog box appears, showing the current bullet symbol selected. You can change the symbol font in the Bullets From drop-down list, adjust the font size percentage in the Size box, or choose a different bullet color in the Special Color drop-down list.

5 Select the bold right arrow from the dialog box.

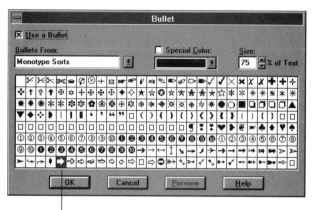

Click the bold right arrow here

6   Click the OK button.

The bullet you selected appears in the first line of text.

Slide View

7   Click the Slide View button.

PowerPoint returns to slide 4 and shows the bullet change.

Change to the next slide

Next Slide

▶   Click the Next Slide button to advance to slide 5.

Adjusting Master Text Indents

PowerPoint uses indent markers to control the distance between bullets and text levels. To work with indented text and bullets, select a text object and show its ruler to make adjustments. Adjusting indents in PowerPoint works the same way it does in Microsoft Word for Windows.

Displaying the Ruler

Slide View

1   Hold down the SHIFT key and click the Slide View button.

The Slide Master appears.

2   Position the pointer anywhere on the first line of text titled "Click to edit Master text styles" in the master text placeholder and click to place the insertion point.

3   From the View menu, choose Ruler.

Your presentation window should look similar to the following illustration:

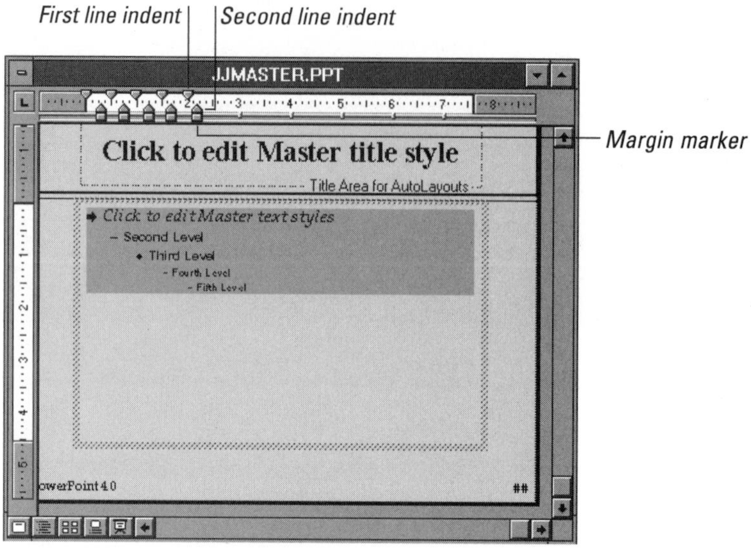

First line indent   *Second line indent*

Margin marker

Setting Indent Markers

The indent markers on the ruler control the five indent levels of the master text object. Each indent level consists of two indent markers (or triangles) and a margin marker (or small box). The upper triangle controls only the first line of the paragraph; the bottom triangle controls the left edge of the paragraph text. Each indent level is set so that the first line extends to the left of the paragraph, with the rest of the paragraph "hanging" below it. This indent setting is called a *hanging indent*.

Adjust indent markers

1   Move your pointer over the bottom triangle of the first indent level.

2   Drag the bottom triangle to the left margin of the ruler.

    When you release the mouse button, the text for the first indent level moves next to the bullet on the left margin.

Your ruler and master text object should look similar to the following illustration:

Drag the bottom triangle to the left margin

Adjust the margin level

1 Slowly drag the margin marker of the first indent level to the 0.5 inch mark on the ruler.

Note If you drag an indent level or margin marker into another indent level, the first indent level (or marker) will push the second indent level until you release the mouse button. To move an indent marker back to its original position, drag the indent level's margin marker or click the Undo button.

Your presentation should look similar to the following illustration:

Drag the margin marker to this position

Moving the first indent marker repositions the left margin of the master text object to the 0.5 inch mark. (Notice the first text level in the master text object.)

TROUBLESHOOTING: **If your ruler looks different** If the ruler on your screen looks different from the one in the above illustration, you might not have moved the indent margin marker. If the indent markers are not aligned over one another, drag one of the markers back to the other.

2   Drag the upper triangle of the first indent marker to the left edge of the ruler.

The first indent level of your ruler is formatted again as a hanging indent.

Your presentation window should look similar to the following illustration:

Drag the upper triangle back to this position

3   In a blank area of the Slide Master, click the right mouse button and then choose Ruler.

The rulers turns off.

4   From the View menu, choose Slides.

PowerPoint returns you to slide 5.

Next Slide

Change to the next slide

▶   Click the Next Slide button to advance to slide 6.

Following the Master

In PowerPoint, you have control of the Master views. Each slide can be individually set to follow the master by clicking the Follow Master button. The Follow Master feature controls the slide color scheme, the slide background, and the display of slide objects from the Slide Master. If you make changes to a slide color scheme or slide background and then decide you don't want the changes, you can set the slide to follow the master.

Change color and shading to follow a master

1   From the Format menu, choose Slide Background.

The Slide Background dialog box appears. The shaded style is set to vertical and the variant is set to the upper right shaded display. Since the current shaded style doesn't match the slide master, the Follow Master button is available.

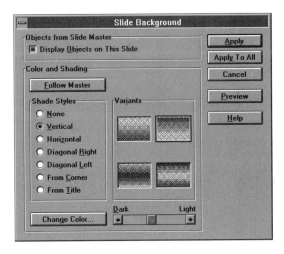

2   Click the Follow Master button.

The Follow Master button is grayed out and the shaded style and variant from the Slide Master are set.

3   Click the Apply button.

The Slide Master background shading is applied to the current slide.

Change background items to follow a master

In PowerPoint, you have the option to display objects from the Slide Master on each slide in your presentation.

1   In a blank area of the slide, click the right mouse button, and choose Slide Background.

2   Click the Display Objects On This Slide check box.

The Display Objects On This Slide option is turned on.

3   Click the Apply button.

All the background items, the PowerPoint 4.0 label, and the page number appear on the slide.

Your presentation window should look similar to the following illustration:

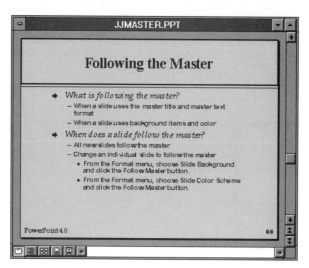

Apply a slide layout

If you make changes to items on a slide and then decide you want the original slide master style back or a different slide layout, you can reapply the slide master layout to that slide using the Slide Layout command. You can also change the current layout of a slide by selecting a new layout from the Slide Layout dialog box.

1 Drag the title object titled "Following the Master" below the main text.

Your presentation window should look similar to the following illustration:

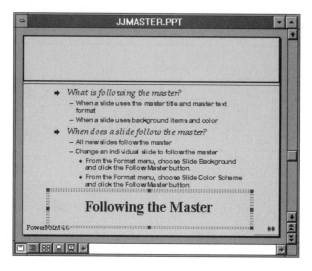

Layout

2   Click the Layout button.

The Slide Layout dialog box appears with the current master style selected.

3   Click the Reapply button.

PowerPoint uses the slide layout to reposition the title object to its original position on the slide.

Next Slide

Change to the next slide

▶   Click the Next Slide button to advance to slide 7.

Understanding and Applying Templates

A template can be any PowerPoint presentation. Applying a template to another presentation copies all the slide, notes, handout, and outline master information to the presentation. A template can be applied to another presentation at any time in the development process, which retroactively applies the master settings to your presentation. You can apply as many templates as you like until you get the one you like the best.

Apply a template

Template

1   Click the Template button.

The Presentation Template dialog box appears.

2   In the Directories box, ensure that the PRACTICE directory is open. If it is not, select the drive where the Step by Step practice files are stored and open the appropriate directories.

3   In the list of file names, select TEMPLT06.PPT.

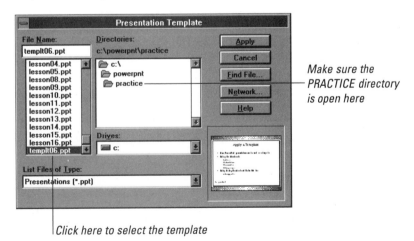

Make sure the PRACTICE directory is open here

Click here to select the template

4 Click the Apply button.

The master information from the Slide, Notes, Handout, and Outline Masters of the template, TEMPLT06.PPT, is applied, or copied, to the masters in your presentation. The text style and format, color scheme, and background items change to match the template. Your content remains the same.

Your presentation window should look similar to the following illustration:

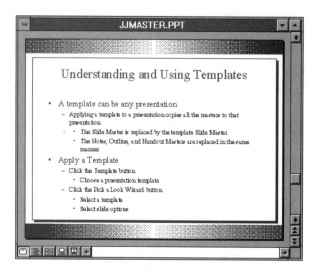

Next Slide

Change to the next slide

▶ Click the Next Slide button to advance to slide 8.

Customizing PowerPoint Defaults

Default settings are the initial attributes that are applied when creating an object. Some examples of PowerPoint default settings include: fill color, shadow, line style, and font style. To find out the current default settings for your presentation, draw an object or create a text object and check the object's attributes.

Change font defaults

1 Position the I-beam over the text "Change Default Settings" in the voice bubble object and click to place the insertion point.

2 From the Format menu, choose Pick Up Text Style.

The font type, style, and size are copied. To change the default text styles, you need to apply the styles to the presentation text defaults.

3 In a blank area, click the right mouse button and choose Apply To Text Defaults.

The text styles are applied to the text defaults.

Text Tool

4 On the Drawing Toolbar, click the Text Tool button.

5 Position the text cursor in the middle of the blank area below the main text and click.

6 Type **Book Antiqua is now the default font**

The font color, shading, type, and size are changed to match the text in the voice bubble object.

7 Select the text object and press the DELETE key.

Change object attribute defaults

Ellipse Tool

1 On the Drawing Toolbar, click the Ellipse Tool button.

2 Position the cross hairs cursor in a blank area below the main text and drag an ellipse.

Notice the current default fill color, shadow, and line style settings.

3 Press the DELETE key.

4 Hold down the SHIFT key and click the voice bubble object.

5 From the Format menu, choose Pick Up Object Style.

The object line style, fill color, shadow color, shadow offset, and text style are copied. To change the default attribute settings, you need to apply the copied object styles to the presentation object defaults.

6 In a blank area of the slide, click the right mouse button and choose Apply To Object Defaults.

Ellipse Tool

7 On the Drawing Toolbar, click the Ellipse Tool button.

8 Position the cross hairs cursor in a blank area below the main text and drag an ellipse.

Because you copied the voice bubble object's styles to the object defaults, the ellipse object has the same attributes as the voice bubble object.

Print the quick-reference notebook presentation

For information on printing a presentation, see Lesson 13.

1 From the File menu, choose Print (CTRL+P).

The Print dialog box appears.

2 Click the drop-down arrow next to Print What.

3 Select Handouts (2 slides per page) from the drop-down list.

4 Click the OK button.

A dialog box appears, giving your printing status.

Save the presentation

Save

▶ On the Standard Toolbar, click the Save button.

No dialog box appears because the presentation already has a name. The current information in your presentation is saved with the same name.

One Step Further

You have learned how to switch to a master, change the master title and master text of your presentation, change bullets, adjust margin indents, follow a master, customize PowerPoint defaults, and apply a template. If you would like to practice these and other basic skills in your practice presentation, try the following:

▶   Change to Notes, Handout, and Outline Master views and add text.

▶   On the Slide Master, change Master text indents and bullets and see how they affect your presentation.

▶   Change Follow Master settings and change your Slide Master to see how they affect your presentation.

▶   Apply other presentations as a template.

▶   Change other defaults and see how they change your presentation.

If You Want to Continue to the Next Lesson

1   From the File menu, choose Close (CTRL+W).

2   If a dialog box appears asking whether you want to save the changes to your presentation, click the No button. You do not need to save the changes you made to the presentation after you printed it.

Choosing this command closes the active presentation; it does not exit PowerPoint.

If You Want to Quit PowerPoint for Now

1   From the File menu, choose Exit (CTRL+Q).

2   If a dialog box appears asking whether you want to save changes to the presentation, click the No button.

Lesson Summary

To	Do this	Button
Switch to Master views	From the View menu, choose Master, and then choose the desired view from the menu or hold down the SHIFT key and click the desired View button.	▢
Add background items to a master	Switch to a master view and add items to the master.	▢
Add the time, date, and page number	From the Insert menu, choose the desired menu item.	▦ ◷ ▦
Format the master title or master text	Select the master title or master text and choose the desired formatting effects.	

To	Do this	Button
Display the text object ruler	From the View menu, choose Ruler or click the right mouse button and choose Ruler from the Shortcut menu.	
Set the indent marker for the first line of text	From the View menu, choose Ruler. Drag the upper triangle.	
Set the indent marker for a paragraph other than the first line of text	From the View menu, choose Ruler. Drag the bottom triangle.	
Adjust a paragraph margin	From the View menu, choose Ruler. Drag the indent margin marker.	
Create a hanging indent	From the View menu, choose Ruler. Position the upper triangle to the left of the bottom triangle.	
Change the bullet format	Click the I-beam cursor in a line of text and choose Bullet from the Format menu.	
Follow the master	From the Format menu, choose Slide Background. Click the Follow Master button.	
Reapply a slide layout	Move to the slide. Click the Layout button, select a layout, and click the Reapply button.	Layout...
Apply a template	Click the Template button. Select the directory that contains the template you want to use, and select the template file. Click the Apply button.	Template...
Customize default settings	Select an object with the default settings you want. From the Format menu, choose Pick Up Object or Text Style. Deselect the object. From the Format menu, choose Apply to Object or Text Defaults.	

For on-line information about	**From the PowerPoint Help menu, choose Contents, select "Using PowerPoint," and then**
Working with the slide master	Select the topic "Creating Presentations and Slides" and click a title under "How to Work with the Slide Master."
Applying a template	Select the topic "Creating Presentations and Slides" and click the title "Applying a Template."
Changing the master title and master text formats	Select the topic "Putting Text on Slides" and click a title under "How to Format Paragraphs."

For more information on	**See the *Microsoft PowerPoint User's Guide***
Masters and templates	Chapter 2, "Creating Presentations and Slides"
Working with slide master text	Chapter 4, "Putting Text on Slides"

Preview of the Next Lesson

In the next lesson, you'll change a color scheme, change colors, and add colors to menus. By the end of the lesson, you'll have produced another presentation for your quick-reference notebook.

Using a Color Scheme

PowerPoint color schemes are sets of professionally balanced colors designed to be used as the primary colors in your slide presentations. A color scheme consists of eight labeled colors: Background, Text and Lines, Shadows, Title Text, Fills, and three Accent colors. Along with the basic eight basic colors are what PowerPoint calls "Other Colors." Other colors will not change when you change a color scheme. You should use one of these colors when the color of an object or picture should never change.

In this lesson, you'll learn how to choose a color scheme, change colors in a color scheme, add a shaded background to a slide, and copy a color scheme to a slide. At the end of the lesson, your presentation will consist of the following slides:

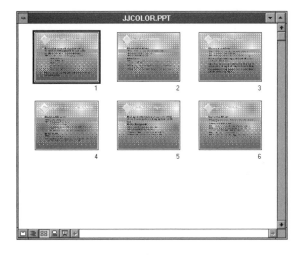

You will learn how to:

- View and choose a color scheme
- Change colors in a color scheme
- Add a shaded background
- Add other colors to the menus
- Copy a color scheme

Estimated lesson time: 20 minutes

Open a presentation

If you haven't already started PowerPoint, do so now. For instructions about starting PowerPoint, see "Getting Ready," earlier in this book.

Open

1 On the Standard Toolbar, click the Open button or select Open an Existing Presentation from the Startup dialog box and click OK.

2 In the Directories box, ensure that the PRACTICE directory is open. If it is not, select the drive where the Step by Step practice files are stored and open the appropriate directories to find the PRACTICE directory.

For information about opening a sample presentation, see Lesson 2.

3 In the list of file names, click LESSON07.PPT.

If you do not see LESSON07.PPT in the list of file names, check to be sure the correct drive and directory are selected. If you need help, see "Getting Ready."

4 Click the OK button.

Your presentation opens to the following slide:

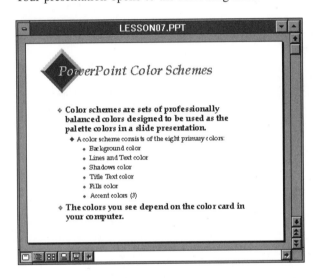

Save the presentation with a new name

Give the presentation a new name so that the changes you make in this lesson do not overwrite the original presentation.

1 From the File menu, choose Save As.

2 In the File Name box, type *your initials***color**

For example, if your initials are J. J., type **jjcolor**

3 Click the OK button.

The Summary Info dialog box appears. If you would like, type in the summary information. Press TAB to move between fields.

4 Click the OK button.

Preview the lesson

The presentation for this lesson contains reference information about PowerPoint colors and color schemes. To preview the information in this lesson, click the Slide Show button and view the on-screen presentation.

Slide Show

1   Click the Slide Show button.

PowerPoint displays the first slide in the presentation.

2   Click to advance to the next slide.

3   Click once for each slide to advance through the rest of the presentation.

After the last slide in the presentation, PowerPoint returns to the first slide.

Next Slide

Change to the next slide

▶   Click the Next Slide button to advance to slide 2.

Choosing a Color Scheme

PowerPoint comes with sets of professionally designed color combinations that look good together. Every presentation, even a new one, has a color scheme. The color scheme could be a set of custom colors (that you've chosen) or the default color scheme. Understanding color schemes helps you create professional-looking presentations.

Look at a color scheme

Next Slide

1   Click the Next Slide button to advance to slide 3.

2   From the Format menu, choose Slide Color Scheme.

The Slide Color Scheme dialog box appears, which shows you the colors currently assigned to each of the color slots for your presentation.

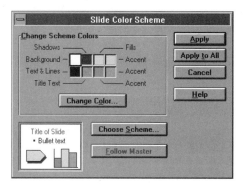

The color scheme for your presentation consists of a Background color, a Text and Lines color, a Shadows color, a Title Text color, a Fills color, and three Accent colors. Each color is placed in a specific slot for a suggested use.

- **Background color**   This color is the canvas color of the slide.
- **Text and Lines color**   This color contrasts with the Background color. It is used for writing text and drawing lines.
- **Shadow color**   This color is generally a darker shade of the background.
- **Title Text color**   This color, like the Text and Lines color, contrasts with the background.
- **Fill color**   This color contrasts with both the Background color and the Text and Lines color.
- **Accent colors**   These colors are designed to work as the colors for other objects.

From the Slide Color Scheme dialog box you can choose a scheme, change a color, shade a background, and apply the color scheme to either the current slide or all the slides in your presentation.

Choose a color scheme

1   Click the Choose Scheme button.

The Choose Scheme dialog box appears.

2   Select the Background color white.

A list of colors for Text & Line appears.

3   Select the Text & Line color blue (the fourth color down in the list).

A visual gallery of four other scheme colors appears.

4   Select the bottom right scheme colors.

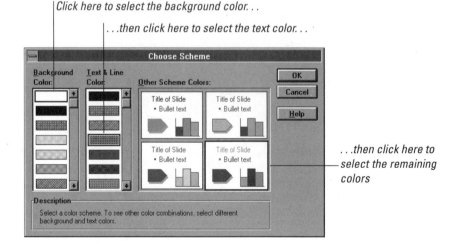

5   Click the OK button.

The Choose Scheme dialog box closes, and the Slide Color Scheme dialog box appears with the new scheme colors.

6   Click the Apply To All button.

The new color scheme is applied to your entire presentation, inclúding your Slide Master.

Next Slide

Change to the next slide

▶   Click the Next Slide button to advance to slide 4.

Changing Colors in a Color Scheme

You can modify any or all the colors within a color scheme to create your own color combinations. Changes made to a color scheme can be applied to the current slide or the entire presentation. As an example, you might want to create a customized color scheme that matches your company's logo. After you have chosen a color scheme you like, you can modify individual colors with the Change Color feature to create the best look for your presentation.

Change colors in a color scheme

1   Position your pointer in a blank area of the slide and click the right mouse button.

A Shortcut menu appears.

2   From the Shortcut menu, choose Slide Color Scheme.

3   In the Change Scheme Colors area, select the red title text color.

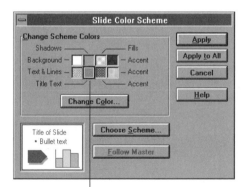

Click here to select the title text color

4   Click the Change Color button.

The Title Text Color dialog box appears.

Tip   You can also double-click the color scheme cell to go directly to the color dialog box.

5   In the Color Palette area, select the maroon color, in the top row of the last column.

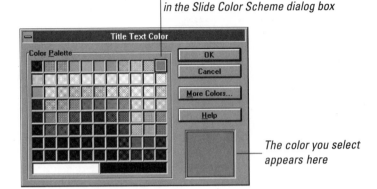

Click here to change the color selected in the Slide Color Scheme dialog box

The color you select appears here

Note   To create a custom color, click the More Colors button in the Title Text Color dialog box and adjust the available options.

---

6   Click the OK button.

The title text color changes to maroon in the color scheme.

7   Click the Apply To All button.

The title text color changes to maroon on every slide in your presentation.

Adding Other Colors to the Menus

For easy color customization, you can add different colors to the toolbar buttons that have color menus—the Text Color and Line Color buttons, for example. Any colors you add to a toolbar button menu remain in the menu even if the color scheme changes.

Add a color to the menus

Text Color

1   On the Formatting Toolbar, click the Text Color button.

Click here to add a color

A drop-down menu appears that looks similar to the following illustration:

2   From the drop-down menu, choose Other Color.

The Other Color dialog box appears.

3   In the Color Palette area, select a color.

4   Click the OK button.

5   On the Formatting Toolbar, click the Text Color button.

The color is added to the drop-down menu.

Text Color

Added colors appear here in
all color drop-down menus

6   Click somewhere on the slide to close the drop-down menu.

Change to the next slide

Next Slide

▶   Click the Next Slide button to advance to slide 5.

Adding a Shaded Background

A shaded background is a visual effect in which a solid color gradually changes from light to dark or dark to light. PowerPoint offers six styles of shaded backgrounds: vertical, horizontal, diagonal right, diagonal left, from corner, and from title. The shading color can be adjusted lighter or darker depending on your needs.

Shade a slide background

1   Position your pointer in a blank area of the slide and click the right mouse button.

2   From the Shortcut menu, choose Slide Background.

The Slide Background dialog box appears.

3   In the Shade Styles area, click the Vertical option button.

Four different vertical shades appear in the Variants area. The upper left variant appears as the default selection.

4   Click the Change Color button.

5   In the Color Palette area, select a light blue color in column 9.

6   Click the OK button.

The color appears in the shade variant boxes.

Click here. . .

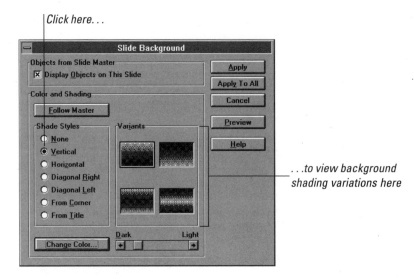

. . .to view background shading variations here

7 In the bottom of the dialog box, click the right scroll arrow four or five times to lighten the shade variants.

8 Click the Apply button.

The new shaded background is applied to the current slide.

Next Slide

Change to the next slide

▶ Click the Next Slide button to advance to slide 6.

Copying a Color Scheme

You can reuse color schemes without having to re-create them. Simply copy or pick up the color scheme from one slide and paste or apply the color scheme to another slide.

Pick up and apply a color scheme

In the Slide Sorter view, the Pick Up Style and Apply Style commands in the Format menu change to Pick Up Color Scheme and Apply Color Scheme. These commands are used to copy a color scheme from one slide and apply it to other selected slides.

Slide Sorter View

1 Click the Slide Sorter View button.

2 Click slide 5 to select it.

3 From the Format menu, choose Pick Up Color Scheme.

The color scheme for slide 5 is picked up and is now ready to be applied to other slides in your presentation or any other open presentation.

Note When you copy a color scheme from one presentation to another, any extra colors on the color scheme menu are not copied.

4 From the Edit menu, choose Select All (CTRL+A).

5 From the Format menu, choose Apply Color Scheme.

The color scheme is applied to all the slides in your presentation.

6 Double-click slide 6.

PowerPoint returns to Slide view.

Print the quick-reference notebook presentation

For information on printing a presentation, see Lesson 13.

1 From the File menu, choose Print (CTRL+P).

The Print dialog box appears.

2 Click the drop-down arrow next to Print What.

3 Select Handouts (2 slides per page) from the drop-down list.

4 Click the OK button.

A dialog box appears, giving your printing status.

Save the presentation

Save

▶ On the Standard Toolbar, click the Save button.

No dialog box appears because the presentation already has a name. The current information in your presentation is saved with the same name.

One Step Further

You have learned to view a color scheme, choose a color scheme, change a color and add other colors to color menus, add a shaded background, and copy a color scheme. If you would like to practice these and other basic skills in your practice presentation, try the following:

▶ Add shaded backgrounds with different shade styles such as Diagonal Right or Diagonal Left, or From Corner or From Title, and change the lightness and darkness of the shade.

▶ Create a custom color and add it to the color menus.

▶ Use the Pick Up Color Scheme command from a different presentation to copy a color scheme, and use the Apply Color Scheme command to paste the color scheme into your presentation.

If You Want to Continue to the Next Lesson

1 From the File menu, choose Close (CTRL+W).

2 If a dialog box appears asking whether you want to save the changes to your presentation, click the No button. You do not need to save the changes you made to the presentation after you printed it.

Choosing this command closes the active presentation; it does not exit PowerPoint.

If You Want to Quit PowerPoint for Now

1   From the File menu, choose Exit (CTRL+Q).

2   If a dialog box appears asking whether you want to save changes to the presentation, click the No button.

Lesson Summary

To	Do this	Button
View a slide color scheme	From the Format menu, choose Slide Color Scheme.	
Choose a slide color scheme	From the Slide Color Scheme dialog box, click the Choose Scheme button. Click a Background color, a Text color, and a set of Other Scheme Colors.	
Change a color in a color scheme	From the Slide Color Scheme dialog box, select a color. Click the Change Color button. Select a new color.	
Add other colors to the menu	On the Formatting Toolbar, click Text Color, and choose Other Color. Select a color. Click the OK button.	
Add a shaded background	From the Format menu, choose Slide Background. Select a Shade Style and Variant.	
Copy a color scheme	From the Slide Sorter view, select a slide with the color scheme you want. From the Format menu, choose Pick Up Color Scheme. Select the slide or slides to apply the color scheme to. From the Format menu, choose Apply Color Scheme.	

For on-line information about	From the PowerPoint Help menu, choose Contents, select "Using PowerPoint," and then
Color schemes	Select the topic "Creating Presentations and Slides" and click a title under "How to Create and Change Color Schemes."

Preview of the Next Lesson

In the next lesson, you'll create and edit a graph, and work with graph data. By the end of the lesson, you'll have produced another presentation for your quick-reference notebook.

4 Adding Graphs and Organizational Charts

Creating and Editing a Graph

To create graphs for your slides, PowerPoint uses an embedded application called Microsoft Graph. Graph uses many of the same features as Microsoft Excel. Adding graphs to a presentation can help communicate your ideas in an effective manner.

A graph is represented by a datasheet and a chart. The datasheet is composed of individual cells that form rows and columns, which in turn make up a group of related data points called a *data series*. The chart is a graphical representation of the information in the data series.

In this lesson, you'll learn how to start Graph from PowerPoint, select individual cells and groups of cells for editing, move through a datasheet, import data from a Microsoft Excel worksheet, enter and edit data in a datasheet, and modify a data series. At the end of the lesson, your presentation will consist of the following slides:

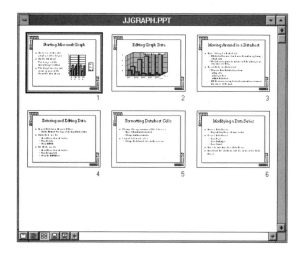

You will learn how to:

- Start Microsoft Graph

- Create and edit a graph

- Select cells in a datasheet

- Import data from Microsoft Excel

- Enter and edit data in a datasheet

- Modify a data series

Estimated lesson time: 25 minutes

Open a presentation

If you haven't already started PowerPoint, do so now. For instructions about starting PowerPoint, see "Getting Ready," earlier in this book.

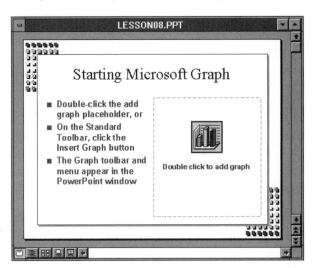

Open

1   On the Standard Toolbar, click the Open button or select Open an Existing Presentation from the Startup dialog box and click OK.

2   In the Directories box, ensure that the PRACTICE directory is open. If it is not, select the drive where the Step by Step practice files are stored and open the appropriate directories to find the PRACTICE directory.

For information about opening a sample presentation, see Lesson 2.

3   In the list of file names, choose LESSON08.PPT.

If you do not see LESSON08.PPT in the list of file names, check to be sure the correct drive and directory are selected. If you need help, see "Getting Ready."

4   Click the OK button.

Your presentation opens to the following slide:

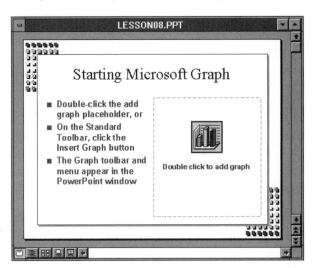

Save the presentation with a new name

Give the presentation a new name so that the changes you make in this lesson do not overwrite the original presentation.

1   From the File menu, choose Save As.

2   In the File Name box, type *your initials***graph**

For example, if your initials are J. J., type **jjgraph**

3   Click the OK button.

The Summary Info dialog box appears. If you would like, type in the summary information. Press TAB to move between fields.

4   Click the OK button.

Preview the lesson

The presentation for this lesson contains reference information about graphing in PowerPoint. To preview the information in this lesson, click the Slide Show button and view the on-screen presentation.

Slide Show

1   Click the Slide Show button.

PowerPoint displays the first slide in the presentation.

2   Click to advance to the next slide.

3   Click once for each slide to advance through the rest of the presentation.

After the last slide in the presentation, PowerPoint returns to the first slide.

Starting Microsoft Graph

For information on linking and embedding , see Lesson 12.

Microsoft Graph is an application that PowerPoint uses to insert a graph in your presentation slide. When you start Microsoft Graph, create a graph, and return to your presentation slide, the graph becomes an *embedded object* in the slide. An embedded object maintains a "link" with its original application for easy editing. You can start Graph by double-clicking a graph placeholder, clicking the Insert Graph button on the Standard Toolbar, or choosing Insert Object from the Edit menu.

Start Graph using a layout

1   Double-click the graph placeholder.

PowerPoint launches Microsoft Graph. The Graph Standard Toolbar and menu appear along with the datasheet and chart.

The datasheet and chart appear with default data and can be modified to meet your specific needs. Changes made to your datasheet appear on the chart.

View Datasheet

2   On the Standard Toolbar, click the View Datasheet button.

The datasheet closes.

Exit Graph

An embedded graph object acts the same as any other PowerPoint object. To exit Graph, simply deselect the graph object.

▶   Position the pointer in a blank area of the presentation window and click.

The PowerPoint toolbars and menu appear. The chart is embedded in the presentation slide after Graph closes.

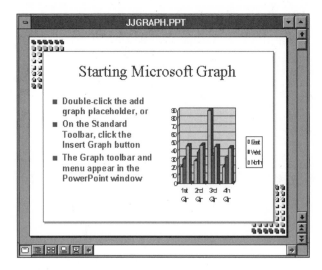

Next Slide

Change to the next slide

▶ Click the Next Slide button to advance to slide 2.

Editing Graph Data

Editing data requires moving through a datasheet and working with individual cells and groups of cells. To view the graph data and the associated chart, you can scroll, resize, and move a datasheet. To make datasheet changes, you can select cells, rows, and columns of data.

Edit a graph

1 Double-click the graph.

The Graph Standard Toolbar and menu appear.

View Datasheet

2 On the Standard Toolbar, click the View Datasheet button.

The datasheet window appears.

Viewing the Datasheet Window

The data entered in the Graph datasheet is plotted on your Graph chart. As you enter data, the datasheet can become large, preventing you from seeing all the data at once. Graph allows you to scroll through the datasheet window to view different areas of the datasheet window.

Use the scroll bars, found on the right and bottom edges of the datasheet window, to move around the datasheet. As you scroll through the datasheet, only the window view changes; an active cell or current selection is not affected by scrolling.

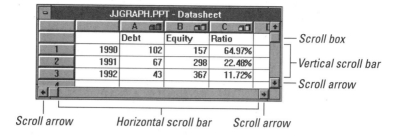

Scroll box — Vertical scroll bar — Scroll arrow — Scroll arrow — Horizontal scroll bar — Scroll arrow

Note   If the Graph default settings have been altered, the Graph datasheet will not look like the above illustration.

Scroll in the datasheet

The following table explains how to scroll in a datasheet to view different cells:

To	Do this
Scroll a row or column at a time	Click a scroll arrow at either end of a scroll bar.
Scroll a window up or down, left or right	Click to either side of the scroll box.
Scroll to a location	Drag the scroll box to the location.

1   Click the scroll arrows to view sections of the datasheet.

2   Drag the scroll boxes to position the datasheet window back to the upper left corner of the datasheet.

Resize the datasheet

You can also resize the datasheet window for more room to work.

1   Position the pointer over the bottom right corner of the datasheet window.

The cursor changes to a two headed diagonal arrow.

2   Drag the lower right corner of the datasheet window to display column D and row 6.

Move the datasheet

As you make changes in the datasheet, the chart also changes. To view changes in the chart, move the datasheet window out of the way.

▶   Drag the datasheet title bar to the top of the presentation window.

Selecting Items in a Datasheet

In a datasheet, using the mouse or keyboard commands, you can select an individual cell, a range of cells, or an entire row or column. When one cell is selected, it is highlighted with a heavy border. When more than one cell is selected, the *active cell* is highlighted with a heavy border and all other selected cells are highlighted in black. To perform most tasks on the datasheet, you must select a specific cell or range of cells.

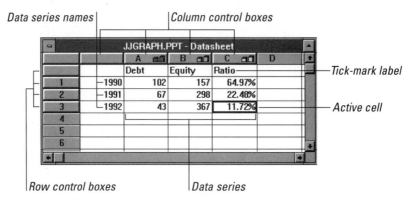

Select a cell

▶ Position the pointer over any cell and click.

A heavy border appears around the cell, indicating that it is selected.

Note   To deselect a cell, a range, a row, a column, or a datasheet, click the pointer away from the selection.

Select a range

Select a range of cells by holding down the SHIFT key and clicking the first and last cells you want to select.

1   Select the cell containing "1990."

2   Hold down the SHIFT key and click the cell containing "367."

A range of cells, 3 x 3, is selected. You can also drag to select a range.

Your datasheet window should look similar to the following illustration:

JJGRAPH.PPT - Datasheet				
	A	B	C	D
	Debt	Equity	Ratio	
1	1990	102	157	64.97%	
2	1991	67	298	22.48%	
3	1992	43	367	11.72%	
4				
5				
6				

Select a row or column

Select a row or column by clicking the row or column control box. Row and column control boxes are the gray boxes located along the left and top edges of the datasheet.

1   Select the row 2 control box to the left of the year "1991."

The entire row is selected.

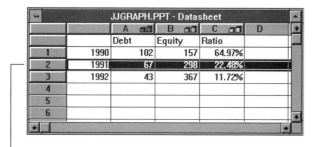

Click the row control box here

2   Select the column B control box above the word "Equity."

The entire column is selected.

Select the entire datasheet

1   Click the upper left corner control box.

The entire datasheet is selected.

2   Click any cell to deselect the datasheet.

Importing Data

In addition to allowing you to type your own data into the datasheet, Graph allows you to import information directly from Microsoft Excel. You can also copy and paste a specified range of data or a complete worksheet into Graph.

Import data from Microsoft Excel

1   Select the blank cell above "1990."

Import Data

2   On the Standard Toolbar, click the Import Data button.

The Import Data dialog box appears. (This dialog box functions just like the Open dialog box.)

3   In the File Name box, select SHEET08.XLS.

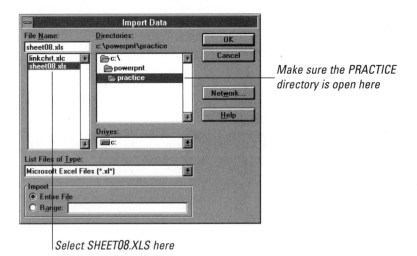

Make sure the PRACTICE directory is open here

Select SHEET08.XLS here

4   Click the OK button.

A Graph dialog box appears, asking to overwrite existing data.

5   Click the OK button.

Your datasheet and chart are updated with the data from your Microsoft Excel worksheet and the existing datasheet is overwritten.

Your datasheet window should look similar to the following illustration:

JJGRAPH.PPT - Datasheet				
	A	B	C	D
	Debt	Equity	Ratio	
1	1990	102	157	64.97%
2	1991	67	298	22.48%
3	1992	43	367	11.72%
4	1993	10	402	1.24%
5				
6				

Changing Datasheet Options

In Graph, you can customize some operations for entering and editing data in the datasheet by changing datasheet option settings.

Change datasheet keyboard options

1   From the Tools menu, choose Options.

The Graph Options dialog box appears with the Datasheet Options tab displayed.

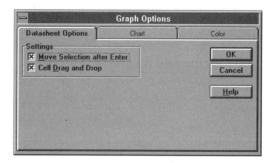

2   In the Settings area, click the Move Selection After Enter check box to turn off the feature.

Now, as you enter data and press the ENTER key, the cell selection will not move.

3   Click the OK button.

Entering and Editing Data

In your datasheet, you'll enter new data and edit existing data that will be used to plot data points on your chart. The chart is updated automatically after the data in the datasheet is entered.

Enter data in the datasheet

1   Select the empty cell below the year "1993."

2   Type **1994** and press ENTER.

Graph places your entry in the cell and activates the data series.

3   Press TAB to move to the next cell (the Debt column).

You can use the ARROW keys to move to an adjacent cell.

4   Type **30** and press TAB.

Graph enters 30 in the datasheet and creates a new column for your graph.

5   Type **200** and press ENTER.

Your datasheet window should look similar to the following illustration:

		A	B	C	D
		Debt	Equity	Ratio	
1	1990	102	157	64.97%	
2	1991	67	298	22.48%	
3	1992	43	367	11.72%	
4	1993	10	402	1.24%	
5	1994	30	200		
6					

JJGRAPH.PPT - Datasheet

Edit data in the datasheet

▶   Type **455** and press ENTER.

Graph replaces the number 200 with the new number.

Formatting a Data Series

In Graph, you can change the format of a number to represent fractions, percentages, monetary currencies, scientific notations, or accounting figures. You can also change the format of the date and time.

Change the font style

1   From the Format menu, choose Font.

The Font dialog box appears.

2   In the Font box, select Times New Roman.

3   Click the OK button.

All of the data in your datasheet changes to the font Times New Roman.

Note   Changing the font characteristics of one cell in your datasheet affects all of the datasheet cells but not the chart text.

Change a number format

1   Select the empty cell below the year "1994."

2   Type **0.0162** and press ENTER.

3   From the Format menu, choose Number.

The Number Format dialog box appears.

4   In the Category box, select Percentage.

The Format Codes list changes to reflect percentage formats.

5   In the Format Codes box, select the format 0.00%.

6   Click the OK button.

The cell format changes from a general format to a percentage format.

Modifying a Data Series

In Graph, you can move and reposition information within the same datasheet to facilitate editing tasks. Graph allows you to copy information to other places in the datasheet. You can also cut information from your datasheet to move it elsewhere.

Move data within the datasheet

1   Select the cell containing 1.62%, if it is not already selected.

2   Position the cursor (which changes to the pointer) over the selection rectangle in the cell.

3   Drag the number to cell C5.

Drag the number from here. . .

		A	B	C	D
		Debt	Equity	Ratio	
1	1990	102	157	64.97%	
2	1991	67	298	22.48%	
3	1992	43	367	11.72%	
4	1993	10	402	1.24%	
5	1994	30	455	1.62%	
6					

JJGRAPH.PPT - Datasheet

. . .to here

Note You can also cut or copy data from a datasheet and paste the information to its new location.

Copy data in the datasheet

1   Select the column A control box above "Debt."

2   On the Standard Toolbar, click the Copy button.

3   Select the empty cell to the right of "Ratio."

4   On the Standard Toolbar, click the Paste button.

Graph duplicates the Debt column in a new column next to the Ratio column.

Clear data from the datasheet

With Graph, you can clear data three ways: clear all data, clear only contents, or clear only formats. When you choose the Clear All command, the data and the format are cleared. The Clear Contents and Clear Formats commands, on the other hand, clear only the content or only the format.

1   With column D selected, choose Clear from the Edit menu, and then choose All.

The data in Column D is cleared.

2   Double-click the column D control box to exclude the column.

Your datasheet window should look similar to the following illustration:

		A	B	C	D
		Debt	Equity	Ratio	
1	1990	102	157	64.97%	
2	1991	67	298	22.48%	
3	1992	43	367	11.72%	
4	1993	10	402	1.24%	
5	1994	30	455	1.62%	
6					

JJGRAPH.PPT - Datasheet

TROUBLESHOOTING: **If you accidentally clear (delete) the correct data**   Immediately select Undo from the Graph Edit menu. The data cleared from your datasheet will be recovered and returned to the datasheet.

Exclude and include data

After entering data in your datasheet, you might want to modify it to produce a better graph. You can exclude and include data by rows and columns, changing the effect of your graph without changing the datasheet information. You can also insert and delete rows and columns to accommodate the information in your datasheet.

1   Select the column C control box above "Ratio."

Copy

Paste

2 From the Data menu, choose Exclude Row/Col.

Graph dims the column heading for "Ratio," indicating the column has been excluded from the datasheet. The data from this column has also been excluded from the chart.

Your datasheet window should look similar to the following illustration:

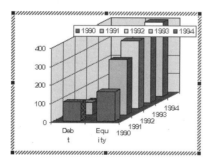

Note An excluded column or row remains excluded until you include the data, import information over the excluded data, or type over the excluded data.

3 Double-click the control box for row 6.

Change a data series view

1 Drag the datasheet title bar to the right side of the window so that you can see the chart in the presentation window.

By Row

2 On the Standard Toolbar, click the By Row button.

The chart view changes from column to row. The datasheet now charts Debt and Equity by year.

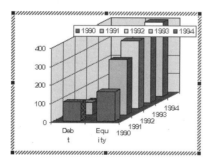

By Column

3 On the Standard Toolbar, click the By Column button.

The datasheet view changes back to column. The data charts the years by Debt and Equity.

4 From the Data menu, choose Include Row/Col.

The Ratio column returns to the datasheet.

Insert columns and rows

Insert a new column to the left of a selected column.

1   Drag the datasheet window back to the middle of your screen.

2   Select the column B control box above "Equity."

3   From the Insert menu, choose Cells.

Graph inserts a new column to the left of the Equity column.

Your datasheet window should look similar to the following illustration:

		A	B	C	D
		Debt		Equity	Ratio
1	1990	102		157	64.97%
2	1991	67		298	22.48%
3	1992	43		367	11.72%
4	1993	10		402	1.24%
5	1994	30		455	1.62%
6					

JJGRAPH.PPT - Datasheet

4   From the Edit menu, choose Delete.

The column created in the previous step is deleted.

Insert and delete a cell

Insert a new cell to the left of a selected cell.

1   Select the cell containing "1990."

2   From the Insert menu, choose Cells.

The Insert dialog box appears.

3   Click the Shift Cells Down option button.

4   Click the OK button.

All the cells in the row shift down when the new cell is inserted.

5   From the Edit menu, choose Delete.

The Delete dialog box appears.

6   Click the Shift Cells Up option button.

7   Click the OK button.

All the cells in the row shift up when the new cell is deleted.

8   Double-click the control box for row 6.

9   On the Standard Toolbar, click the View Datasheet button.

View Datasheet

Exit Graph

▶ Position your pointer in a blank area of the presentation window and click.

The PowerPoint toolbars and menu appear.

Print the quick-reference notebook presentation

For information on printing a presentation, see Lesson 13.

1 From the File menu, choose Print (CTRL+P).

The Print dialog box appears.

2 Click the drop-down arrow next to Print What.

3 Select Handouts (2 slides per page) from the drop-down list.

4 Click the OK button.

A dialog box appears, giving your printing status.

Save the presentation

Save

▶ On the Standard Toolbar, click the Save button.

No dialog box appears because the presentation already has a name. The current information in your presentation is saved with the same name.

One Step Further

You have learned to select and scroll on a datasheet, edit and move data in Graph, import data from a Microsoft Excel worksheet, and modify a data series. If you'd like to practice these and other basic skills in your practice presentation, try the following:

▶ Exclude the Ratio column and select a 3-D Area graph from the Galleries box in the AutoFormat dialog box.

▶ Add additional data series and data points.

▶ Reposition one or more data series and notice how these actions affect the graph.

▶ If you have a copy of Microsoft Excel, import a worksheet and create a chart with the data.

If You Want to Continue to the Next Lesson

1 From the File menu, choose Close (CTRL+W).

2 If a dialog box appears asking whether you want to save the changes to the presentation, click the No button. You do not need to save the changes you made to the presentation after you printed it.

Choosing this command closes the active presentation; it does not exit PowerPoint.

If You Want to Quit PowerPoint for Now

1 From the File menu, choose Exit (CTRL+Q).

2 If a dialog box appears asking whether you want to save changes to the presentation, click the No button.

Lesson Summary

To	Do this	Button
Start Graph using a slide layout	Click the Layout button and select Graph Layout. Double-click the graph placeholder.	
Start Graph using a toolbar button	On the Standard Toolbar, click the Graph Tool button. A full-size graph appears.	
Scroll through a datasheet	Click the datasheet scroll bars.	
Select a cell	Move your pointer to the cell and click.	
Select a cell range	Hold down the SHIFT key and click the cells you want to select, or drag across a group of cells.	
Select a row or column	Move the pointer to the row or column control box and click.	
Select all the cells in the datasheet	Click the upper left corner control box.	
Enter data	Select the cell, type the data, and press ENTER or TAB.	
Edit data	Select the cell and type the new information.	
Move data	Drag the selection rectangle to a new location.	
Import data	On the Standard Toolbar, click the Import Data button.	
Exclude or include data	Select the row or column. From the Data menu, choose Exclude Row/Col or Include Row/Col.	

To	Do this	Button
Insert rows, columns, or cells	Select the cells you want to insert. From the Insert menu, choose Cells. Click the Entire Row, Enitre Column, Shift Cells Right, or Shift Cells Down option button.	
Delete rows, columns, or cells	Select the cells you want to delete. From the Edit menu, choose Delete. Click the Entire Row, Enitre Column, Shift Cells Left, or Shift Cells Up option button.	
Exit Graph	Deselect the graph object.	

For on-line information about	**From the PowerPoint Help menu, choose Contents, select "Using PowerPoint," and then**
Creating and editing a graph	Select the topic "Adding Visuals to Slides" and click the title "Inserting a Graph" or "Editing a Graph."

For on-line information about	**From the Graph Help menu, choose Contents, select "The Datasheet," and then**
Editing Graph data	Select the topic "Working in the Datasheet."
Formatting Graph data	Select the topic "Formatting Data in the Datasheet."

For more information on	**See the *Microsoft PowerPoint User's Guide***
Creating and editing a graph	Chapter 5, "Adding Visuals to Slides"

Preview of the Next Lesson

In the next lesson, you'll learn to change a graph format, add titles and data labels, change the axis scale, and work with the legend. By the end of the lesson, you'll have produced another presentation for your quick-reference notebook.

Formatting a Graph

In Microsoft Graph you can change the appearance of your graphs at any time. Simply double-click the graph you would like to change. You can control the way your graph looks by changing various feature settings such as the chart type, 3-D view, Autoformat, font styles, arrows, and legends.

In this lesson, you'll learn how to edit a graph from PowerPoint, format graph axis scales and data series, change a graph chart type and 3-D view, work with a legend, apply and format arrows, and change graph colors. At the end of the lesson, your presentation will consist of the following slides:

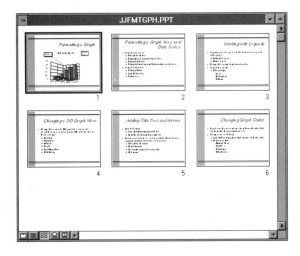

You will learn how to:

- Edit a graph from PowerPoint

- Change axis scales and data series number formats

- Format a data series with a pattern and show data labels

- Format a legend

- Change a graph's 3-D view

- Add title text and an arrow to your graph

- Change graph colors

Estimated lesson time: 35 minutes

Open a presentation

If you haven't already started PowerPoint, do so now. For instructions about starting PowerPoint, see "Getting Ready," earlier in this book.

Open

1   On the Standard Toolbar, click the Open button or select Open an Existing Presentation from the Startup dialog box and click OK.

2   In the Directories box, ensure that the PRACTICE directory is open. If it is not, select the drive where the Step by Step practice files are stored and open the appropriate directories to find the PRACTICE directory.

For information about opening a sample presentation, see Lesson 2.

3   In the list of file names, click LESSON09.PPT.

If you do not see LESSON09.PPT in the list of file names, check to be sure the correct drive and directory are selected. If you need help, see "Getting Ready."

4   Click the OK button.

Your presentation opens to the following slide:

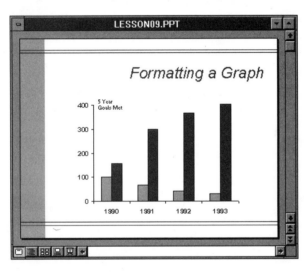

Save the presentation with a new name

Give the presentation a new name so that the changes you make in this lesson do not overwrite the original document.

1   From the File menu, choose Save As.

2   In the File Name box, type *your initials***fmtgph**

For example, if your initials are J. J., type **jjfmtgph**

3   Click the OK button.

The Summary Info dialog box appears. If you would like, type in the summary information. Press TAB to move between fields.

4   Click the OK button.

Preview the lesson

The presentation for this lesson contains reference information about formatting a graph in PowerPoint. To preview the information in this lesson, click the Slide Show button and view the on-screen presentation.

Slide Show

1 Click the Slide Show button.

PowerPoint displays the first slide in the presentation.

2 Click to advance to the next slide.

3 Click once for each slide to advance through the rest of the presentation.

After the last slide in the presentation, PowerPoint returns to the first slide.

Formatting Graph Axes and Data Series

Graph data is plotted on axes based on specified scales. You can format axes independently to achieve desired effects. Two-dimensional (2-D) graphs have two axes: a y-axis and an x-axis. The x-axis plots horizontally, and the y-axis plots vertically. Three-dimensional (3-D) graphs have three axes: an x-axis (category axis), a y-axis (series axis), and a z-axis (value axis).

Format an axis's pattern, scale, and numbers

Graph formats axis scales with different line and tick-mark styles, text orientations, font characteristics, and scale sizes.

1 Double-click the graph.

The Graph toolbar and menus appear.

2 Position the pointer over the vertical axis line (or scale values) and click to select the y-axis.

Edit handles appear on both ends of the axis.

3 From the Format menu, choose Selected Axis.

The Format Axis dialog box appears. In this dialog box, you can customize the axis pattern, scale, font, numbers, and alignment.

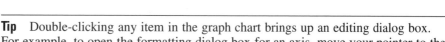
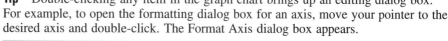

Tip Double-clicking any item in the graph chart brings up an editing dialog box. For example, to open the formatting dialog box for an axis, move your pointer to the desired axis and double-click. The Format Axis dialog box appears.

4 Click the Patterns tab, if it is not already selected.

5 In the Axis area, click the Weight drop-down arrow and select the bottom weight.

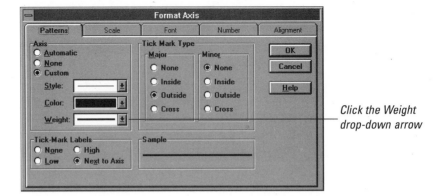

Click the Weight drop-down arrow

6 Click the Scale tab.

The scale settings appear.

7 In the Maximum box, double-click the number 400.

The number 400 is selected.

8 Type **500**

9 Click the Number tab.

The number settings appear.

10 In the Category box, scroll to the bottom of the list and select Currency.

The list of Format Codes changes to reflect currency formats. In the Format Codes box, the currency format $#,##0;($#,##0) is selected by default.

11 Click the OK button.

The y-axis pattern weight changes to a thicker line style, the maximum y-axis scale changes to 500, and the tick-mark label format changes to include dollar signs.

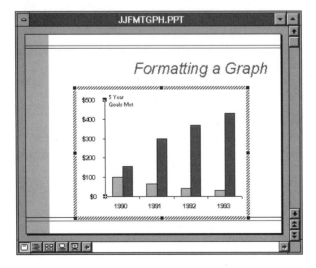

Note   The line weight change appears when you close Graph.

Format a data series pattern and show data labels

With Graph, you can format a data series chart pattern, color, and line style and show the data labels.

1   Double-click the Equity data series (the blue columns).

The Format Data Series dialog box appears. In this dialog box, you can customize the data series patterns, axis, y error bars, and data labels.

2   Click the Patterns tab, if it is not already selected.

The pattern settings appear.

3   In the Area area, click the Pattern drop-down arrow and select a pattern.

The current column pattern appears in the sample area.

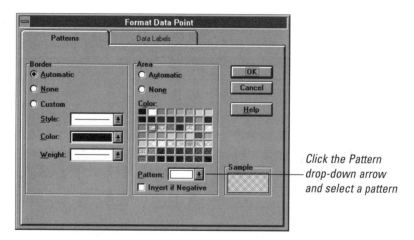

Click the Pattern drop-down arrow and select a pattern

4   Click the Data Labels tab.

The data label settings appear.

5   In the Data Labels area, click the Show Value option button.

6   Click the OK button.

The data series changes from a solid to a pattern, and shows the data values.

7   From the Format menu, choose Selected Data Labels.

The Format Data Labels dialog box appears.

8   Click the Font tab.

9   In the Color box, click the drop-down arrow and select red from the top row.

Tip   You can set an attribute back to its default setting by changing the attribute to Automatic.

10   Click the OK button.

Your graph chart should look similar to the following illustration:

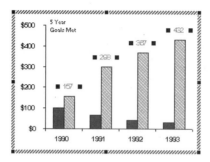

Practice for a moment

▶   Select the other axis and change the pattern, scale, and numbers to match what you have already completed.

▶   Select the other data series and change the pattern, axis, and data labels to match what you have already done.

Formatting a Graph Chart

The Graph gallery allows you to choose the format for your graph. There are 12 graph categories, including two-dimensional graphs and three-dimensional graphs, for a total of 84 different formats.

Change the chart type

Chart Type

1   On the Standard Toolbar, click the Chart Type drop-down arrow.

The Chart Type menu appears, displaying seven two-dimensional and seven three-dimensional graph formats. The Chart Type menu is a "tear-off" menu, meaning you can drag it to another place in the PowerPoint window.

2   Drag the Chart Type menu to the right of the presentation window.

3   Select the Surface Chart (the sixth chart down in the right column).

Add gridlines

Vertical Gridlines

Horizontal Gridlines

1   On the Standard Toolbar, click the Vertical Gridlines button.

Vertical gridlines appear across the back of the graph to give a visual guide of the data values.

2   On the Standard Toolbar, click the Horizontal Gridlines button.

Horizontal gridlines appear across the back of the graph to give a visual guide of the data series.

Your graph chart should look similar to the following illustration:

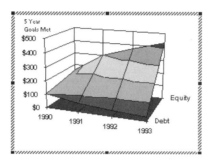

Change the graph format

1   From the Format menu, choose AutoFormat.

The AutoFormat dialog box appears with graph formats and galleries.

2   In the Galleries box, select 3-D Column.

3   Select format number 6, if it is not already selected.

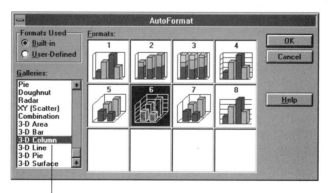

Select 3-D Column here

4   Click the OK button.

Your graph chart should look similar to the following illustration:

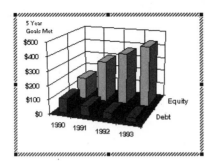

Working with Legends

Legends represent data series markers in a graph using color or patterns. Each color or pattern corresponds to a specific data series name in the graph. Graph legends can be positioned automatically or manually. Legends can be formatted with different colors, font styles, and patterns. Data series names and category names supply text for the legend.

Add a legend

Legend

▶   On the Standard Toolbar, click the Legend button.

Graph places the legend in its default position on the right side of the chart area and resizes the chart to accommodate the legend.

Change the legend's appearance

1   From the Format menu, choose Selected Legend.

The Format Legend dialog box appears.

2   Click the Patterns tab.

The pattern settings appear.

3   In the Border area, click the Shadow check box.

The Sample area shows the results of your changes.

4   Click the Font tab.

The font settings appear.

5   In the Font box, select Book Antiqua.

6   In the Size box, select 16.

7   Click the Placement tab.

The placement settings appear.

8   In the Type area, click the Corner option button.

9   Click the OK button.

Graph applies all three changes (shadow, font, and position) to your legend, as shown in the following illustration:

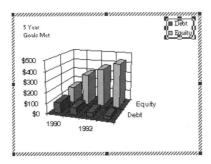

Tip   You can also move the legend manually in the graph window by dragging it.

Changing a Graph's 3-D View

You can give your graph a dynamic look by changing the 3-D view. With Graph, you have control of the elevation, rotation, position, and perspective of a 3-D chart using the 3-D View command.

Format a graph's 3-D view

1   From the Format menu, choose 3-D View.

The Format 3-D View dialog box appears. The Format 3-D View dialog box allows you to change six options:

- **Elevation**   The elevation controls the height at which you view your graph. All 3-D graphs, except for 3-D pie graphs, can range from -90 degrees to +90 degrees.

- **Rotation**   This option controls the rotation of the plot area around the z–axis (vertical axis). You can rotate your graph from 0 degrees to 360 degrees.

- **Perspective**   Use this option to change the distance perspective. More perspective makes data markers at the back of the graph smaller than the markers at the front of the graph.

- **Right Angle Axes**   This option controls the orientation of the axes. Select the check box to show axes at right angles to each other. Clearing the check box shows the axes in perspective.

- **Auto Scaling**   Use this option when changing from a 2-D graph to a 3-D graph. When the Auto Scaling feature is turned off, 3-D graphs sometimes are smaller.

- **Height**   This option controls the height of the z-axis and the walls relative to the length of the x-axis or to the width of the base of the graph. The height is measured based on a percentage of the x-axis length.

2   To view the chart, drag the Format 3-D View title bar to the upper right corner of your screen.

3   Click the down Elevation button until the Elevation box shows -5.

In the Graph dialog box, the view box shows the results of your format changes.

4   Click the Apply button.

The chart changes elevation.

5   Click the left Rotation button until the Rotation box shows 30.

6   Click the down Perspective button until the Perspective box shows 50.

The Format 3-D View dialog box should look similar to the following illustration:

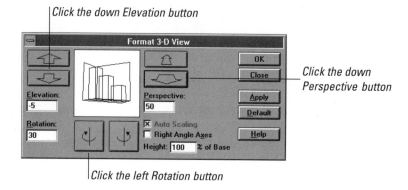

Click the down Elevation button

Click the down Perspective button

Click the left Rotation button

7   Click the OK button.

Your graph chart should look similar to the following illustration:

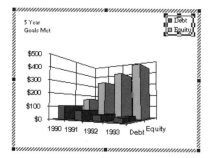

Practice for a moment

▶   From the Format 3-D View dialog box, change the elevation, rotation, and perspective options as desired and look at the results on your graph.

▶   When you are finished, click the Default button to restore the graph's previous settings.

Adding Title Text and Arrows

Graph uses arrows to call out important information or connect unattached text to a specific data marker on the graph chart. Graph arrows are objects that you can modify just as you would any other PowerPoint object.

Add title text

1   From the Insert menu, choose Titles.

The Titles dialog box appears.

2   In the Attach Text To area, click the Chart Title check box.

3   Click the OK button.

4   Position the cursor over the word "Title" and double-click to select the word.

5   Type **Debt and Equity**

Add a border and shadow to text

Drawing

1   On the Standard Toolbar, click the Drawing button.

The Drawing Toolbar appears below the Standard Toolbar. With the Drawing Toolbar, you can add and format shapes on your graph.

2   Position the cursor over the text "5 Year Goals Met" and click to select the object.

Drop Shadow

3   On the Drawing Toolbar, click the Drop Shadow button.

4   Position the cursor in a blank area of the graph and click to deselect the text object.

Add an arrow

Arrow

1   On the Drawing Toolbar, click the Arrow button.

2   Drag the cursor from the right corner of the text box "5 Year Goals Met" to a point near the top of the "1992 Equity" column.

The arrow appears selected with resize handles, indicating that the arrow can be edited.

Your graph chart should look similar to the following illustration:

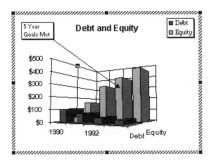

Note Clicking outside the arrow deselects the arrow and simultaneously selects another item in the chart.

Change an arrow

When an arrow is added to a graph, it is selected for editing purposes. Each time you format the arrow later, you must select it by clicking it or using the UP ARROW key or the DOWN ARROW key. The arrow is currently selected.

1 From the Format menu, choose Selected Object.

The Format Object dialog box appears.

Note The available options in the Format Object dialog box change depending on the item selected in your graph.

2 In the Line area, click the Color drop-down arrow and select red from the top row.

3 In the Line area, click the Weight drop-down arrow and select the third weight line.

4 Click the OK button.

Graph changes the arrow color and weight.

Changing Graph Colors

The color scheme of the active PowerPoint presentation determines the Graph color scheme.

Change a chart's fill color

1 From the Tools menu, choose Options.

The Graph Options dialog box appears.

2 Click the Color tab.

The graph color options appear.

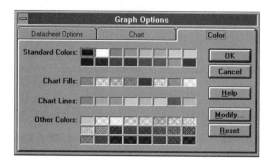

The following table shows how the elements of the presentation color scheme correspond to the elements of the graph color scheme.

PowerPoint Color Scheme	Graph Color Scheme
Background	Second item in the top row of the Standard Colors palette
Lines and Text	First item in the top row of the Standard Colors palette
Fills	First item in the Chart Fills palette
Accents	Second, third, and fourth items in the Chart Fills palette
Shadows	Fifth item in the Chart Fills palette
Title Text	Sixth item in the Chart Fills palette

3   In the Chart Fills palette, click the first color box.

4   Click the Modify button.

The Color Picker dialog box appears.

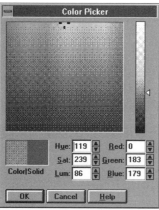

 Tip   Double-clicking any color on the Color tab in the Graph Options dialog box opens the Color Picker dialog box.

5   Move the pointer anywhere in the color box and click.

The color in the Color|Solid box changes as you move the pointer.

6 Click the OK button.

The Color Picker dialog box closes. In the Graph Options dialog box, the chart fill color changes to the color you selected.

7 Click the OK button.

Your presentation window should look similar to the following illustration:

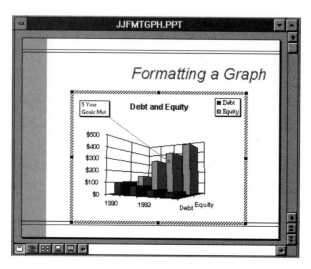

Exit Graph

▶ Position your pointer in a blank area of the presentation window and click.

Print the quick-reference notebook presentation

For information on printing a presentation, see Lesson 13.

1 From the File menu, choose Print (CTRL+P).

The Print dialog box appears.

2 Click the drop-down arrow next to Print What.

3 Select Handouts (2 slides per page) from the drop-down list.

4 Click the OK button.

A dialog box appears, giving your printing status.

Save the presentation

Save

▶ On the Standard Toolbar, click the Save button.

No dialog box appears because the presentation already has a name. The current information in your presentation is saved with the same name.

Register Today!

Return the
Microsoft® PowerPoint® 4 for Windows™
Step by Step
registration card for:

✔ special book upgrade offers

✔ a Microsoft Press® catalog

✔ exclusive offers on specially priced books

U.S. and Canada addresses only. Fill in information below and mail postage-free. Please mail only the bottom half of this page.

1-55615-622-7A   *Microsoft PowerPoint 4 for Windows Step by Step Owner Registration Card*   **WP5**

_____
NAME

_____
COMPANY (if applicable)

_____
ADDRESS

_____

_____
CITY   STATE   ZIP

Your feedback is important to us.

Include your daytime telephone number, and we may call to find out how you use *Microsoft PowerPoint 4 for Windows Step by Step* and what we can do to make future editions even more useful. If we call you, we'll send you a **FREE GIFT** for your time!

(   )
_____
DAYTIME TELEPHONE NUMBER

Lost in the Jungle of Computerland?
Need Some Friendly Help?

Let Microsoft Press Field Guides be your desktop companions. These handy, task-oriented
guidebooks are organized in easy-to-remember sections with rich cross-referencing for easy lookup.
Look for the friendly guy in the pith helmet to show you the way.

Field Guide to Microsoft® Excel 5 for Windows™
Stephen L. Nelson
208 pages   4³/₄ x 8 $9.95 ($12.95 Canada)   ISBN 1-55615-579-4

Field Guide to Microsoft® Word 6 for Windows™
Stephen L. Nelson
208 pages   4³/₄ x 8 $9.95 ($12.95 Canada)   ISBN 1-55615-577-8

Field Guide to Microsoft Access® for Windows™
Stephen L. Nelson
208 pages   4³/₄ x 8 $9.95 ($12.95 Canada)   ISBN 1-55615-581-6
Available April 1994

*Microsoft*Press

Microsoft Press® books are available wherever quality books are sold and through CompuServe's Electronic Mall—GO MSP.
*Call 1-800-MSPRESS for direct ordering information or for placing credit card orders.**
Please refer to BBK when placing your order. Prices subject to change.
*In Canada, contact Macmillan Canada, Attn: Microsoft Press Dept., 164 Commander Blvd., Agincourt, Ontario, Canada M1S 3C7, or call (416) 293-8464, ext. 340.
Outside the U.S. and Canada, write to International Coordinator, Microsoft Press, One Microsoft Way, Redmond, WA 98052-6399.

NO POSTAGE
NECESSARY
IF MAILED
IN THE
UNITED STATES

BUSINESS REPLY MAIL
FIRST-CLASS MAIL   PERMIT NO. 53   BOTHELL, WA

POSTAGE WILL BE PAID BY ADDRESSEE

MICROSOFT PRESS REGISTRATION
MICROSOFT POWERPOINT 4 FOR WINDOWS
  STEP BY STEP
PO BOX 3019
BOTHELL WA   98041-9910

One Step Further

You have learned to edit and format a graph chart, format axes scales, format a legend, add and move arrows, and change graph colors. If you'd like to practice these and other basic skills in your practice presentation, try the following:

▶   Change the Gallery setting to other 3-D graphs and format the 3-D view.

▶   Apply different borders, patterns, and characteristics to your legend.

▶   Add drawing and text objects, and change the object fill, position, and style.

▶   Add arrows to your graph, and change the line pattern and style using the patterns from the Format menu.

▶   Change the format of your axes using the Select Axis command from the Format menu.

If You Want to Continue to the Next Lesson

1   From the File menu, choose Close (CTRL+W).

2   If a dialog box appears asking whether you want to save changes to the presentation, click the No button. You do not need to save the changes you made to the presentation after you printed it.

Choosing this command closes the active presentation; it does not exit PowerPoint.

If You Want to Quit PowerPoint for Now

1   From the File menu, choose Exit (CTRL+Q).

2   If a dialog box appears asking whether you want to save changes to the presentation, click the No button.

Lesson Summary

To	Do this	Button
Edit a graph from PowerPoint	Double-click the graph.	
Change chart formats	On the Standard Toolbar, click the Chart Type drop-down arrow and select a chart type.	
Change the 3-D format of a graph	From the Format menu, choose 3-D View.	
Add or delete a legend	On the Standard Toolbar, click the Legend button.	

To	Do this	Button
Format a legend	Select the legend. From the Format menu, choose Selected Legend.	
Move a legend	Drag the legend for manual placement, or from the Format Legend dialog box, click the Placement tab.	
Change a numeric format	Select an axis. From the Format menu, choose Number.	
Change datasheet font styles	Select an axis. From the Format menu, choose Font.	
Change tick-mark labels	Select an axis. From the Format Legend dialog box, click the Placement tab.	
Change a graph color	From the Tools menu, choose Options and click the Color tab.	
Add an arrow	On the Drawing Toolbar, click the Arrow button. Drag an arrow.	
Exit Graph	Deselect the graph object.	

For on-line information about	From the PowerPoint Help menu, choose Contents, select "Using PowerPoint," and then
Creating and editing a graph	Select the topic "Adding Visuals to Slides" and click the title "Inserting a Graph" or "Editing a Graph."

For on-line information about	From the Graph Help menu, choose Contents, select "Charts," and then
Working with chart types	Select the topic "Working With Chart Types and AutoFormats."
Changing data in a chart	Select the topic "Changing Data in a Chart."
Formatting a chart	Select the topic "Formatting a Chart."

For more information on	See the *Microsoft PowerPoint User's Guide*
Formatting a graph	Chapter 5, "Adding Visuals to Slides"

Preview of the Next Lesson

In the next lesson, you'll create, edit, and format an organizational chart, and work with chart information. At the end of the lesson, you'll have another presentation for your quick-reference notebook.

Creating an Organizational Chart

To create organizational charts for your slides, PowerPoint uses an embedded application called Microsoft Organization Chart. An embedded object maintains a "link" with its original application for easy editing. For more information on linking and embedding, see Lesson 12, "Linking Information with Other Applications."

In this lesson, you'll learn how to start Organization Chart from PowerPoint, create an organizational chart, enter and edit chart text, format chart text and chart boxes, and return to your presentation. At the end of the lesson, your presentation will consist of the following slides:

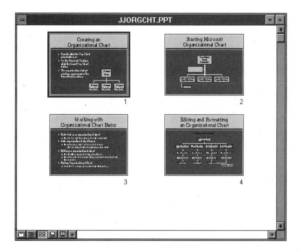

You will learn how to:

- Start Microsoft Organization Chart

- Create an organizational chart

- Enter and edit chart text

- Exit Organization Chart

- Edit an organizational chart from PowerPoint

- Format chart text and chart boxes

Estimated lesson time: 35 minutes

Open a presentation

If you haven't already started PowerPoint, do so now. For instructions about starting PowerPoint, see "Getting Ready," earlier in this book.

Open

1   On the Standard Toolbar, click the Open button or select Open an Existing Presentation from the Startup dialog box and click OK.

2   In the Directories box, ensure that the PRACTICE directory is open. If it is not, select the drive where the Step by Step practice files are stored and open the appropriate directories to find the PRACTICE directory.

For information about opening a sample presentation, see Lesson 2.

3   In the list of file names, click LESSON10.PPT.

If you do not see LESSON10.PPT in the list of file names, check to be sure the correct drive and directory are selected. If you need help, see "Getting Ready."

4   Click the OK button.

Your presentation opens to the following slide:

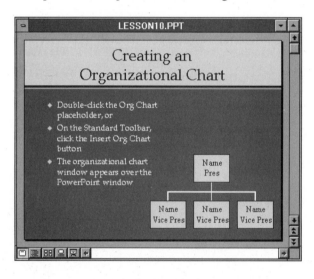

Save the presentation with a new name

Give the presentation a new name so that the changes you make in this lesson do not overwrite the original document.

1   From the File menu, choose Save As.

2   In the File Name box, type *your initials***orgcht**

For example, if your initials are J. J., type **jjorgcht**

3   Click the OK button.

The Summary Info dialog box appears. If you would like, type in the summary information. Press TAB to move between fields.

4   Click the OK button.

Preview the lesson

The presentation for this lesson contains reference information about creating organizational charts in PowerPoint. To preview the information in this lesson, click the Slide Show button and view the on-screen presentation.

Slide Show

1   Click the Slide Show button.

PowerPoint displays the first slide in the presentation.

2   Click to advance to the next slide.

3   Click once for each slide to advance through the rest of the presentation.

After the last slide in the presentation, PowerPoint returns to the first slide.

Starting Microsoft Organization Chart

Microsoft Organization Chart is an application that PowerPoint uses to embed organizational chart objects in your presentation slides. Starting Organization Chart creates an embedded object you can edit at any time. You can start Organization Chart by double-clicking the org chart placeholder, clicking the Insert Org Chart button on the Standard Toolbar, or choosing the Object command from the Insert menu and selecting Microsoft Organization Chart 1.0.

Next Slide

1   Click the Next Slide button to advance to slide 2.

2   Double-click the org chart placeholder.

PowerPoint launches Organization Chart.

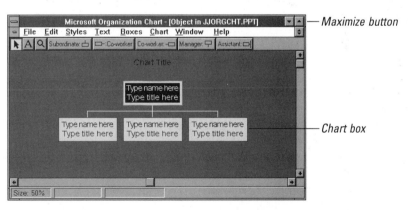

The chart displayed in the organizational chart window represents the chart that will be embedded in your PowerPoint presentation. The chart appears with a template that can be modified to meet your specific needs. The top level chart box appears selected (highlighted in black).

Resize the organizational chart window

▶   Click the organizational chart window's Maximize button.

The entire chart appears in full view.

Working with Organization Chart Basics

The basics of chart design include entering and changing chart text, changing the chart style, and modifying the chart format, shape, and color. Start with the organizational chart template; fill in the sample chart boxes and add new chart boxes to create your own organizational chart.

Select and deselect organizational chart boxes

To enter, edit, or format a chart, you select text chart boxes in the chart template. A text chart box is selected when the box is highlighted. You can select chart boxes by clicking an individual box, dragging a selection rectangle around a set of boxes, or choosing commands from the Select submenu such as All, All Managers, Branch, or Lowest Level.

1   Position the pointer over any of the lower level chart boxes and click to select it.

2   From the Edit menu, choose Select and then choose Lowest Level.

All three chart boxes in the lowest level are selected.

3   Click a blank area of the chart window to deselect the chart boxes.

4   From the Edit menu, choose Select and then choose All Managers.

The top chart box is selected.

Enter information into an organizational chart

1   Position the pointer (which changes to an I-beam) over the top chart box and click to place the insertion point.

A larger text box appears with placeholder text, as shown in the following illustration:

2   Drag to select the first line of the box.

3   Type *your name*.

4   Press TAB and type **CEO**

You can also use the UP ARROW and DOWN ARROW keys to move between lines of placeholder text.

5   Press TAB and type **President** to replace <Comment1>.

6   Click a blank area of the chart window to deselect the chart box.

Your organizational chart should look similar to the following illustration:

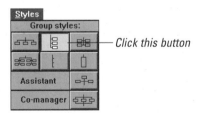

Add and delete chart boxes

Assistant

1   On the Standard Toolbar, click the Assistant button.

2   Position the cursor (which changes to a small chart box) over the top chart box and click to add an assistant chart box.

Co-worker

3   On the Standard Toolbar, click the left Co-worker button.

4   Position the cursor (which changes to a small chart box) over the lower left chart box and click to add a new chart box.

5   Press the DELETE key.

The selected chart box is deleted.

Change the chart style

Subordinate

1   On the Standard Toolbar, click the Subordinate button.

2   Position the cursor (which changes to a small chart box) over the lower left chart box and click to add a new chart box.

3   From the Styles menu, click the middle button in the top row.

The chart box changes to the selected style.

Your organizational chart should look similar to the following illustration:

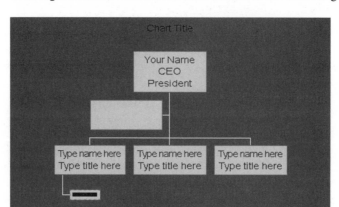

Practice for a moment

▶   Select different chart box types from the toolbar and add new chart boxes.

▶   Select chart boxes and enter your own organizational chart information.

▶   Select different chart boxes and change the chart style.

Exiting Organization Chart

When exiting Organization Chart, you can either update your presentation with changes you've made or ignore the changes. You can also update your presentation with changes you've made to a chart without exiting Organization Chart.

Exit Organization Chart and update your presentation

1   From the File menu, choose Exit and Return to JJORGCHT.PPT.

An Organization Chart dialog box appears.

2   Click the Yes button to update your presentation.

Organization Chart embeds the chart in your slide.

Your presentation window should look similar to the following illustration:

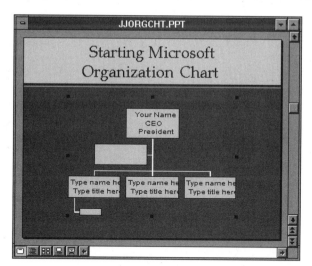

Note   If you wish to update your PowerPoint presentation and continue to work in Organization Chart, choose Update from the File menu. This positions your chart on the slide and lets you make additional changes while still working.

Next Slide

Change to the next slide

▶   Click the Next Slide button to advance to slide 3.

Editing and Rearranging an Organizational Chart

After you have created an organizational chart in your PowerPoint slide, you can edit it much like other embedded objects. You edit the chart from PowerPoint by double-clicking the organizational chart object.

Edit the organizational chart from PowerPoint

Next Slide

1   Click the Next Slide button to advance to slide 4.

2   Double-click the organizational chart object.

The organizational chart window appears.

3   Click the organizational chart window's Maximize button.

The entire chart appears in full view.

Edit the chart's title text

1 Position the pointer (which changes to an I-beam cursor) to the left of the "Chart Title" text.

2 Drag to select the "Chart Title" text.

3 Type **Parnell Aerospace**

Important Before you begin the next section, read all the steps carefully so you understand what happens when you rearrange a chart box.

Rearrange organizational chart boxes

1 Position the pointer over the chart box titled "Brian Gibson."

2 Drag and place the chart box on the chart box titled "Bruce Craig."

While dragging, the cursor changes to a four-headed arrow. When you place one chart box on another, the four-headed arrow changes to one of the following cursors.

- A left arrow when positioned over the left side of the chart box.

- A right arrow when positioned over the right side of the chart box.

- A small chart box when positioned over the bottom of the chart box.

To cancel the operation, release the mouse button when the pointer is not positioned over a chart box.

3 When the four-headed arrow changes to a small chart box, release the mouse button.

The chart box is moved to a new position in the organizational chart.

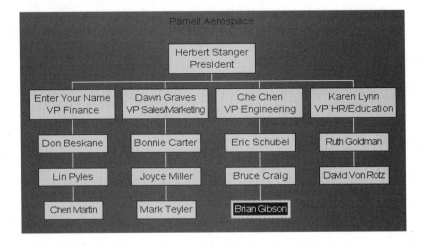

Formatting an Organizational Chart

In Organization Chart, you can format text and individual chart boxes or entire groups of chart boxes. You can format title text, add a shadow to a chart box, change the thickness of connecting lines, and add a text label.

Format the organizational chart title text

1   Drag to select the chart title text "Parnell Aerospace."

2   From the Text menu, choose Font.

   The Font dialog box appears.

3   In the Font Style box, select Bold Italic.

4   In the Size box, select 20 points.

5   Click the OK button.

Format organizational chart boxes

1   From the Edit menu, choose Select Levels.

   The Select Levels dialog box appears.

2   Press TAB and type **2**

3   Click the OK button.

   The top two levels of the chart are selected.

4   From the Boxes menu, choose Box Shadow and then click the bottom button in the first column.

— Click this button

   The top two levels of the chart are formatted with a box shadow.

5   Click a blank area of the chart window to deselect the chart boxes.

Format organizational chart connecting lines

1   From the Edit menu, choose Select and then choose Connecting Lines.

   The chart's connecting lines are selected.

2   From the Boxes menu, choose Line Thickness and then choose 2 pt.

3   Click a blank area in the chart window to deselect the connecting lines.

   The line thickness changes from hairline to 2 point.

Add a connecting line to the organizational chart

Connecting Line

1 From the Chart menu, choose Show Draw Tools (CRTL+D).

The Drawing Tools appear on the right side of the Standard Toolbar.

2 On the Standard Toolbar, click the Connecting Line Tool button.

3 Position the cross hairs cursor over the right side of the chart box titled "Brian Gibson."

4 Drag to the lower middle of the chart box titled "David Von Rotz."

The dotted line connects the right side of the chart box titled "Brian Gibson" to the bottom of the chart box titled "David Von Rotz."

5 Click a blank area of the chart window to deselect the connecting lines.

Add a text label to the organizational chart

Text Tool

1 On the Standard Toolbar, click the Text Tool button.

2 Position the I-beam cursor below the connecting line you just created and click to place the insertion point.

3 Type **15 Employees** and press ENTER.

4 Type *the current date*.

5 Click a blank area of the chart window to deselect the text box.

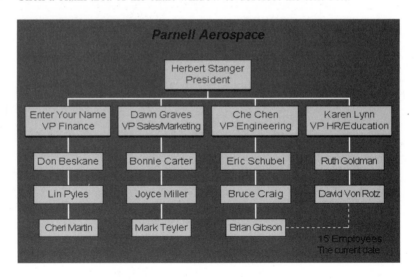

Exit Organization Chart and update your presentation

1   From the File menu, choose Exit and Return to JJORGCHT.PPT.

An Organization Chart dialog box appears.

2   Click the Yes button to update your presentation.

Organization Chart embeds the updated chart in your slide.

3   Click a blank area of the slide to deselect the org chart.

Your presentation window should similar to the following illustration:

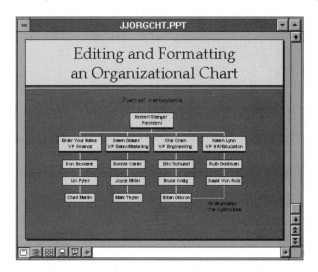

Print the quick-reference notebook presentation

For information on printing a presentation, see Lesson 13.

1   From the File menu, choose Print (CTRL+P).

The Print dialog box appears.

2   Click the drop-down arrow next to Print What.

3   Select Handouts (2 slides per page) from the drop-down list.

4   Click the OK button.

A dialog box appears, giving your printing status.

Save the presentation

Save

▶   On the Standard Toolbar, click the Save button.

No dialog box appears because the presentation already has a name. The current information in your presentation is saved with the same name.

One Step Further

You have learned to start Organization Chart, create an organizational chart using basic features, exit Organization Chart, and edit an organizational chart from PowerPoint. If you'd like to practice these and other basic skills in your practice presentation, try the following:

▶   On a blank slide, create an organizational chart using the Org Chart button.

▶   Change the chart style and add chart boxes of different types.

▶   Create an organizational chart for your company or department.

If You Want to Continue to the Next Lesson

1   From the File menu, choose Close (CTRL+W).

2   If a dialog box appears asking whether you want to save the changes to the presentation, click the No button. You do not need to save the changes you made to the presentation after you printed it.

Choosing this command closes the active presentation; it does not exit PowerPoint.

If You Want to Quit PowerPoint for Now

1   From the File menu, choose Exit (CTRL+Q).

2   If a dialog box appears asking whether you want to save changes to the presentation, click the No button.

Lesson Summary

To	Do this	Button
Start Organization Chart using a slide layout	Click the Layout button and select the Org Chart layout. Double-click the org chart placeholder.	
Start Organization Chart using a toolbar button	On the Standard Toolbar, click the Org Chart button. A full-size organizational chart appears.	
Select a chart box	Move the pointer over a chart box and click.	
Add a chart box	On the Standard Toolbar, click a chart box type button. Position the cursor over a chart box and click.	

To	Do this	Button
Enter text into a chart	Select a chart box, place the insertion point, drag the I-beam to select the sample text, and type new text into the chart box.	
Change the chart style	Select a chart box. From the Styles menu, choose a new style.	
Update your presentation without leaving Organization Chart	From the File menu, choose Update.	
Exit Organization Chart	From the File menu, choose Exit and Return.	
Edit a chart from PowerPoint	Double-click the chart.	
Rearrange a chart box	Drag a deselected chart box on top of another chart box.	
Add a chart box shadow	Select a chart box. From the Boxes menu, choose a box shadow style.	
Format chart connecting lines	From the Edit menu, choose Select and then choose Connecting Lines. From the Boxes menu, choose a Line format.	
Add a connecting line	On the Standard Toolbar, click the Connecting Line Tool button. Drag a connecting line between two chart boxes.	
Add a text label	On the Standard Toolbar, click the Text Tool button. Click in a blank area of the chart window and type the text.	A

For on-line information about	From the PowerPoint Help menu, choose Contents, select "Using PowerPoint," and then
Creating an organizational chart	Select the topic "Adding Visuals to Slides" and click a title under "How to Create Organizational Charts."

For on-line information about	From the Organizational Chart Help menu, choose Index and then
Creating and updating charts	Select the topic "Creating and updating charts" and click the title "Basic chart operations."
Working with boxes and lines	Select the topic "Creating and updating charts" and click the title "Working with boxes and lines."
Working with text	Select the topic "Creating and updating charts" and click the title "Working with text."

For more information on	See the *Microsoft PowerPoint User's Guide*
Creating an organizational chart	Chapter 5, "Adding Visuals to Slides"

Preview of the Next Lesson

In the next lesson, you'll learn how to insert clip art; insert sound and movies, and WordArt; insert, recolor, and crop pictures; and rescale objects. At the end of the lesson, you'll have another presentation for your quick-reference notebook.

5 Inserting and Linking Information

Inserting Information into PowerPoint

You can insert information into PowerPoint in several ways. The most straightforward way is to copy and paste the information. You can copy and paste text, objects, and slides within a presentation, among presentations, and into other Windows-based applications. PowerPoint uses the Windows Clipboard, which stores the copied information, to paste information into PowerPoint presentations. Another way to insert information into PowerPoint is to use commands on the Insert menu and the Standard Toolbar, which allow you to insert clip art, sound, movies, pictures, or objects.

In this lesson, you'll learn how to insert clip art, sound, WordArt, and a picture in a slide; scale an object; and crop and recolor a picture. At the end of the lesson, your presentation will consist of the following slides:

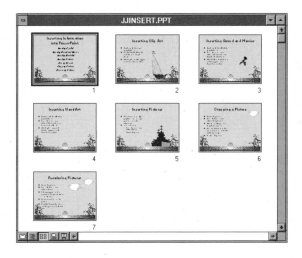

You will learn how to:

- Insert clip art in a slide

- Insert a sound or movie

- Insert WordArt

- Insert a picture

- Scale an object

- Crop and recolor a picture

Estimated lesson time: 20 minutes

Open a presentation

If you haven't already started PowerPoint, do so now. For instructions about starting PowerPoint, see "Getting Ready," earlier in this book.

Open

1   On the Standard Toolbar, click the Open button or select Open an Existing Presentation from the Startup dialog box and click OK.

2   In the Directories box, ensure that the PRACTICE directory is open. If it is not, select the drive where the Step by Step practice files are stored and open the appropriate directories to find the PRACTICE directory.

For information about opening a sample presentation, see Lesson 2.

3   In the list of file names, click LESSON11.PPT.

If you do not see LESSON11.PPT in the list of file names, check to be sure the correct drive and directory are selected. If you need help, see "Getting Ready."

4   Click the OK button.

Your presentation opens to the following slide:

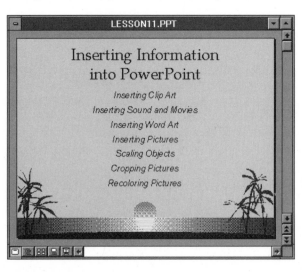

Save the presentation with a new name

Give the presentation a new name so that the changes you make in this lesson do not overwrite the original presentation.

1   From the File menu, choose Save As.

2   In the File Name box, type y*our initials***insert**

For example, if your initials are J. J., type **jjinsert**

3   Click the OK button.

The Summary Info dialog box appears. If you would like, type in the summary information. Press TAB to move between fields.

4   Click the OK button.

Preview the lesson

The presentation for this lesson contains reference information about inserting information into PowerPoint. To preview the information in this lesson, click the Slide Show button and view the on-screen presentation.

Slide Show

1   Click the Slide Show button.

   PowerPoint displays the first slide in the presentation.

2   Click to advance to the next slide.

3   Click once for each slide to advance through the rest of the presentation.

   After the last slide in the presentation, PowerPoint returns to the first slide.

Next Slide

Change to the next slide

▶   Click the Next Slide button to advance to slide 2.

Inserting Clip Art

PowerPoint comes with more than 1100 professionally designed pieces of clip art to use in your presentations. The Microsoft ClipArt Gallery makes it easy to find a clip art category and image that best meet your needs. You can access the ClipArt Gallery by double-clicking a clip art placeholder or clicking the Insert Clip Art button on the Standard Toolbar.

Insert clip art in a slide

1   Double-click the clip art placeholder.

   The Microsoft ClipArt Gallery dialog box appears with a visual preview list of the clip art images.

Note   The first time you open the Microsoft ClipArt Gallery, PowerPoint needs to build an index of the pictures in the gallery. At the dialog box, click the New button to build the index and then click the Yes button to continue. Because there are over 25 clip art categories, building the clip art index takes a few minutes.

---

2   In the Choose A Category To View Below box, click the down scroll arrow and select Transportation.

   A visual preview of images appears for the transportation category.

3   In the visual preview box, click the down scroll arrow several times and select the sailboat.

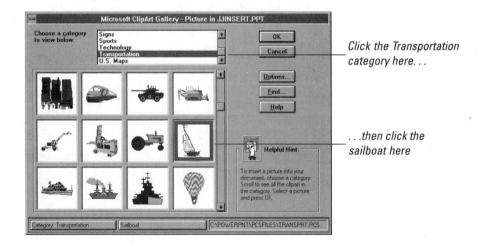

Click the Transportation category here. . .

. . .then click the sailboat here

4 Click the OK button.

The clip art image is placed in the clip art placeholder.

Create a new clip art category

1 Double-click the sailboat object.

The Microsoft ClipArt Gallery dialog box appears.

2 Click the Sailboat button located at the bottom of the dialog box.

The Edit Picture Information dialog box appears.

3 In the Category area, type **Recreation** in the New box.

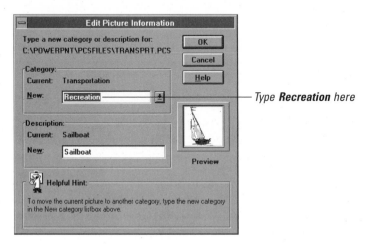

Type **Recreation** here

4 Click the OK button.

The Edit Picture Information dialog box closes. Notice the Category button at the bottom of the dialog box now says "Recreation."

5 Click the OK button.

Move the clip art on the slide

1 With the sailboat object selected, click the DOWN ARROW key until the sailboat object sits in the water.

2 Click a blank area of the slide to deselect the sailboat object.

Your presentation window should look similar to the following illustration:

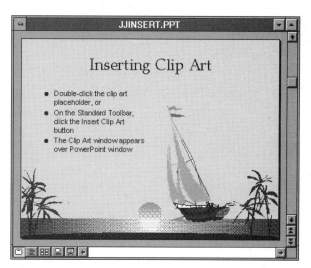

Next Slide

Change to the next slide

▶ Click the Next Slide button to advance to slide 3.

Inserting Sound and Movies

With PowerPoint, you can play sounds and movies during your presentations. You can insert a sound or movie by double-clicking an object placeholder or choosing Object from the Insert menu and selecting the Sound or Media Clip object type. PowerPoint inserts sounds and movies as objects, which can be changed and edited. To play sounds, you'll need sound hardware installed on your computer.

Insert a sound in a slide

1 Double-click the object placeholder.

The Insert Object dialog box appears showing a list of object types.

2 In the Object Type box, click the down scroll arrow and select Sound.

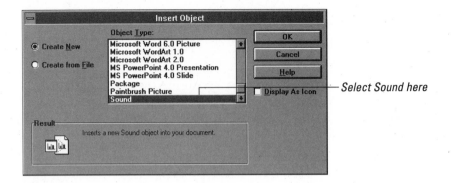

Select Sound here

3 Click the OK button.

The Sound Recorder dialog box appears.

4 From the Edit menu, choose Insert File.

The Insert File dialog box appears. (This dialog box functions just like the Open dialog box.)

5 In the Directories box, double-click the PRACTICE directory.

6 In the list of file names, click SEAGUL.WAV.

If you do not see SEAGUL.WAV in the list of file names, ensure that the correct drive and directory are selected. If you need help, see "Getting Ready."

7 Click the OK button.

8 Click the Play button.

Click the Play button

9 From the File menu, choose Exit.

A Sound Recorder dialog box appears, asking to update the sound in JJINSERT.PPT.

10 Click the Yes button.

A small sound icon appears on your slide. Because the sound icon is an object, you can scale it to a bigger size.

11 From the Draw menu, choose Scale.

12 In the Scale To box, type **400**

13 Click the OK button.

Play sounds in PowerPoint

1   Click the sound object.

2   From the Tools menu, choose Play Settings.

The Play Settings dialog box appears.

3   In the Start Play area, click the Ends, Plus option button and type **4** in the Seconds box.

Click the option button here...

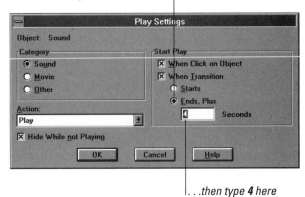

*...then type **4** here*

4   Click the OK button.

5   Click the Slide Show button.

Slide Show

The sound plays 4 seconds after the transition.

6   Press the ESC key to stop the slide show.

Change to the next slide

Next Slide

▶   Click the Next Slide button to advance to slide 4.

Inserting WordArt

You can insert fancy or stylized text into your presentation with Microsoft WordArt. The objects you create in Microsoft WordArt are embedded in your slide and can be moved around and edited anytime. You can insert WordArt by double-clicking an object placeholder or choosing Object from the Insert menu.

Insert WordArt in a slide

1   Double-click the object placeholder.

The Insert Object dialog box appears displaying a list of object types.

2   In the Object Type box, click the down scroll arrow and select Microsoft WordArt 2.0.

3   Click the OK button.

The WordArt toolbar and menus appear. The Enter Your Text Here dialog box is placed on your slide, as shown in the following illustration:

4   In the Enter Your Text Here dialog box, type **Sunset** and press ENTER.

5   Type **Sailing** and press ENTER.

6   Type **Adventures**

7   Click the Update Display button.

The text you typed is updated in the placeholder.

Format the WordArt text

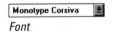

Font

1   On the Formatting Toolbar, click the Font drop-down arrow and select Monotype Corsiva.

The WordArt object changes to the Monotype Corsiva font.

Format

2   On the Formatting Toolbar, click the Format drop-down arrow and select the Curve Up symbol, as shown in the following illustration:

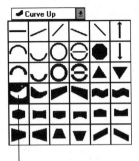

Select the Curve Up symbol here

Shading

3   On the Formatting Toolbar, click the Shading button.

The Shading dialog box appears.

4 In the Color area, click the Foreground drop-down arrow and select Blue.

5 Click the OK button.

The Shading dialog box closes.

Shadow

6 On the Formatting Toolbar, click the Shadow button and select the second symbol in the top row, as shown in the following illustration:

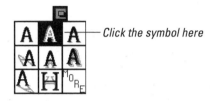

Click the symbol here

Exit WordArt

▶ Position your pointer in a blank area of the presentation window and click.

The PowerPoint toolbars and menus appear.

Next Slide

Change to the next slide

▶ Click the Next Slide button to advance to slide 5.

Inserting a Picture

If you have pictures—scanned photographs and line art, photos and artwork from CDs or other applications—you can insert them into PowerPoint with the Picture command from the Insert menu. PowerPoint can insert fourteen different graphic formats. A list can be found in Appendix A, "Installing PowerPoint."

Insert a picture

1 From the Insert menu, choose Picture.

The Insert Picture dialog box appears. (This dialog box functions just like the Open dialog box.)

2 In the Directories box, double-click the PRACTICE directory.

3 In the list of file names, click SHIP.WMF.

If you do not see SHIP.WMF in the list of file names, ensure that the correct drive and directory are selected. If you need help, see "Getting Ready."

4 Click the OK button.

A ship object appears on the slide.

Your presentation window should look similar to the following illustration:

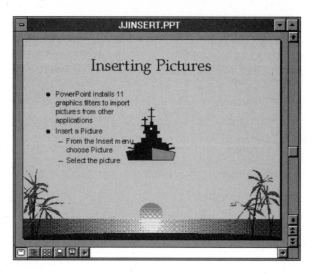

Scaling an Object

Scaling means resizing an entire object by a certain percentage. With the Scale command you can resize an object numerically instead of dragging its resize handle. An object can be scaled relative to the original picture size if the appropriate check box in the Scale dialog box is turned on.

Scale an object

1 Select the ship object, if it's not already selected.

2 From the Draw menu, choose Scale.

The Scale dialog box appears.

3 In the Scale To box, type **170**

The scale size is applied to the object after you type a new percentage. You can click the Preview button to view the object before leaving the dialog box.

*Type **170** here*

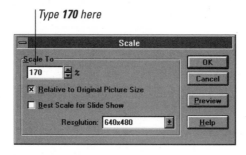

4   Click the OK button.

5   Drag the ship object to the top edge of the water.

6   Click a blank area of the slide to deselect the object.

Your presentation window should look similar to the following illustration:

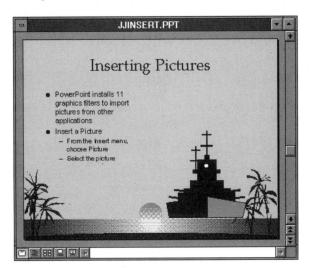

Tip   PowerPoint remembers the original size of a picture or text object. If you accidently change an object to the wrong size, set the scale back to 100% relative to its original size.

Next Slide

Change to the next slide

▶   Click the Next Slide button to advance to slide 6.

Cropping a Picture

Sometimes you need only a portion of a picture in your presentation. With the Crop Picture command, you can cover portions of a picture so you don't see all of it on the screen. The picture is not altered, just covered up.

Crop a picture

1   Select the clouds object.

2   From the Tools menu, choose Crop Picture.

The pointer changes to the Cropping tool.

Cropping Tool

3   Position the center of the Cropping tool over the left middle resize handle.

4   Drag to the right to crop the left cloud.

While you're dragging, a dotted outline appears to show you the cropped area. The Cropping tool also changes to a constrain cursor, indicating the direction that you're cropping.

5   Click a blank area of the slide to turn off the Cropping tool.

The Cropping tool changes to the pointer. Your presentation window should look similar to the following illustration:

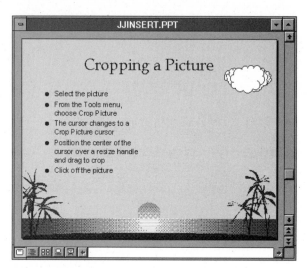

Next Slide

Change to the next slide

▶   Click the Next Slide button to advance to slide 7.

Recoloring a Picture

Pictures can be recolored to follow a new color scheme. The Recolor Picture command displays a dialog box with a preview of the picture and a list of all the colors in the picture. Each color in the list can be individually changed.

Recolor a picture

1   Select the clouds object.

2   From the Tools menu, choose Recolor.

The Recolor Picture dialog box appears.

3   Under New, click the drop-down arrow next to the black color.

A color menu appears.

4   Select the light blue color.

The color swatch changes to light blue. An X appears in the check box to the left, indicating you changed a color.

5   Click the Preview button to see your changes.

Click the drop-down arrow here
and select the light blue color

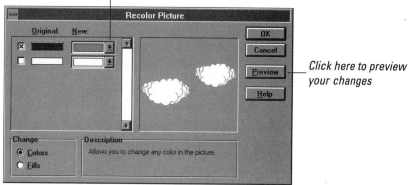

Click here to preview
your changes

6   Click the OK button.

PowerPoint recolors the clouds object.

Print the quick-reference notebook presentation

For information
on printing a
presentation, see
Lesson 13.

1   From the File menu, choose Print (CTRL+P).

The Print dialog box appears.

2   Click the drop-down arrow next to Print What.

3   Select Handouts (2 slides per page) from the drop-down list.

4   Click the OK button.

A dialog box appears, giving your printing status.

Save the presentation

Save

▶   On the Standard Toolbar, click the Save button.

No dialog box appears because the presentation already has a name. The current information in your presentation is saved with the same name.

One Step Further

You have learned how to add clip art, sound, WordArt, and a picture to your presentation; scale objects; and insert, crop, and recolor pictures. If you'd like to practice these and other basic skills in your practice presentation, try the following:

▶ Insert a movie object into your presentation, if you have a movie available.

▶ Insert a picture.

▶ Scale the objects.

▶ Crop and recolor the objects.

If You Want to Continue to the Next Lesson

1　From the File menu, choose Close (CTRL+W).

2　If a dialog box appears asking whether you want to save the changes to your presentation, click the No button. You do not need to save the changes you made to the presentation after you printed it.

　　Choosing this command closes the active presentation; it does not exit PowerPoint.

If You Want to Quit PowerPoint for Now

1　From the File menu, choose Exit (CTRL+Q).

2　If a dialog box appears asking whether you want to save changes to the presentation, click the No button.

Lesson Summary

To	Do this	Button
Add clip art	On the Standard Toolbar, click the Insert Clip Art button or double-click the clip art placeholder. Select an image and click the OK button.	
Insert a sound	From the Insert menu, choose Object. In the Object Type box, select Sound. Click the OK button. Insert a sound and click the OK button.	
Insert WordArt text	From the Insert menu, choose Object. In the Object Type box, select Microsoft WordArt 2.0. Click the OK button. Create the WordArt and click a blank area of the presentation window.	

To	Do this	Button
Insert a picture	From the Insert menu, choose Picture. Select a picture file and click the OK button.	
Scale an object	Select the object. From the Draw menu, choose Scale. Type a percentage.	
Crop a picture	From the Tools menu, choose Crop Picture. Drag a resize handle.	
Recolor a picture	From the Tools menu, choose Recolor. Click the drop-down arrow for each color and select a new one from the list. Click the Preview button to view your changes. Click the OK button.	

For on-line information about	From the PowerPoint Help menu, choose Contents, select "Using PowerPoint," and then
Inserting clip art	Select the topic "Adding Visuals to Slides" and click a title under "How to Add Clip Art to Your Slides."
Inserting a picture	Select the topic "Adding Visuals to Slides" and click a title under "Inserting Pictures on Your Slides."
Inserting WordArt	Select the topic "Adding Visuals to Slides" and click a title under "How to Create Special Effects Using WordArt."
Inserting a movie	Select the topic "Using PowerPoint with Other Applications" and click a title under "How to Insert Movies."

For on-line information about	From the WordArt Help menu, choose Contents and then
Entering and editing text	Select the topic "Typing and Editing Text in WordArt."
Adding special effects to text	Select the topic "Adding Special Effects to Text in WordArt."

For more information on	See the *Microsoft PowerPoint User's Guide*
Inserting clip art, pictures, and embedded objects	Chapter 5, "Adding Visuals to Slides"
Working with embedded objects	Chapter 7, "Using PowerPoint with Other Applications"

Preview of the Next Lesson

In the next lesson, you'll link an object from a source document and a picture from a file to your presentation, update changes to a linked object, cancel a link, and embed an object in a PowerPoint slide. By the end of the lesson, you'll have produced another presentation for your quick-reference notebook.

Linking Information with Other Applications

With PowerPoint's OfficeLinks, you can copy, link, or embed information from other applications. To make updating easier, link or embed an object instead of just copying it. When you link an object, the object is stored in its source document, where it was created. Your presentation becomes one of several users of the information and can be automatically updated when others update the source document. Your presentation stores only a representation of the original document. When you embed an object, the object becomes a part of your presentation. You are the only user of the information. With either an embedded or linked object, you just double-click the object to open it for editing.

In this lesson, you'll learn how to create a link to a Microsoft Excel chart object and a picture; update and change a link; embed a Microsoft Excel worksheet and a Microsoft Word table; create a report in Microsoft Word; and send a presentation with Microsoft Mail. At the end of the lesson, your presentation will consist of the following slides:

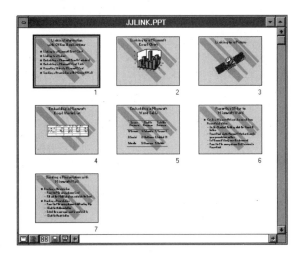

You will learn how to:

- Link a object to a PowerPoint slide

- Edit a link

- Link a picture to a slide

- Embed an object in a slide

- Report slides to Microsoft Word

- Send a presentation with Microsoft Mail

Estimated lesson time: 30 minutes

Open a presentation

If you haven't already started PowerPoint, do so now. For instructions about starting PowerPoint, see "Getting Ready," earlier in this book.

Open

1   On the Standard Toolbar, click the Open button or select Open an Existing Presentation from the Startup dialog box and click OK.

2   In the Directories box, ensure the PRACTICE directory is open. If it is not, select the drive where the Step by Step practice files are stored and open the appropriate directories to find the PRACTICE directory.

For information about opening a sample presentation, see Lesson 2.

3   In the list of file names, click LESSON12.PPT.

If you do not see LESSON12.PPT in the list of file names, check to be sure the correct drive and directory are selected. If you need help, see "Getting Ready."

4   Click the OK button.

Your presentation opens to the following slide:

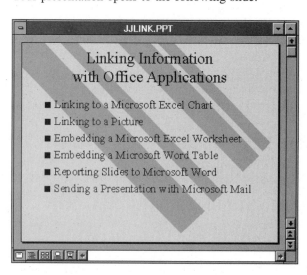

Save the presentation with a new name

Give the presentation a new name so that the changes you make in this lesson do not overwrite the original presentation.

1   From the File menu, choose Save As.

2   In the File Name box, type *your initials***link**

For example, if your initials are J. J., type **jjlink**

3   Click the OK button.

The Summary Info dialog box appears. If you would like, type in the summary information. Press TAB to move between fields.

4   Click the OK button.

Preview the lesson

The presentation for this lesson contains reference information about linking information with other applications. To preview the information in this lesson, click the Slide Show button and view the on-screen presentation.

Slide Show

1   Click the Slide Show button.

PowerPoint displays the first slide in the presentation.

2   Click to advance to the next slide.

3   Click once for each slide to advance through the rest of the presentation.

After the last slide in the presentation, PowerPoint returns to the first slide.

Change to the next slide

Next Slide

▶   Click the Next Slide button to advance to slide 2.

Linking and Embedding in This Lesson

For some sections in this lesson, you'll need Microsoft Excel version 5.0 for Windows and Microsoft Word version 6.0 for Windows. If you don't have these applications, you can use the same techniques with other Windows-based applications that support linking and embedding, or you can simply read the lesson to learn the concepts.

Linking to a Microsoft Excel Chart

For information on Microsoft Excel, see your Microsoft Excel documentation.

To ensure that your presentation always shows the latest information, you can create a link between a source document, such as a Microsoft Excel chart object, and your PowerPoint presentation. To create a link, select the source document information you want to link, choose the Copy command, return to your PowerPoint presentation, and choose the Paste Special command.

Link a Microsoft Excel chart to a slide

1   Press CTRL+ESC to display the Task List.

The Task List dialog box appears.

2   Select Program Manager and click the Switch To button.

3   Locate and start Microsoft Excel.

Microsoft Excel

4   Open the Excel chart document LINKCHRT.XLC.

Make sure the PRACTICE directory is open. If it is not, select the drive where the Step by Step practice files are stored and open the appropriate directories. If you do not see LINKCHRT.XLC in the list of file names, check to be sure the correct drive and directory are selected. If you need help, see "Getting Ready."

5   Click the OK button.

A dialog box appears, asking you to update document links.

6   Click the No button.

7   Click a blank area in any corner of the chart window to select the chart.

     Black resize handles appear around the chart.

Copy

8   On the Standard Toolbar, click the Copy button.

     A selection box appears around the chart.

9   Switch to your PowerPoint presentation.

Tip   For a quick way to switch to PowerPoint or any other Windows-based application, hold down the ALT key and then press the TAB key. A billboard with an application icon and name appears. Continue to press TAB until the PowerPoint icon and name appear. Release the ALT and TAB keys to switch to PowerPoint.

10   From the Edit menu, choose Paste Special.

     The Paste Special dialog box appears with the Microsoft Excel 5.0 Chart Object selected.

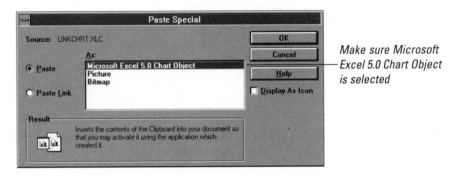

Make sure Microsoft Excel 5.0 Chart Object is selected

The Paste Special dialog box appears with a list of different data types in which the object on the Windows Clipboard can be pasted to a PowerPoint slide. The selected data type, Microsoft Excel 5.0 Chart Object, is the data type currently placed on the Windows Clipboard.

11   Click the Paste Link option button.

12   Click the OK button.

     The Microsoft Excel chart appears on the PowerPoint slide.

Scale the chart from Microsoft Excel

1   From the Draw menu, choose Scale.

     The Scale dialog box appears.

2   In the Scale To box, type **200**

3   Click the OK button.

Editing a Link

Once a link is created, you must decide whether information should be updated automatically or manually. All links are initially set as automatic links. You can change a link in a destination document from automatic to manual so you can control when the information is updated. You may want to make a link manual if the document does not need to be updated very often or if you have several links in the document. With a manual link, an update from the source document is not made until you request it.

Update an automatically linked Microsoft Excel chart

Chart Type

1   Double-click the linked Microsoft Excel chart.

The chart appears. PowerPoint toolbars and menus change to Microsoft Excel toolbars and menus.

2   On the Chart Toolbar, click the Chart Type drop-down arrow and select the 3-D pie chart (the fifth chart down in the right column).

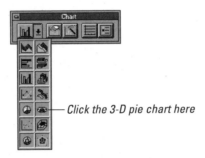

— Click the 3-D pie chart here

The chart changes to a 3-D pie chart.

3   Switch back to PowerPoint.

Use ALT+TAB to switch applications. The PowerPoint toolbars and menu appear. The Excel chart automatically updates the PowerPoint slide to show the 3-D pie chart.

Change an automatic link to a manual link

1   From the Edit menu, choose Links.

The Links dialog box appears. The Links dialog box shows the current type of linked file, the name of the file, and the type of link (automatic or manual).

2   Click the Manual option button.

```
┌─────────────────────────────────────────────────────────────┐
│ ─                              Links                          │
│                                                              │
│  Links:                    Type        Update    ┌─────────┐ │         Be sure this link
│  D:\...                    Chart        Manual    │  Close  │ │         is selected
│                                                   └─────────┘ │
│                                                   ┌─────────┐ │
│                                                   │Update Now│ │
│                                                   └─────────┘ │
│                                                   ┌─────────┐ │
│                                                   │Open Source│ │
│                                                   └─────────┘ │
│                                                   ┌─────────┐ │
│                                                   │Change Source...│ │
│                                                   └─────────┘ │
│                                                   ┌─────────┐ │
│                                                   │Break Link│ │
│                                                   └─────────┘ │
│  Source:   D:\PP4LESNS\LINKCHRT.XLCILINKCHRT.XLC             │
│  Type:     Microsoft Excel 5.0 Chart                         │
│  Update:      ○ Automatic       ⦿ Manual     ┌─────────┐    │
│                                               │  Help   │    │
│                                               └─────────┘    │
└─────────────────────────────────────────────────────────────┘
```

Click the Manual option button

The type of link changes from automatic to manual. The next time the Excel chart changes, PowerPoint will not automatically update the chart in your presentation.

3   Click the Close button.

Update a manually linked Microsoft Excel chart

1   Double-click the Microsoft Excel chart.

The chart appears.

Tip   If you switch among Microsoft applications often, use the Microsoft Toolbar application buttons by choosing the Toolbars command from the View menu. The application you're switching to must be open.

Chart Type

2   On the Chart Toolbar, click the Chart Type drop-down arrow and select the 3-D column chart (the third chart down in the right column).

The Excel chart changes to a column chart.

3   Switch back to PowerPoint.

Use ALT+TAB to switch applications. The linked Excel chart is not updated to the 3-D column chart.

4   From the Edit menu, choose Links.

Tip   To update more than one link, hold down the CTRL key and click each link. To update a contiguous set of links, select the first link and then hold down the SHIFT key and select the last link.

5   Click the Update Now button.

The link to the chart is updated.

6   Click the Close button.

Your presentation window should look similar to the following illustration:

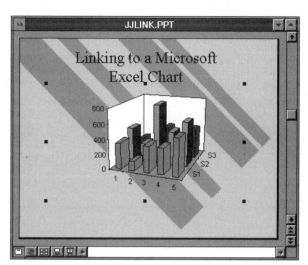

7   Switch to Excel.

Use ALT+TAB to switch applications.

8   From the File menu, choose Close.

A Excel dialog box appears.

9   Click the No button to ignore changes to LINKCHRT.XLC.

10   Switch to PowerPoint.

Use ALT+TAB to switch applications.

Change a link

When you link data into a PowerPoint presentation, PowerPoint attaches the path and name of the source document to the linked information. It uses this information to locate the source data that appears in your document. If you change the name of the source document or move the source document to a different directory or network drive, you must change the links to include the new name or path of the source document.

1   From the Edit menu, choose Links.

The Links dialog box appears.

2   Select the link if its not already selected.

3   Click the Change Source button.

4   In the Directories box, ensure that the PRACTICE directory is open. If it is not, select the drive where the Step by Step practice files are stored, and open the appropriate directories to find the PRACTICE directory.

5   In the list of file names, select LINKNEW.XLC.

6   Click the OK button.

7   Click the No button to cancel re-establishing links.

The link to the chart changes from LINKCHRT.XLC to LINKNEW.XLC.

8   Click the Close button.

Your presentation window should look similar to the following illustration:

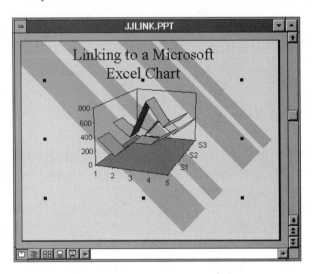

Note   You can cancel or break a link permanently so that the information in the destination document is no longer updated from the source document. From the Edit menu, choose Links, select the linked file, and click the Break Link button.

Next Slide

Change to the next slide

▶   Click the Next Slide button to advance to slide 3.

Linking a Picture to a Slide

Pictures from other applications can be linked to a PowerPoint slide. Changes made to a linked picture are sent automatically to PowerPoint as soon as they are available. This ensures that your presentation always shows the latest information.

Link a picture to a slide

1   From the Insert menu, choose Picture.

The Insert Picture dialog box appears. (This dialog box functions just like the Open dialog box.)

2   In the Directories box, ensure that the PRACTICE directory is open. If it is not, select the drive where the Step by Step practice files are stored and open the appropriate directories to find the PRACTICE directory.

3   In the list of file names, click LINK1.WMF.

If you do not see LINK1.WMF in the list of file names, check to be sure the correct drive and directory are selected. If you need help, see "Getting Ready."

4   Click the Link To File check box.

Be sure LINK1.WMF is selected...

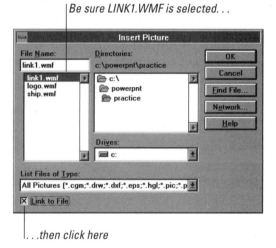

...then click here

An X in the Link To File check box creates a link to the picture, LINK1.WMF.

5   Click the OK button.

Your presentation window should look similar to the following illustration:

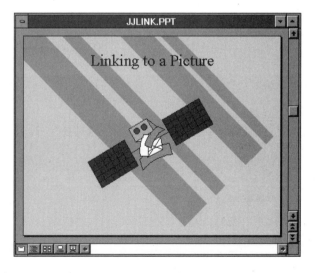

Next Slide

Change to the next slide

▶ Click the Next Slide button to advance to slide 4.

Embedding a Microsoft Excel Worksheet

For information on creating a Microsoft Excel worksheet, see your Microsoft Excel documentation.

You can embed an object in a PowerPoint slide to create a direct link with the embedded application that can be edited from your presentation. To embed an object, choose the Object command and select an object—for example, Microsoft Excel 5.0 Sheet. To edit an embedded object, double-click the embedded object in your PowerPoint slide, edit it, and deselect the object to return to PowerPoint. The changes you make to the embedded object are made on your PowerPoint slide.

Embed a Microsoft Excel worksheet object in a slide

PowerPoint simplifies the process of embedding a Microsoft Excel worksheet into your presentation by providing a special toolbar button. The Insert Microsoft Excel Worksheet button allows you to select a specific worksheet size to embed so that you can work with only the area you want.

Insert Microsoft Excel Worksheet

1 On the Standard Toolbar, click the Insert Microsoft Excel Worksheet button.

Click here to insert a Microsoft Excel worksheet

2 Click the lower right corner cell and drag down to select a 5 x 5 Sheet.

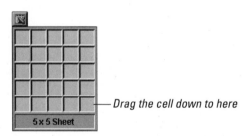

—— *Drag the cell down to here*

A blank Microsoft Excel worksheet, titled Sheet1, appears.

3 Type the following text in the Excel worksheet.

	A	B	C	D	E
1		Mercury	Columbia	Voyager	Totals
2	Proposed	75.5	150.8	125.6	351.9
3	Actual	110.4	270.3	204.8	585.5
4	Difference	34.9	119.5	79.2	233.6
5					

Sheet1

Use the Arrow keys to move from cell to cell.

4 Drag to select the 5 x 5 worksheet of data.

Copy

5 On the Standard Toolbar, click the Copy button.

6 From the Insert menu, choose Worksheet.

A new worksheet, titled Sheet2, appears. You can switch between two or more worksheets in the same embedded object.

Paste

7 On the Standard Toolbar, click the Paste button.

8 Click a blank area of the slide to deselect the embedded object.

The worksheet appears on the PowerPoint slide. Since the slide view scale is set to 50%, the worksheet appears small. Next, you can scale the worksheet in the same way as any other object.

9 From the Draw menu, choose Scale.

The Scale dialog box appears.

10 In the Scale To box, type **200**

11 Click the OK button.

12 Drag the embedded Excel worksheet object to the center of the side.

Tip To embed an object from a specific file you have already created, choose Object from the Insert menu, click the Create From File option button, click the Browse button, and select a file.

Format an embedded object

1 On the Drawing+ Toolbar, click the Fill Color button.

Fill Color

| *Click here to change the fill color*

2 From the Fill Color drop-down menu, select magenta (the third color in the second row).

Shadow Color

Line Color

3   On the Drawing+ Toolbar, click the Shadow Color button.

4   From the Fill Color drop-down menu, select dark blue (the second color in the first row).

5   On the Drawing+ Toolbar, click the Line Color button.

6   From the Line Color drop-down menu, select dark blue (the second color in the first row).

Your presentation window should look similar to the following:

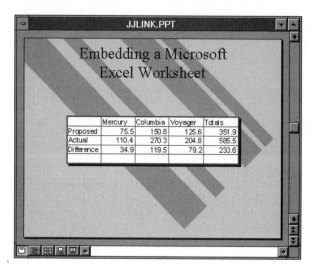

Update an embedded Microsoft Excel object

1   Double-click the embedded Microsoft Excel worksheet.

Excel opens to Sheet2.

2   Drag the resize bar to the right to display the entire Sheet1 tab.

Drag the resize bar to this position

3   Click the Sheet1 tab button.

4   Select cell C3 and type **286.7**

5   Select cell C4 and type **135.9**

Your worksheet should look similar to the following illustration:

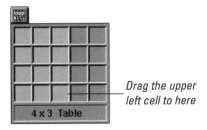

	A	B	C	D	E
1		Mercury	Columbia	Voyager	Totals
2	Proposed	75.5	150.8	125.6	351.9
3	Actual	110.4	286.7	204.8	601.9
4	Difference	34.9	135.9	79.2	250
5					

Sheet2 \ **Sheet1**

6   Click a blank area of the slide to deselect the embedded object.

The PowerPoint toolbars and menus return and the embedded Excel worksheet is updated on the slide.

Tip   To change an embedded object from one embedded application to another, select the object, choose Edit Object from the Edit menu, and then choose Convert.

Next Slide

Change to the next slide

▶   Click the Next Slide button to advance to slide 5.

Embedding a Microsoft Word Table

For information on Microsoft Word, see your Microsoft Word documentation.

With the Insert Microsoft Word Table feature, you can use all the power of Microsoft Word 6.0 or later to create a table in PowerPoint. Simply click the Insert Microsoft Word Table button drag a table size. PowerPoint inserts a blank table for you to fill in with your text.

Insert a Microsoft Word table

Insert Microsoft Word Table

1   On the Standard Toolbar, click the Insert Microsoft Word Table button.

PowerPoint launches Microsoft Word and inserts your presentation slides with the same title text and main text format into a blank Word document.

2   Click the upper left corner cell and drag to select a 4 x 3 Table.

Drag the upper left cell to here

4 x 3 Table

A blank Word table appears in the middle of the slide and the Word toolbar appears above the presentation window.

3 Type the following text in the Word table.

Use the TAB key to move from cell to cell.

Format a Microsoft Word table

1 Drag to select the top row of text in the table.

2 On the Formatting Toolbar, click the Bold button and the Center button.

Bold *Center*

The selected table text format changes to bold and aligns to the center of the individual cells.

3 On the Formatting Toolbar, click the Font drop-down arrow and select Arial.

4 On the Formatting Toolbar, click the Borders button.

Borders

The Borders Toolbar appears below the Formatting Toolbar.

Line Style

5 On the Borders Toolbar, click the Line Style drop-down arrow and select the 3 pt line.

The current line style changes to a 3 point line (a point is 1/72 of an inch thick).

Top Border

6 On the Borders Toolbar, click the Top Border button.

The top border of the cell is formatted with the current line style.

7 Drag to select the bottom three rows of text in the table.

8 On the Formatting Toolbar, click the Numbering button.

Numbering

The Table Numbering dialog box appears with the Number Down Columns option button selected.

9 Click the OK button.

Numbers appears in front of each table entry.

10 On the Borders Toolbar, click the Top Border button.

Top Border

A border line is placed on the table.

11 On the Borders Toolbar, click the Bottom Border button.

Bottom Border

12 Click a blank area of the slide to deselect the embedded object.

The PowerPoint toolbars and menus return and the embedded Word table is updated on the slide.

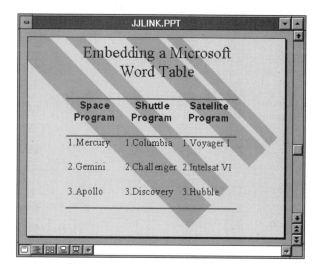

13   From the Window menu, choose Fit to Page to resize the presentation window.

Next Slide

Change to the next slide

► Click the Next Slide button to advance to slide 6.

Reporting Slides to Microsoft Word

With the Report It feature, you can insert your presentation slides directly into Microsoft Word 6.0. Click the Report It button on the Standard Toolbar, and PowerPoint does the rest. PowerPoint launches Microsoft Word and inserts the title text and main text of each slide in your presentation into a blank Word document.

Report It to Microsoft Word

1   On the Standard Toolbar, click the Report It button.

Report It

PowerPoint launches Microsoft Word and inserts your presentation slides with the title text and main text format into a blank Word document.

2   Click the OK button to close the Tip Of The Day dialog box, if necessary.

3   From the File menu, choose Save As.

4   In the File Name box, type *your initials***link**

For example, if your initials are J. J., type **jjlink**

5   In the Drives box, ensure that drive C is selected, if that is where you stored your Step by Step practice files. If you need assistance, see "Getting Ready," earlier in this book.

6   In the Save File as Type box, click the drop-down arrow and select Word Document.

7   In the Directories box, ensure that the PRACTICE directory is selected. If it is not, select it by double-clicking it.

8   Click the OK button.

Word saves your presentation slide text in a document called JJLINK.DOC in your Step by Step practice directory.

9   From the File menu, choose Exit.

Word closes and you return to PowerPoint.

Next Slide

Change to the next slide

▶   Click the Next Slide button to advance to slide 7.

Sending a Presentation with Microsoft Mail

If you see the Send command on the File menu, Microsoft Mail or another compatible mail package is installed. With Microsoft Mail, you can send your presentations to someone using electronic mail. You can either send a presentation to one person or you can route a presentation to more than one person, using the Add Routing Slip command.

To send and route presentations, the sender and the receiver must have PowerPoint and Microsoft Mail or another mail package installed.

Send a presentation

When you send a presentation directly to another person, the file is saved as an attachment to a note.

1   From the File menu, choose Send.

A dialog box appears so that you can identify the person who is to receive your presentation.

Tip   If you send mail from PowerPoint often, add the Send Mail button and the Routing Slip button to a PowerPoint toolbar by choosing the Customize command from the Tools menu and dragging the buttons to a toobar.

2   Complete the address information.

3   Click the Send button.

Route a presentation

You can send one or more copies of the same presentation to a small group for an important review before you give the presentation by using the Routing Slip command.

1   From the File menu, choose Add Routing Slip.

The Add Routing Slip dialog box appears.

2   Click the Address button.

The Address dialog box appears.

3   Select the recipient names and click the Add button.

4   Click the OK button.

5   In the Subject and Message text boxes, type the subject and any message you want to send with the presentation.

6   Click the All At Once option button.

This option routes multiple copies of the presentation to all recipients at the same time.

7   Click the Route button.

8   Click the Yes button to confirm that you want to route the presentation.

Print the quick-reference notebook presentation

For information on printing a presentation, see Lesson 13.

1   From the Print menu, choose Print (CTRL+P).

The Print dialog box appears.

2   Click the drop-down arrow next to Print What.

3   Select Handouts (2 slides per page) from the drop-down list.

4   Click the OK button.

A dialog box appears, giving your printing status.

Save the presentation

Save

▶   On the Standard Toolbar, click the Save button.

No dialog box appears because the presentation already has a name. The current information in your presentation is saved with the same name.

One Step Further

You have learned how to create a link to a document and picture; update, change, and cancel a link; and embed an object in a PowerPoint slide. If you'd like to practice these and other basic skills in your practice presentation, try the following:

▶   Create a link to Paintbrush. Open and close documents and presentations with links.

▶   Create, change, and cancel links to pictures.

▶   Insert other objects from your system.

If You Want to Continue to the Next Lesson

1   From the File menu, choose Close (CTRL+W).

2   If a dialog box appears asking whether you want to save the changes to your presentation, click the No button. You do not need to save the changes you made to the presentation after you printed it.

   Choosing this command closes the active presentation; it does not exit PowerPoint.

If You Want to Quit PowerPoint for Now

1   From the File menu, choose Exit (CTRL+Q).

2   If a dialog box appears asking whether you want to save changes to the presentation, click the No button.

Lesson Summary

To	Do this	Button
Link to an object	Switch to the source document. Copy the object. Switch to PowerPoint. From the Edit menu, choose Paste Special. Click the Paste Link button and then click the OK button.	
Edit a link to an object	Double-click the object in PowerPoint. Make the changes to the document. From the File menu, choose Exit.	
Change a link to automatic or manual	From the Edit menu, choose Links. Select the link. Click the Automatic option button or the Manual option button.	
Change a link's source	From the Edit menu, choose Links. Select the link. Click the Change Source button. Select the new file to link. Click the Update Now button.	
Link a picture	From the Insert menu, choose Picture. Select a picture. Click the Link To File box.	

To	Do this	Button
Embed an object	From the Insert menu, choose Object. Select the object to embed. Create or modify the object. Click back in PowerPoint.	
Edit an embedded an object	Double-click the embedded object. Make changes to the object. Click back in PowerPoint.	
Insert a Microsoft Excel worksheet	On the Standard Toolbar, click the Insert Microsoft Excel Worksheet button and select a worksheet size.	
Insert a Microsoft Word table	On the Standard Toolbar, click the Insert Microsoft Word Table button and select a table size.	
Report your slides to Word	On the Standard Toolbar, click the Report It button.	
Send a presentation	From the File menu, choose Send. Fill out the Send dialog box and click the Send button.	
Route a presentation	From the File menu, choose Add Routing Slip. Fill out the Add Routing Slip dialog box and click the Route button.	

For on-line information about	From the PowerPoint Help menu, choose Contents, select "Using PowerPoint," and then
Understanding embedded and linked objects	Select the topic "Using PowerPoint with Other Applications" and click a title under "Understanding Embedded and Linked Objects."
Working with embedded objects	Select the topic "Using PowerPoint with Other Applications" and click a title under "How to Work with Embedded Objects."
Working with linked objects	Select the topic "Using PowerPoint with Other Applications" and click a title under "How to Work with Linked Objects."
Sending mail from PowerPoint	Select the topic "Using PowerPoint with Other Applications" and click a title under "How to Send and Route Mail."

For more information on	See the *Microsoft PowerPoint User's Guide*
Working with linked and embedded objects	Chapter 7, "Using PowerPoint with Other Applications"

Preview of the Next Lesson

In the next lesson, you'll print presentation slides, speaker's notes, audience handouts, and an outline. By the end of the lesson, you'll have produced another presentation for your quick-reference notebook.

6 Printing and Producing a Presentation

Setting Up Your Slides and Printing

PowerPoint allows you to print your presentation slides, speaker's notes, audience handouts, and outlines. PowerPoint also includes a way to create an output file that can be sent to a service bureau for imaging to 35mm slides. Printing in PowerPoint offers a number of options: paper size, page orientation, range of pages, printers, and several output alternatives.

In this lesson, you'll learn how to choose a printer, change a slide format using the slide options, set up a presentation for printing, and print slides, speaker's notes, an outline, and audience handouts. At the end of the lesson, your presentation will consist of the following slides:

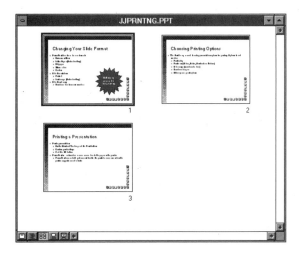

You will learn how to:

- Choose a printer
- Change a presentation slide format
- Print presentation slides
- Print speaker's notes
- Print an outline
- Print audience handouts

Estimated lesson time: 30 minutes

Open a presentation

If you haven't already started PowerPoint, do so now. For information about starting PowerPoint, see "Getting Ready," earlier in this book.

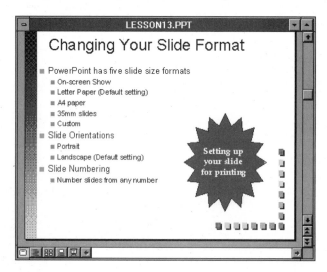

Open

1   On the Standard Toolbar, click the Open button or select Open an Existing Presentation from the Startup dialog box and click OK.

2   In the Directories box, ensure that the PRACTICE directory is open. If it is not, select the drive where the Step by Step practice files are stored and open the appropriate directories to find the PRACTICE directory.

For information about opening a sample presentation, see Lesson 2.

3   In the list of file names, click LESSON13.PPT.

If you do not see LESSON13.PPT in the list of file names, check to be sure the correct drive and directory are selected. If you need help, see "Getting Ready."

4   Click the OK button.

Your presentation opens to the following slide:

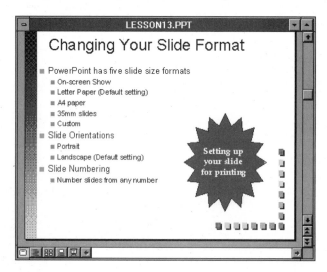

Save the presentation with a new name

Give the presentation a new name so that the changes you make in this lesson do not overwrite the original presentation.

1   From the File menu, choose Save As.

2   In the File Name box, type *your initials***prntng**

For example, if your initials are J. J., type **jjprntng**

3   Click the OK button.

The Summary Info dialog box appears. If you would like, type in the summary information. Press TAB to move between fields.

4   Click the OK button.

Preview the lesson

The presentation for this lesson contains reference information about setting up your slides and printing. To preview the information in this lesson, click the Slide Show button and view the on-screen presentation.

Slide Show

1   Click the Slide Show button.

PowerPoint displays the first slide in the presentation.

2   Click to advance to the next slide.

3   Click once for each slide to advance through the rest of the presentation.

After the last slide in the presentation, PowerPoint returns to the first slide.

Choosing a Printer

Presentations print to the default printer unless you select a special printer. Your default printer is set up in the Windows Control Panel. You can choose a printer other than the default printer for slides and for notes, handouts, and outlines.

1   Make sure your printer is turned on and connected to your computer.

2   From the File menu, choose Print.

The Print dialog box appears.

3   Click the Printer button.

The Print Setup dialog box appears.

4   In the Printers area, select your default printer.

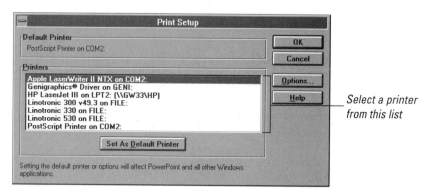

Select a printer from this list

TROUBLESHOOTING: **If your printer is not available in the list of printers** See Appendix B, "Installing and Selecting a Printer," for information on how to install and select a printer.

5 Click the OK button.

The Print Setup dialog box closes.

6 In the Print dialog box, click the Cancel button.

Changing a Slide Format

The slide format determines the size and orientation of your printed slides. For a new presentation, PowerPoint opens with default slide format settings: Letter Paper (10 inches wide by 7.5 inches tall), landscape orientation, and slide numbers starting at one. If you need to change these slide format settings, it's a good idea to set the slide format before you design your presentation. Changing the orientation or slide size for an existing presentation might change the scaling of objects on the slide.

Change the slide size

1 From the File menu, choose Slide Setup.

The Slide Setup dialog box appears.

2 In the Slide Sized For box, click the drop-down arrow and select Letter Paper (8.5 x 11 in).

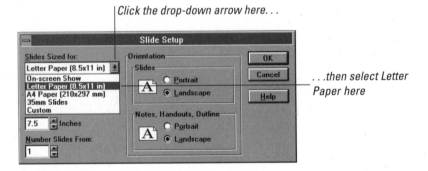

Click the drop-down arrow here. . .

. . .then select Letter Paper here

PowerPoint has five slide size formats to choose from: On-screen Show, Letter Paper (8.5 x 11 in), A4 Paper (210 x 297 mm), 35mm Slides, and Custom.

- **On-screen Show** Use this setting when designing an on-screen presentation or printing overhead transparencies on U.S. letter paper.

- **Letter Paper (8.5 x 11 in)** Use this setting when designing a presentation for U.S. letter paper (8.5 x 11 in).

- **A4 Paper (210 x 297 mm)**   Use this setting when printing to (international) A4 paper (210 x 297 mm or 10.83 x 7.5 in).

- **35mm Slides**   Use this setting when designing a presentation for 35mm slides.

- **Custom**   Use this setting when designing a presentation with a special size. Select the height and width of the slide by clicking the up arrow or down arrow button or positioning the cursor and typing a size. Anytime the height and width numbers do not match one of the three standard sizes, the format is a custom size format.

Note   The slide orientation should not be changed from landscape (7.5 x 10 in) to portrait (10 x 7.5 in) for existing presentations, because objects on the slides will shift or scale to the new slide size. Slide orientation should be changed before beginning a new presentation.

---

3   Click the OK button.

The slide size changes to Letter Paper (8.5 x 11 in).

4   From the Window menu, choose Fit To Page.

Your presentation window should look similar to the following illustration:

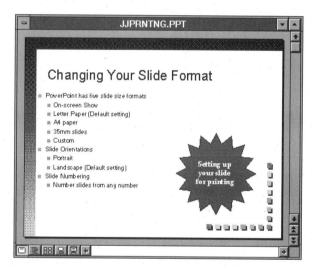

Change the notes, handouts, and outline orientation

Notes Pages View

1 Click the Notes Pages View button.

2 From the File menu, choose Slide Setup.

The Slide Setup dialog box appears.

3 In the Orientation area for Notes, Handouts, Outline, click the Portrait option button.

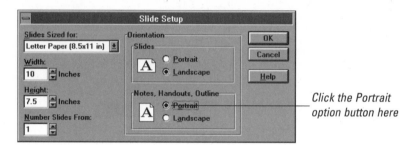

Click the Portrait option button here

PowerPoint has two orientation settings—one for slides and another for notes, handouts, and outlines—so that you don't have to change the orientation when you are printing more than one view.

4 Click the OK button.

The Note Pages view changes orientation from landscape to portrait.

Slide View

5 Click the Slide View button.

Change to the next slide

Next Slide

▶ Click the Next Slide button to advance to slide 2.

Printing in PowerPoint

PowerPoint allows you to print your presentation in four different ways: You can print slides, speaker's notes, audience handouts, and the outline. A printing sample of your practice presentation looks similar to the following illustrations:

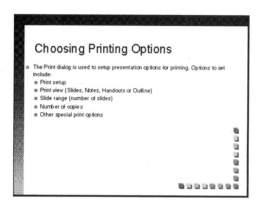

Slide (landscape)

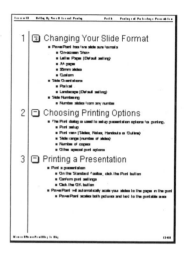

Outline

Notes Page

Handout Page

Printing Slides, Notes, Handouts, and Outlines

You can print slides, speaker's notes, audience handouts, and your outline as it appears in Outline view using the Print command from the File menu. The Print dialog box allows you to specify print options such as what to print, the print range, the number of copies, whether to print black and white, and whether to scale to fit the paper.

Printing Presentation Slides

In PowerPoint, your presentation slides automatically scale to the printer you have selected. Using scalable fonts such as TrueType fonts allows you to print your presentation on different printers with the same great results.

Print slides

1   From the File menu, choose Print.

The Print dialog box appears.

2   Click the drop-down arrow next to Print What.

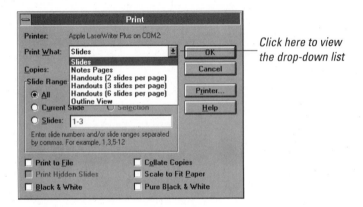

Click here to view the drop-down list

Six print format options are available.

- **Slides**   Prints your slides as they appear on the screen, one per page.

- **Notes Pages**   Prints the speaker's notes pages that correspond to the slide numbers selected in the Print Range area.

- **Handouts (2 slides per page)**   Prints two slides per page.

- **Handouts (3 slides per page)**   Prints three slides per page.

- **Handouts (6 slides per page)**   Prints six slides per page.

- **Outline View**   Prints your outline according to your view scale setting. What you see in Outline view is what you get on the printout. You can print titles and bodies, or titles only with formatting or without formatting.

For information about slide builds, see Lesson 15.

Note   If your presentation contains slides with build points, the Slides print option changes to Slides (with Builds) and Slides (without Builds). The Slides (with Builds) option prints each build point on a separate page. The Slides (without Builds) option prints the complete slide on one page.

3   Select the Slides printing option to close the drop-down list.

4   Click the OK button.

A print dialog box appears, giving your printing status.

Printing Speaker's Notes

You can print speaker's notes in the same way you print presentation slides. A reduced image of the presentation slide prints on each notes page.

Print speaker's notes with options

1   From the File menu, choose Print.

The Print dialog box appears.

2   Click the drop-down arrow next to Print What and select Notes Pages.

3   In the Slide Range area, click the Slides option button.

The insertion point appears to the left of the number 1 already in the range box.

4   Type **2-3,**

The numbers 2-3,1 appear in the slide range. PowerPoint will print slides 2 and 3, and then print slide 1. You can print slides in any order by entering slide numbers and ranges separated by commas.

5   Click the Black & White check box.

Six print options are available at the bottom of the dialog box.

- **Print to File**   Use this option to print slides to a presentation file to create 35mm slides using a personal film recorder. This option can also be used to send a presentation to a Genigraphics service center. See Lesson 14, "Producing 35mm Slides" for more information on Genigraphics.

- **Print Hidden Slides**   Use this option to print all hidden slides.

- **Black & White**   Use this option to turn all fills to white (or black and white, if patterned). Unbordered objects that have no text appear with a thin black frame.

- **Collate Copies**   Use this option to print multiple copies of your presentation. This option is usually available for laser printers only.

Tip   When printing multiple copies of your presentation, turn off the Collate Copies printing option for faster results.

- **Scale to Fit Printer**   Use this only if the paper in the printer does not correspond to the slide size and orientation settings. This option scales slides automatically to fit the paper size in the printer.

- **Pure Black & White**   Use this option when printing draft copies of your presentation on a color printer. This option turns all color fills to white, turns all text and lines to black, adds outlines or borders to all filled objects, and renders pictures in grayscale.

6   Click the OK button.

A print dialog box appears, giving your printing status.

Printing Handouts

You can print handouts in three different formats: 2 slides per page, 3 slides per page, and 6 slides per page. Add the handouts you print to your quick-reference notebook.

Print the quick-reference notebook presentation

1   From the File menu, choose Print (CTRL+P).

The Print dialog box appears.

2   Click the drop-down arrow next to Print What.

3   Select Handouts (2 slides per page) from the drop-down list.

4   Click the OK button.

A dialog box appears, giving your printing status.

Printing an Outline

PowerPoint prints the outline of your presentation as it appears in Outline view. The text format and current view scale you see on-screen in Outline view are what you'll get when the outline prints. The current view of your presentation slides will not affect the printout.

Print an outline of your presentation

1   From the View menu, choose Outline.

Zoom Control

2   On the Standard Toolbar, click the Zoom Control drop-down arrow and select 50%.

3   From the File menu, choose Print.

The Print dialog box appears.

4   Click the drop-down arrow next to Print What.

5   Select Outline View from the drop-down list.

6   In the Slide Range area, click the All option button.

7   Click the Black & White check box to turn off the option.

8   Click the OK button.

A print dialog box appears, giving your printing status.

9   Click the Slide View button.

Slide View

Save the presentation

▶   On the Standard Toolbar, click the Save button.

Save

No dialog box appears because the presentation already has a name. The current information in your presentation is saved with the same name.

One Step Further

You have learned in this lesson to set your slide format and set up your presentation for printing. If you'd like to practice these and other basic skills in your practice presentation, try the following:

▶   From the Slides Sized for box, select A4 Paper, change the orientation or the width and height settings, and look at your slide to see what changed.

▶   Print your practice presentation using the different print options from the Print dialog box found in the File menu.

▶   Print your presentation in the different views: Notes Pages, Handouts, Outline View, and Slides with and without builds.

If You Want to Continue to the Next Lesson

1   From the File menu, choose Close (CTRL+W).

2   If a dialog box appears asking whether you want to save the changes to your presentation, click the No button. You do not need to save the changes you made to the presentation after you printed it.

Choosing this command closes the active presentation; it does not exit PowerPoint.

If You Want to Quit PowerPoint for Now

1   From the File menu, choose Exit (CTRL+Q).

2   If a dialog box appears asking whether you want to save changes to the presentation, choose the No button.

Lesson Summary

To	Do this	Button
Choose a printer	From the File menu, choose Print. In the Print dialog box, click the Printer button.	
Change the slide format	From the File menu, choose Slide Setup and then select a slide format.	
Print slides	From the File menu, choose Print. Click the Print What drop-down arrow and select Slides.	
Print notes pages	From the File menu, choose Print. Click the Print What drop-down arrow and select Notes Pages.	
Print audience handouts	From the File menu, choose Print. Click the Print What drop-down arrow and select Handouts (2, 3, or 6 slides per page).	
Print an outline	From the File menu, choose Print. Click the Print What drop-down arrow and select Outline view.	
Print a black and white presentation	From the File menu, choose Print. Click the Black & White check box.	
Print the current slide	From the File menu, choose Print. Click the Current Slide option button.	

For on-line information about	**From the PowerPoint Help menu, choose Contents, select "Using PowerPoint," and then**
Printing a presentation	Select the topic "Notes, Handouts, Slide Shows, and Printing" and click the title "How to Print a Presentation."

For more information on	**See the *Microsoft PowerPoint User's Guide***
Printing a presentation	Chapter 6, "Notes, Handouts, Slide Shows, and Printing"

Preview of the Next Lesson

In the next lesson, you'll learn how to produce 35mm slides, how to you save your presentation with the Genigraphics driver, and how to send a presentation to Genigraphics using the GraphicsLink application. By the end of the lesson, you'll have produced another presentation for your quick-reference notebook.

Producing 35mm Slides

PowerPoint makes the process of producing 35mm slides from your presentations easier than ever. Your PowerPoint application connects to Genigraphics, a computer graphics company that can produce professional 35mm slides from your presentations. You can send your presentations via modem or on disk to a Genigraphics Service Center that will image your PowerPoint slides directly to 35mm color slides.

In this lesson, you'll learn how to select the Genigraphics Driver, set slide and Genigraphics print options, and complete job instructions and billing information. You'll also start GraphicsLink and send a presentation file. At the end of the lesson, your presentation will consist of the following slides:

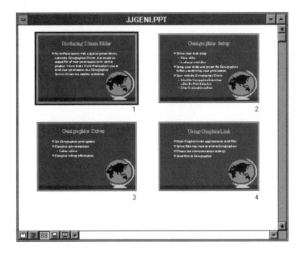

You will learn how to:

- Select the Genigraphics Driver
- Set slide and Genigraphics print options
- Complete job instructions and billing information
- Open and send files with GraphicsLink

Estimated lesson time: 25 minutes

Open a presentation

If you haven't already started PowerPoint, do so now. For instructions about starting PowerPoint, see "Getting Ready," earlier in this book.

Open

1   On the Standard Toolbar, click the Open button or select Open an Existing Presentation from the Startup dialog box and click OK.

2   In the Directories box, ensure that the PRACTICE directory is open. If it is not, select the drive where the Step by Step practice files are stored and open the appropriate directories to find the PRACTICE directory.

For information about opening a sample presentation, see Lesson 2.

3   In the list of file names, select LESSON14.PPT.

If you do not see LESSON14.PPT in the list of file names, check to be sure the correct drive and directory are selected. If you need help, see "Getting Ready."

4   Click the OK button.

Your presentation opens to the following slide:

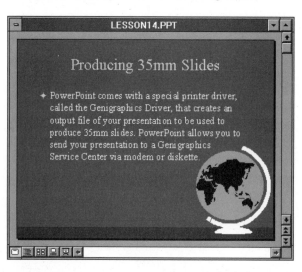

Save the presentation with a new name

Give the presentation a new name so that the changes you make in this lesson do not overwrite the original presentation.

1   From the File menu, choose Save As.

2   In File Name box, type *your initials***geni**

For example, if your initials are J. J., type **jjgeni**

3   Click the OK button.

The Summary Info dialog box appears. If you would like, type in the summary information. Press TAB to move between fields.

4   Click the OK button.

Preview the lesson

The presentation for this lesson contains reference information about Genigraphics. To preview the information in this lesson, click the Slide Show button and view the presentation.

Slide Show

1   Click the Slide Show button.

PowerPoint displays the first slide in the presentation.

2   Click to advance to the next slide.

3   Click once for each slide to advance through the rest of the presentation.

After the last slide in the presentation, PowerPoint returns to the first slide.

Next Slide

Change to the next slide

▶   Click the Next Slide button to advance to slide 2.

Setting Up the Genigraphics Driver

Before you send a presentation to a Genigraphics Service Center, you must set the appropriate PowerPoint settings. PowerPoint comes with a special printer driver, called the Genigraphics Driver, which you must select before you can send your presentation. Selecting the Genigraphics Driver includes choosing specific options that are designed to make the process easier.

Set up the slides

1   From the File menu, choose Slide Setup.

The Slide Setup dialog box appears.

2   In the Slides Sized for box, click the drop-down arrow and select 35mm Slides.

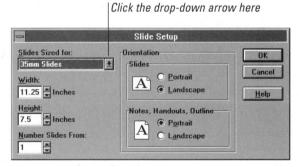

3   Click the OK button.

Fit the slides to the window

▶   From the Window menu, choose Fit To Page.

Your presentation window expands to encompass the larger slide format.

Choose the Genigraphics Driver and setup options

1 From the File menu, choose Print.

The Print dialog box appears.

2 Click the Printer button.

The Print Setup dialog box appears.

3 In the Printers area, select the Genigraphics® Driver on GENI.

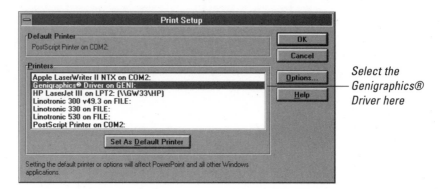

Select the Genigraphics® Driver here

The Genigraphics Driver sets the aspect ratio and image size of the slides.

TROUBLESHOOTING: **If the Genigraphics Driver doesn't appear in the Printers list** Click the Cancel button and reinstall the Genigraphics Driver. Double-click the PowerPoint Setup icon in the Microsoft Office group and install the Genigraphics Driver and GraphicsLink application.

4 Click the Options button.

The Genigraphics Setup dialog box appears.

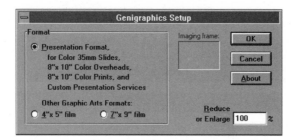

The Genigraphics Setup dialog box allows you to choose from three Genigraphics formats. **Do not** change the default format setting.

- **Presentation Format** Use this format for 35mm slides, 8" x 10" overheads and prints, and custom presentations.

- **4" x 5" film** Use this setting when you want to work with color on printed materials, such as brochures.

- **7" x 9" film**   Used this format when you want enlarge your presentation for display.

Tip   To prepare an existing presentation for Genigraphics, select Presentation Format in the Genigraphics Setup dialog box.

5   Click the OK button.

The Genigraphics Setup dialog box closes.

6   Click the OK button.

The Print Setup dialog box closes. The Genigraphics Driver and printer options are set up to create 35mm slides.

7   Click the Cancel button.

The Genigraphics Driver is set up. In the next section, you'll create the 35mm slides.

Change to the next slide

Next Slide

▶   Click the Next Slide button to advance to slide 3.

Creating a Genigraphics Presentation

With the Genigraphics Driver selected and your slides set up for 35mm slides, you are ready to save your presentation with the Genigraphics Driver. To save your presentation, simply print your presentation. However, saving with the Genigraphics Driver requires you to fill out job instructions and billing information.

Save your presentation to create 35mm slides

1   From the File menu, choose Print.

The Print dialog box appears, displaying Slides in the Print What box and the Genigraphics Driver on GENI as the printer.

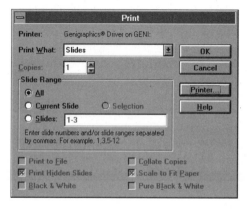

TROUBLESHOOTING: **If your Print dialog box does not look like the dialog box shown above**   Click the Printer button and follow the steps in the "Setting Up the Genigraphics Driver" section earlier in this lesson.

2   In the Slide Range area, click the All option button, if it is not already selected.

All the other settings in the Print dialog box are set correctly.

3   Click the OK button.

The Genigraphics Job Instructions dialog box appears. This dialog box provides Genigraphics with instructions on how to process your order.

4   In the Copies box next to 8" x 10" Overheads, double-click the 0.

5   Type **2**

The information in the Copies box now tells Genigraphics to send you one set of 35mm slides on plastic mounts and two sets of 8" x 10" overheads.

6   Insert a blank, formatted disk into drive A (or drive B).

7   In the Send Via area, click the Diskette option button.

This option saves your presentation to a disk as a Genigraphics file.

8   In the Return Via area, click the Mail option button.

Your order will be returned to you through the mail when Genigraphics has completed the necessary work.

9   In the Save As box, double-click JJGENI and type **jj35mm**

The Genigraphics Job Instructions dialog box should look similar to the following illustration:

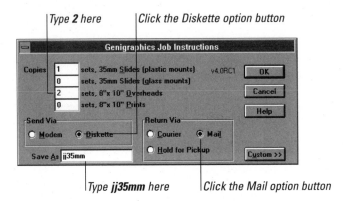

Note   You can customize your Genigraphics order by clicking the Custom button in the Genigraphics Job Instructions dialog box.

10   Click the OK button.

Because you saved your file to a disk, the standard Save As dialog box appears. Selecting the modem option button in the Genigraphics Job Instructions dialog box would save your file to the Genigraphics directory in your Windows 3.1 system folder.

11   In the Drives box, click the down arrow and select drive A (or drive B, depending on where your disk is located).

12   Click the OK button.

A print status dialog box appears, and then the Genigraphics Billing Information dialog box appears.

Complete the billing information

The Genigraphics Billing Information dialog box requires you to fill in information for your Genigraphics Service Center.

To successfully save your presentation, enter the required basic information. The small x located to the left of some boxes identifies information that is always required by the Genigraphics Service Center.

1   Type **Spinning Globes Inc.** in the Company box and press TAB.

2   Type **Darlene Garcelon** in the Contact box and press TAB twice.

3   Type **One World Way** in the Street Address box and press TAB twice.

4   Type **Hemisphere** in the City box and press TAB.

5   Type **CA** in the State box and press TAB.

6   Type **91234** in the Zip box and press TAB.

7   Type **(510) 555-1234**

8   In the Billing area, click the COD option button.

The Genigraphics Billing Information dialog box should look similar to the following illustration:

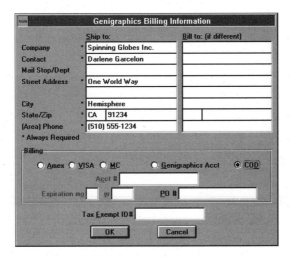

9   Click the OK button.

A Genigraphics Driver dialog box appears, telling you your presentation has been saved with the file name JJ35MM.GNA.

10   Click the OK button.

Your presentation is saved on the disk and can now be sent to the Genigraphics imaging facility.

For all users, mail your Genigraphics file to:

Genigraphics Corp./Central Imaging Facility
4155 Willow Lake Blvd.
Will Lake Business Park - Bldg. 9
Memphis, TN 38118
Tel: 1-800-638-7348 or 901-795-6431

Next Slide ·

Change to the next slide

▶   Click the Next Slide button to advance to slide 4.

Using GraphicsLink

GraphicsLink is a telecommunications program that comes with PowerPoint. It enables you to send your presentation files by modem to a Genigraphics Service Center. GraphicsLink allows you to keep track of all presentation files, their job descriptions, and their billing information.

Switch to Program Manager

1   Press CTRL+ESC to display the Task List dialog box.

The Task List dialog box appears. (PowerPoint is still open. More than one application can be open at the same time.)

2   Select Program Manager and click the Switch To button.

Start GraphicsLink and select the file

GraphicsLink

1   Double-click the GraphicsLink icon in the Microsoft Office program group window.

The GraphicsLink window appears.

2   From the GraphicsLink File menu, choose Switch Directory (CTRL+D).

The Switch Directory dialog box appears.

3   In the Directories box, select [-a-] or [-b-], depending on where your disk is located.

4   Click the OK button.

5   In the Files box, select JJ35MM.GNA, if it is not already selected.

Your GraphicsLink window should look similar to the following illustration:

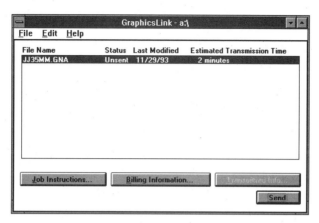

6   Click the OK button.

The GraphicsLink window displays your presentation.

Transmit the presentation

1   From the GraphicsLink File menu, choose Communications Setup.

The Communications Setup dialog box appears.

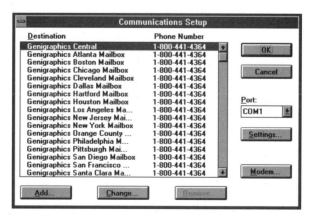

2   Select the closest Genigraphics Service Center location listed in the Communications Setup dialog box.

For users outside the United States, modem your Genigraphics file to 1-800-441-4364.

3 Click the OK button.

The Communications Setup dialog box closes. To actually send your presentation with the GraphicsLink application, click the Send button in the GraphicsLink window. A Send Status dialog box appears, showing you the progress of your transmission. After your transmission is final, a transmission summary appears on your screen, telling you the results of your transmission.

Note A $.50 (U.S.A.) per minute charge for transmission of your files will be added to your invoice. When a file has been successfully transmitted to a Genigraphics Service Center, the .GNA file is deleted and replaced with a .GNX file. This new file contains a job report and transmission summary report, which give you an accurate record of all your Genigraphics orders.

---

4 From the File menu choose Exit.

The GraphicsLink window closes.

5 Press CTRL+ESC to display the Task List dialog box.

The Task List dialog box appears.

6 Select Microsoft PowerPoint and click the Switch To button.

Your presentation window reappears.

Print the quick-reference notebook presentation

For information on printing a presentation, see Lesson 13.

1 From the File menu, choose Print (CTRL+P).

The Print dialog box appears.

2 Click the Printer button.

3 In the Printers area, select the default printer.

4 Click the OK button.

The Print Setup dialog box closes.

5 Click the drop-down arrow next to Print What.

6 Select Handouts (2 slides per page) from the drop-down list.

7 Click the OK button.

A dialog box appears, giving your printing status.

Save the presentation

Save

▶ On the Standard Toolbar, click the Save button.

No dialog box appears because the presentation already has a name. The current information in your presentation is saved with the same name.

One Step Further

You have learned to set up your slides and printer for Genigraphics, save a presentation file with the Genigraphics format, set Genigraphics options, and use GraphicsLink to send your file. If you'd like to practice these and other basic skills in your practice presentation, try the following:

▶   Select the Modem option button from the Send Via box in the Genigraphics Job Instructions dialog box. Find the file in the Windows directory.

▶   Prepare and send a presentation to a Genigraphics Service Center. Pricing for each 35mm slide starts at $9.95. For a complete price list of Genigraphics Desktop Images Services, call 1-800-638-7348.

If You Want to Continue to the Next Lesson

1   From the File menu, choose Close (CTRL+W).

2   If a dialog box appears asking whether you want to save the changes to the presentation, click the No button.

If You Want to Quit PowerPoint for Now

1   From the File menu, choose Exit (CTRL+Q).

2   If a dialog box appears asking whether you want to save changes to the presentation, click the No button.

Lesson Summary

To	Do this	Button
Select the Genigraphics Driver	From the File menu, choose Print. In the Printer area, select Genigraphics Driver. Click the OK button.	
Select the Genigraphics setup options	From the Print Setup dialog box, click the Options button.	
Set up the Genigraphics slide options	From the File menu, choose Slide Setup. Select 35mm Slides.	
Save your presentation with the Genigraphics format	Select the Genigraphics Driver. On the Standard Toolbar, click the Print button.	
Fill out the Genigraphics Job Instructions dialog box	Select the Genigraphics Driver. On the Standard Toolbar, click the Print button. The dialog box appears. Enter the job instructions.	

To	Do this	Button
Fill out the Genigraphics Billing Information dialog box	From the Genigraphics Job Instructions dialog box, click the OK button and enter the billing information.	
Use the GraphicsLink application	From Program Manager, double-click the GraphicsLink icon.	
Select your phone number and modem	From the GraphicsLink File menu, choose Communications Setup.	

For on-line information about	From the PowerPoint Help menu, choose Contents, select "Reference Information," and then
Creating a 35mm presentation	Select the topic "Genigraphics Help," and click the title "Genigraphics Driver — The Basics."
Sending slides to Genigraphics	Select the topic "Genigraphics Help," and click the title "GraphicsLink — The Basics."

Preview of the Next Lesson

In the next lesson, you'll learn how to produce an electronic presentation by adding slide transitions and timings, building slides, rehearsing timings, and using the PowerPoint Viewer. By the end of the lesson, you'll have produced another presentation for your quick-reference notebook.

Producing an Electronic Presentation

In PowerPoint you can display your presentations on your computer using Slide Show. The Slide Show feature turns your computer into a projector that displays your presentation slide by slide. A slide show can also operate continuously, unattended, to show a presentation.

In this lesson, you'll learn how to draw on a slide during a slide show, hide a slide from a slide show, add slide transitions, and add a bullet point transition called a *build slide*. You'll also set slide timings, rehearse your slide show, and show presentations with the PowerPoint Viewer. At the end of the lesson, your presentation will consist of the following slides:

You will learn how to:

- Draw freehand in a slide show

- Set slide transitions and timings

- Rehearse a slide show

- Create a build slide

- Hide a slide

- Show presentations with the PowerPoint Viewer

Estimated lesson time: 20 minutes

Open a presentation

If you haven't already started PowerPoint, do so now. For instructions about starting PowerPoint, see "Getting Ready," earlier in this book.

Open

1   On the Standard Toolbar, click the Open button or select Open an Existing Presentation from the Startup dialog box and click OK.

2   In the Directories box, ensure that the PRACTICE directory is open. If it is not, select the drive where the Step by Step practice files are stored and open the appropriate directories to find the PRACTICE directory.

For information about opening a sample presentation, see Lesson 2.

3   In the list of file names, click LESSON15.PPT.

If you do not see LESSON15.PPT in the list of files names, check to be sure the correct drive and directory are selected. If you need help, see "Getting Ready."

4   Click the OK button.

Your presentation opens to the following slide:

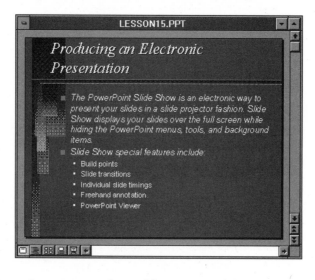

Save the presentation with a new name

Give the presentation a new name so that the changes you make in this lesson do not overwrite the original document.

1   From the File menu, choose Save As.

2   In the File Name box, type *your initials***sldsho**

For example, if your initials are J. J., type **jjsldsho**

3   Click the OK button.

The Summary Info dialog box appears. If you would like, type in the summary information. Press TAB to move between fields.

4   Click the OK button.

Drawing Freehand in Slide Show

During a slide show presentation, you can draw freehand lines, circles, and arrows to emphasize your message. You simply move the mouse to display the pointer, click the annotation icon, and then draw. When you finish drawing, you click the annotation icon again to continue the presentation.

Draw a freehand line

Slide Show

1   Click the Slide Show button.

PowerPoint displays the first slide in the presentation.

2   Move the mouse to display the pointer.

Annotation

3   Click the Annotation icon in the lower right corner of the screen.

The pointer changes to a pencil cursor. Now you are ready to draw on the slide.

4   Position the pencil cursor under the bullet next to the text "PowerPoint Viewer."

The text "PowerPoint Viewer" is the last line of text on the slide.

5   Drag a line under the line "PowerPoint Viewer."

Use slide show controls

During a slide show presentation, you have the ability to erase annotation drawings or blank out the presentation screen at any time to make a point.

1   Press the E key to erase the annotation drawing.

2   Press the W key to make the screen white.

You can press the W key again to restore the screen.

3   Press the B key to blacken the screen.

Press the B key again to restore the screen.

Exit Annotation

4   Click the Exit Annotation icon to turn off annotation.

The pencil cursor changes back to the pointer.

5   Press the RIGHT ARROW key or the PAGE DOWN key to advance to the next slide.

You can press the LEFT ARROW key or PAGE UP key to return to the previous slide.

6   Click once for each slide to advance through the rest of the presentation.

After the last slide in the presentation, PowerPoint returns to the current view.

Change to the next slide

Next Slide

▶   Click the Next Slide button to advance to slide 2.

Viewing Slides in Slide Sorter View

In Slide Sorter view, you can view your presentation slides with or without slide formatting. For some presentations with shaded backgrounds, the slide text might be difficult to read. If you turn off the Show Formatting feature in Slide Sorter view, PowerPoint displays your presentation slides with black title text on a white background, without formatting.

Change the slide formatting

Slide Sorter View

Show Formatting

1   Click the Slide Sorter View button.

Notice all of the formatting styles are visible on the slides.

2   On the Slide Sorter Toolbar, click the Show Formatting button.

Click here to turn off formatting

All of the formatting information is turned off.

Note   When the Show Formatting feature is turned off, transition and build effects do not display in Slide Sorter view.

---

3   Drag slide 3, titled "Slide Transition and Timings," between slide 1 and slide 2.

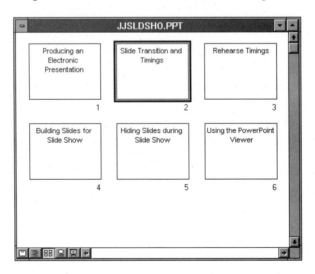

Show Formatting

4   On the Slide Sorter Toolbar, click the Show Formatting button again.

The slides' formatting information is turned back on.

Setting Slide Transitions and Timings

A slide transition is the visual effect given to a slide as it moves on and off the screen during a slide show. Slide transitions include such effects as Checkerboard Across, Cover Down, Cut, and Split Vertical Out; there are a total of 46 slide transition effects. You can set a transition for one slide or a group of slides by selecting the slides and applying the transition.

Slide timing refers to the time a slide appears on the screen. As with transitions, you can set slide timings for one slide or a group of slides depending on how many slides you have selected when you apply the slide timing.

Apply a slide transition

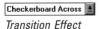

Transition Effect

1   On the Slide Sorter Toolbar, click the Transition Effect drop-down arrow and select Checkerboard Across.

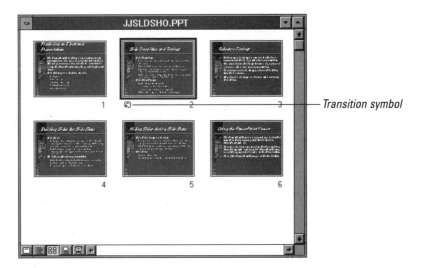

— *Transition symbol*

PowerPoint places a transition symbol below the lower left corner of slide 2. This tells you a slide transition has been applied to this slide.

Slide Show

2   Click the Slide Show button.

Slide Show displays slide 2 with the Checkerboard Across effect.

3   Press the ESC key.

PowerPoint returns you to slide 2.

Apply multiple transitions and timings

1   From the Edit menu, choose Select All (CTRL+A).

2   On the Slide Sorter Toolbar, click the Transition button or from the Slide menu, choose Transition.

Transition

The Transition dialog box appears. The option boxes in the Transition dialog box are blank when multiple slides are selected that have different transition settings. The Transition dialog box should look similar to the following illustration:

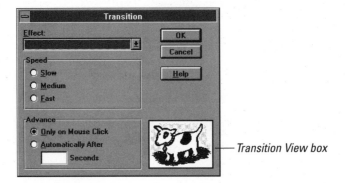

— *Transition View box*

3 Click the Effect drop-down arrow, and select Random Transition.

The Transition View box demonstrates the transition effect.

4 Click the Slow option button to set the transition speed.

5 In the Advance box, click the Automatically After Seconds option button.

6 Type **4**

There are two ways to advance your slide show, automatically or by mouse click.

■ The automatic advance timing feature moves your slides through the slide show automatically, keeping the slide on the screen the length of time designated in the Advance box.

■ The mouse click manually moves your slides through the slide show.

The Transition dialog box should look similar to the following illustration:

Click the Slow option button here

Click here to view the drop-down list

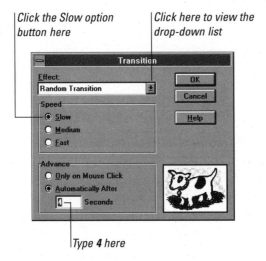

Type 4 here

Tip In Slide Show, a mouse click always advances a slide, even if the timing set in the transition box has not elapsed. Conversely, holding down the mouse button prevents a timed transition from occurring until you release the mouse button, even if the set timing has elapsed.

7 Click the OK button.

All the slides in your presentation now have a transition symbol and a slide time (:04), as shown in the following illustration:

Slide Show

8 Click the Slide Show button.

Slide Show runs through your presentation, using the slide time and transition you set in the Transition dialog box.

Setting Rehearsed Slide Timings

You can also set slide timings using the Rehearse Timing button. If you are unsure of how fast to set the slide timings of your presentation, you can rehearse your slide show and adjust your timings appropriately for each slide.

Important Before you begin this section, read all the steps carefully so you understand what happens when you click the Rehearse Timing button.

Rehearse Timing

1 On the Slide Sorter Toolbar, click the Rehearse Timing button.

Slide Show begins, displaying a Time button in the lower left corner of the screen, as in the following illustration:

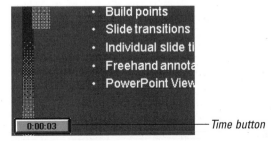
Time button

The Time button begins running as soon as the first slide appears. As soon as you feel the timing is adequate to read and view the information, click the Time button to move to the next slide.

2   Click the Time button to select a new slide timing or press the O key to use the original timings for each slide in the presentation.

At the end of the slide rehearsal, a confirmation dialog box appears with the total time for the slide show.

3   Click the Yes button to save the new slide timings.

Your slides now display the new slide time settings.

4   Click a blank area of the presentation window to deselect all the slides.

Setting Build Slides for a Slide Show

All bullet point subparagraphs move with the major bullet points.

In a slide show, you can have slide bullet points transition one at a time on the screen. The transition of each bullet point onto the slide is called a *build slide*. You can build bullet points for a slide show using 30 different transition effects. The Build feature can be applied only in the Slide Sorter view and Slide view.

Create a build slide

1   Click slide 4.

2   Click the Slide View button.

Slide View

3   From the Tools menu, choose Build.

The Build dialog box appears.

4   Click the drop-down arrow under the Dim Previous Points check box, and select dark green (the second color in the top row).

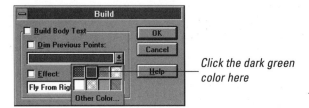

Click the dark green color here

The Build Body Text check box and the Dim Previous Points check box are turned on. The bullet points will change to dark green as they dim during your slide show when each new build point appears.

5   Click the drop-down arrow under the Effect check box.

6   Click the down scroll arrow and select Dissolve.

7   Click the OK button.

8   From the View menu, choose Slide Show.

The Slide Show dialog box appears.

9   In the Slides box, click the From option button.

10   Press the TAB key to switch to the To text box and type **4**

The Slide Show dialog box should look similar to the following illustration:

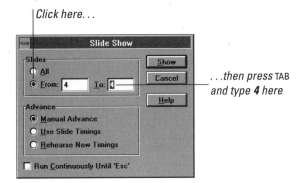

11   Click the Show button.

Slide Show runs slide 4 with the new build effects, using the slide timing set in the slide show rehearsal.

Create multiple build slides

1   From the View menu, choose Slide Sorter.

2   From the Edit menu, choose Select All (CTRL+A).

Build

3   On the Slide Sorter Toolbar, click the Build button.

The Build dialog box appears. The option boxes in the Build dialog box are grayed out when multiple slides are selected that have different build settings.

4   Click the drop-down arrow under the Dim Previous Points check box, and select dark green.

The Build Body Text check box and the Dim Previous Points check box are turned on.

5   Click the drop-down arrow under the Effect check box and select Random Effects.

6   Click the OK button.

All of the slides now have build symbols below their lower left corners next to the transition symbols, signifying that they all have builds.

Note   Applying builds to multiple slides might affect how long you want the slide to stay on the screen during a slide show. Slide timings are divided equally among the builds for each slide, and you might need to adjust the slide timing to adequately show your build points. For example, if you have a slide with four build points and a slide timing of 8 seconds, each build point will have 2 seconds on the screen.

Slide Show

7   Click the Slide Show button.

The build slides appear during the on-screen presentation.

8   Click in a blank area of the presentation window to deselect all the slides.

Hiding a Slide During a Slide Show

You might want to customize an on-screen presentation for a specific audience. With PowerPoint, you can hide the slides you don't want to use during a slide show by using the Hide Slide command.

Hide a slide during a slide show

1   Click slide 5.

Hide Slide

2   On the Slide Sorter Toolbar, click the Hide Slide button.

A hide symbol appears over the slide number, as shown in the following illustration:

🔁 ⠿ :16   🟥 —*Hide symbol*

3   Click a blank area of the presentation window to deselect slide 5.

Slide Show

4   Click the Slide Show button.

Slide 5 doesn't appear during the on-screen presentation.

5   Click slide 4.

6   Click the Slide Show button.

Hide

7   Move the mouse and click the Hide icon next to the Annotation icon or press the H key to show the hidden slide.

8   Press the ESC key to stop the slide show.

Creating a Drill Down Document

You can add "drill down" documents that allow you to review material in another application during a slide show. For example, you might drill down or branch to a Microsoft Excel worksheet or a PowerPoint slide to provide more detail on a topic.

Create a drill down document

1 From the Insert menu, choose Object.

The Insert Object dialog box appears.

2 Click the Create From File option button.

3 Click the Browse button.

The Browse dialog box appears.

4 In the Source box, select SLDSHOW1.PPT and click the OK button.

5 Click the Display As Icon check box.

The Insert Object dialog box should look similar to the following illustration:

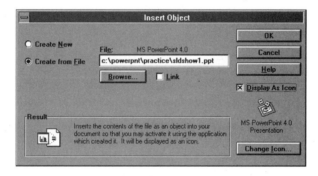

6 Click the OK button.

A small PowerPoint icon is placed on your presentation slide.

Slide Show

7 Click the Slide Show button.

8 Click the PowerPoint icon displayed on the slide.

The slide show branches to display the slides from SLDSHOW1.PPT.

9 Click to advance through the drill down presentation back to the original slide.

10 Press the ESC key to exit the slide show.

Using the PowerPoint Viewer

If the PowerPoint Viewer is not installed, see Appendix A for more information.

PowerPoint comes with a special application called the PowerPoint Viewer, which allows you to show a slide show on a computer that does not have PowerPoint installed. You can freely install the PowerPoint Viewer program on any compatible system. To install the program, choose Run from the File menu in Program Manager and type **a:\vsetup** (or **b:\vsetup**) in the File Name text box.

Showing Presentations with the PowerPoint Viewer

PowerPoint
Viewer

1   Press ALT+TAB to switch to the Program Manager.

2   Double-click the PowerPoint Viewer icon from the Microsoft Office program group window.

The Microsoft PowerPoint Viewer dialog box appears.

3   In the Directories box, ensure that the PRACTICE directory is open. If it is not, select the drive where the Step by Step practice files are stored, and open the appropriate directories to find the PRACTICE directory.

4   In the File Name box, select SLDSHOW1.PPT.

Use the down arrow in the scroll bar to find your practice presentation if you do not see it in the list.

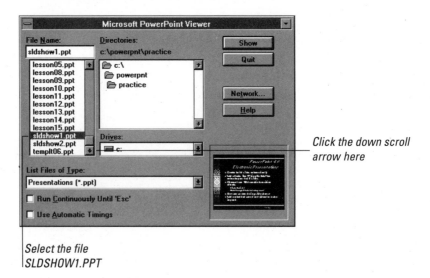

Click the down scroll arrow here

Select the file SLDSHOW1.PPT

5   Click the Show button.

PowerPoint shows SLDSHOW1.PPT—a presentation with PowerPoint samples. The PowerPoint Viewer responds to the same PowerPoint keyboard and mouse commands. When the slide show ends, the Microsoft PowerPoint Viewer dialog box reappears on your screen.

Show a list of presentations

With the PowerPoint Viewer, you can show multiple presentations one after another using a playlist file. The playlist can contain Windows PowerPoint files, Macintosh PowerPoint files, and even other playlists (filename.lst). You can create a playlist file with the Windows Notepad application. Simply save the file with a (.lst) extension.

1   Under List Files of Type, click the drop-down arrow.

2   Select Play Lists (*.lst).

3   In the File Name box, select SHOWLIST.LST.

4 Click the Show button.

The PowerPoint Viewer shows SLDSHOW1.PPT and SLDSHOW2.PPT in order.

5 Click the Quit button to exit the PowerPoint Viewer.

Switch back to PowerPoint

▶ Switch back to your PowerPoint presentation.

Use ALT+TAB to switch applications. The PowerPoint toolbars and menu appear.

Print the quick-reference notebook presentation

For information on printing a presentation, see Lesson 13.

1 From the File menu, choose Print (CTRL+P).

The Print dialog box appears.

2 Click the drop-down arrow next to Print What.

3 Select Handouts (2 slides per page) from the drop-down list.

4 Click the OK button.

A dialog box appears, giving your printing status.

Save the presentation

Save

▶ On the Standard Toolbar, click the Save button.

No dialog box appears because the presentation already has a name. The current information in your presentation is saved with the same name.

One Step Further

You have learned to produce and present a slide show in PowerPoint using build points, transitions, and timings. If you'd like to practice these and other basic skills in your practice presentation, try the following:

▶ Practice freehand drawing and slide show commands during a slide show.

▶ Apply different transition and build effects to individual slides and rehearse your presentation's slide timings with build slides.

▶ Use the PowerPoint Viewer to show your presentation on a compatible computer that does not have PowerPoint installed.

If You Want to Continue to the Review & Practice

1 From the File menu, choose Close (CTRL+W).

2 If a dialog box appears asking whether you want to save the changes to the presentation, click the No button.

If You Want to Quit PowerPoint for Now

1 From the File menu, choose Exit (CTRL+Q).

2 If a dialog box appears asking whether you want to save changes to the presentation, click the No button.

Lesson Summary

To	Do this	Button
Run a slide show	Click the Slide Show button.	
Stop a slide show	Press the ESC key.	
Do freehand drawing in a slide show	Click the Slide Show button. Click the annotation icon, and then draw. Click the exit annotation icon (arrow) to exit.	
Show formatting in Slide Sorter view	On the Slide Sorter Toolbar, click the Show Formatting button.	
Apply a transition	Select the slides. On the Slide Sorter Toolbar, click the Transition button, or choose Transitions from the Slide menu.	
Rehearse slide timings	On the Slide Sorter Toolbar, click the Rehearse Timing button.	
Apply builds to slides	Select one or more slides. On the Slide Sorter Toolbar, click the Build button.	
Hide a slide	On the Slide Sorter Toolbar, click the Hide Slide button.	
Run the PowerPoint Viewer	Double-click the PowerPoint Viewer icon in Program Manager. Select a presentation and click the Show button.	
Show more than one presentation in succession	Using the Windows Notepad, create a playlist (*.lst) file that includes a list of the presentation file names.	

For on-line information about	From the PowerPoint Help menu, choose Contents, select "Using PowerPoint," and then
Producing an electronic presentation	Select the topic "Notes, Handouts, Slide Shows, and Printing" and click the title "How to Create and Run Slide Shows."

Review & Practice

In the lessons, you learned to create presentations by working with slides, an outline, text, drawings, masters, color schemes, graphs, organizational charts, information from other sources, printing, 35mm slides, and slide shows. If you want to practice these skills and test your understanding, you can work through the Review & Practice section following this lesson.

Review & Practice

Practice the skills you learned in the lessons by working through this Review & Practice section. You'll use PowerPoint to create a presentation.

Scenario

You are an account manager in a financial firm and have many years of experience working directly with personal investment portfolios. Due to a merger with another firm, your job gets phased out. The thought of starting your own company has crossed your mind many times, but it never seemed like the right time.

You and a partner decide to start a financial firm called Ferguson and Bardell. To develop a solid customer base and market your new company, you need to create an investment presentation that portrays stability and confidence, yet can be customized for specific customer needs.

After recently learning PowerPoint techniques, you realize creating a presentation with PowerPoint is easy and effective. In this section, you pick a look for your presentation, enter and modify an outline, add your logo, insert an Microsoft Excel worksheet to analyze data, insert a chart to show the investment process, add a graph to show risks versus rewards, insert a Microsoft Word table to show market statistics, and print the final product. To impress clients, change the blank and white template to color and give an on-screen electronic presentation.

You will review and practice how to:

- Create a new presentation using the Pick a Look Wizard
- Enter and modify your ideas
- Add a logo and change the presentation's look
- Insert an Excel worksheet
- Create a process chart with Microsoft Organizational Chart
- Create a graph
- Insert a Word table
- Print and save the presentation
- Change the presentation template
- Give an on-screen electronic presentation

Estimated practice time: 30 minutes

Step 1:   Start a New Presentation Using the Pick a Look Wizard

Since you are a financial expert and not an artist, use PowerPoint's Pick a Look Wizard to help you customize the look of your presentation.

1   Start PowerPoint.

2   Select the Pick a Look Wizard option and then click the OK button.

3   Click the Next button.

4   Select the Black and White Overheads option and then click the Next button.

5   Select the World option and then click the Next button.

6   Click the Audience Handout Pages check box, click the Outline Pages check box, click the Speaker's Notes check box, and then click the Next button.

7   Click the Page Number check box and then click the Next button.

8   Click the Finished button.

For more information on	See
Creating a new presentation	Lesson 2

Step 2:   Enter and Modify Your Ideas

Modify the presentation content to meet your specific needs.

1   Click the title object and type **Investment Presentation**

2   Click the sub title object and type **Prepared for <client name>**

3   Click the Outline View button.

4   Click the New Slide button and enter the following information:

2 □ Overview
   • Investment Review
     – Where are you today?
     – Where do you want to be tomorrow?
   • Investing for Your Future
     – Review Historical Returns
     – Investment Selection

3 □ Investment Review
   • Current Financial Status

4 □ Investment Process

5 □ Risk vs Rewards

6 □ Selecting Markets

7 □ Recomendations

5   Double-click slide 2.

For more information on	See
Entering text in Slide view and Outline view	Lessons 2 and 3

Step 3:   Add a Logo and Change the Presentation's Look

Insert your company logo and adjust the look of the slide master.

1   Hold down the SHIFT key and click the Slide View button

2   From the Insert menu, choose Picture and select LOGO.WMF.

3   Scale the logo to 20% and move to the top center of the slide above the title.

4   Place the insertion point in the first line of the master text.

5   From the Format menu, choose Bullet and select the check mark (✔).

6   Click the Slide View button.

7   Click the Next Slide button to advance to slide 3.

For more information on	See
Inserting a picture	Lesson 11
Changing the slide master	Lesson 6

Step 4:   Insert a Microsoft Excel Worksheet

Insert an Excel worksheet to analyze the current financial status of the client.

1   Click the Insert Microsoft Excel Worksheet button and drag a 7 x 5 Sheet.

2   Enter in the following information:

Current Income	Value	% Total	Tax	Non Tax
Stocks				
Bonds				
Cash				
Other Income				
Deferred Income				
Totals				

3   Click a blank area of the presentation window to return to PowerPoint.

4   Select the worksheet object and move it to the center of the slide.

5   From the Draw menu, choose Scale and type **200**

6   On the Drawing+ Toolbar, click the Fill Color button and select a color.

7   On the Drawing+ Toolbar, click the Shadow Color button and select a color.

8   Click the Next Slide button to advance to slide 4.

For more information on	See
Inserting a Microsoft Excel worksheet	Lesson 12

Step 5:   Create a Process Chart with Organizational Chart

To map out the investment process, create a chart in Microsoft Organizational Chart.

1   Click the Layout button and select the Org Chart slide layout.

2   Double click the org chart placeholder and create the following chart:

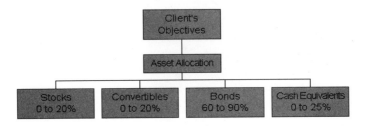

Investment Reveiw Process

3   Select all the boxes and add a box shadow.

4   From the File menu, choose Exit and Return to Presentation.

5   Click the Next Slide button to advance to slide 5.

For more information on	See
Creating an organizational chart	Lesson 10

Step 6:   Create a Graph

To show the market trends, create a graph with the risks versus the rewards.

1   Click the Layout button and select the Graph slide layout.

2   Double click the graph placeholder and enter the following data:

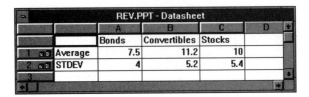

3   Select the data series on the chart and display the data labels.

4   Click a blank area of the presentation window to return to PowerPoint.

5   Click the Next Slide button to advance to slide 6.

For more information on	See
Working with Graph	Lessons 8 and 9

Step 7: Insert a Microsoft Word Table

To show the market statistics, create a Word table with market numbers.

1 Click the Layout button and select the Table slide layout.

2 Double click the table placeholder and create the following 5 x 6 table:

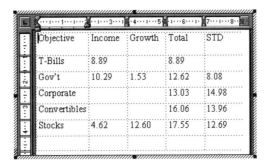

Objective	Income	Growth	Total	STD
T-Bills	8.89		8.89	
Gov't	10.29	1.53	12.62	8.08
Corporate			13.03	14.98
Convertibles			16.06	13.96
Stocks	4.62	12.60	17.55	12.69

3 Select column 1 and choose Cell Height And Width from the Table menu.

4 Click the up arrow until the column width is 2.2 and click the OK button.

5 Select the table data.

6 Use the Formatting Toolbar to change the font style and format.

7 Use the Borders Toolbar to change the line style and border format.

8 Click a blank area of the presentation window to return to PowerPoint.

9 Drag the elevator to go back to slide 1.

For more information on	See
Inserting a Word table	Lesson 12

Step 8: Print and Save the Presentation

Now you are finished, so print and save your presentation.

1 From the File menu, choose Print.

2 Click the Print What drop-down arrow and select Slides.

3 Click the OK button.

4 On the Standard Toolbar, click the Save button.

5 Ensure that the PRACTICE directory is open.

6 In the File Name box, type a *filename* and click the OK button.

For more information on	See
Printing a presentation	Lesson 2
Saving a presentation	Lesson 1

Step 9: Change the Presentation Template

Let's change this black and white presentation to color so that you can give an on-screen slide show presentation.

1   Click the Template button.

2   Double-click the SLDSHOW directory and select WORLDS.PPT.

3   Click the Apply button.

For more information on	See
Applying a template	Lesson 6

Step 10: Give an On-screen Electronic Presentation

Give an on-screen presentation to a client at your office using a big-screen projector.

1   Click the Slide Sorter button.

2   From the Edit menu, choose Select All.

3   On the Slide Sorter Toolbar, click the Transition Effects drop-down arrow and select Checkerboard Down.

4   On the Slide Sorter Toolbar, click the Build Effects drop-down arrow and select Fly From Top.

5   Click the Slide Show button.

6   Click each slide to advance through the slide show presentation.

7   Click the Annotation icon and underline and circle important points. Click the Annotation icon again to turn the feature off.

For more information on	See
Giving a slide show presentation	Lesson 15

If You Want to Quit PowerPoint for Now

1   From the File menu, choose Exit (CTRL+Q).

2   If a dialog box appears asking whether you want to save changes to the presentation, click the Yes button.

Appendixes

Installing PowerPoint

The Microsoft PowerPoint Setup program copies the PowerPoint program, the PowerPoint Viewer, the GraphicsLink program, and other files to your hard disk. Before you can start using PowerPoint, you must install it using the PowerPoint Setup program.

Hardware and Software Requirements

To use PowerPoint, your computer system must meet the following minimum requirements:

- Personal computer using an 80386 or higher microprocessor (an 80486 or higher microprocessor is recommended).

- Microsoft MS-DOS operating system 3.1 or later (MS-DOS version 5.0 or later is recommended).

- Microsoft Windows operating system version 3.1 or later; or Microsoft Windows for Workgroups operating system version 3.1 or later; or Microsoft Windows NT operating system version 3.1 or later.

- Minimum 4 MB of memory (8 MB recommended).

- Hard disk and a 3.5-inch high-density 1.44 MB floppy disk drive.

- Microsoft Mouse or other mouse that is compatible with Microsoft Windows 3.1.

- VGA, XGA, or any video adapter supported by Microsoft Windows 3.1 or later (except EGA, CGA, and Hercules monochrome). A color monitor and 256-color video adapter are recommended.

The following equipment is optional:

- Printer and/or film recorder compatible with Microsoft Windows 3.1.

- Microsoft Windows Graphical Environment for Pen Computing.

PowerPoint Installation Considerations

Before you install PowerPoint, you need to determine which type of installation is best for you. If you are an individual PowerPoint user, you need to install PowerPoint on your hard disk using the high-density disks. This type of installation is called a *local single-user* installation. If you are a network administrator, you can install PowerPoint on a network file server or a shared directory. This type of installation is called an *administrator* installation. If PowerPoint is installed on a network and you are connected to the network, you can either install PowerPoint on your hard disk or run PowerPoint off the network. Installing PowerPoint on your hard disk off a network is known as a *workstation* or *shared* installation.

All three types of installations are discussed briefly in this appendix.

Local Single-User Installation

For a detailed explanation of PowerPoint Setup, see your PowerPoint documentation.

The following Setup procedure covers the basics of setting up PowerPoint on a local single-user system. The options you choose during Setup determine the amount of disk space needed to install PowerPoint onto your hard disk. The PowerPoint Setup options are as follows:

Typical (Requires 22 MB)   Installs the most commonly used PowerPoint components, including the templates, typical clip art, basic TrueType fonts, spelling checker, WordArt, Microsoft Organization Chart, and Microsoft Graph.

Custom/Complete (Requires 33 MB)   With this option you can either install PowerPoint completely (Complete) or with only the options you want (Custom). If you choose Custom Installation, PowerPoint asks you which components you want to install in the Complete/Custom dialog box. As you install components, PowerPoint keeps track of the disk space it needs to successfully complete the installation.

Laptop (Requires 11 MB)   Installs the minimum set of components required to run PowerPoint. This option takes up the least amount of hard disk space.

Note   A fourth installation option is available when you install PowerPoint from a network. This option, called "Workstation," is discussed later in this appendix.

Set up PowerPoint on your hard disk

1   If Windows is not currently running, type **win** at the MS-DOS prompt.

-or-

If Windows is running, close all open applications.

2   Insert the PowerPoint Setup disk (Disk 1) in drive A (or drive B if you are using the B drive).

3   From the Program Manager File menu, choose Run.

The Run dialog box appears.

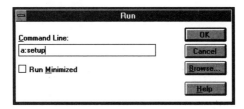

4   Type **a:setup** (or **b:setup** if you are using the B drive) and click the OK button.

A dialog box appears telling you to quit all open applications before proceeding with Setup. If there is a previous version of PowerPoint on your system, you can replace it or install PowerPoint version 4 in a different directory.

5   Click the OK button to continue Setup.

The Name and Organization Information dialog box appears. If the information is not correct, type in the correct information.

6   Click the OK button.

A dialog box appears telling you where PowerPoint will be installed.

7   Click the OK button to accept the destination directory.

-or-

Click the Change Directory button and select a different directory.

A dialog box appears showing you the PowerPoint installation options.

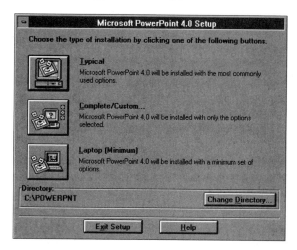

8   Click the installation option that best meets your needs. To complete all the lessons in this book, the Complete/Custom installation is recommended.

- If you click the Typical Installation button, the Choose Program Group dialog box appears.

- If you click the Complete/Custom Installation button, the Complete\Custom dialog box appears.

- If you click the Laptop Installation button, the Choose Program Group dialog box appears.

Note   If you click either the Typical Installation button or the Laptop Installation button, skip steps 9 and 10.

---

9   To install PowerPoint completely, click the Continue button.

-or-

To customize your installation of PowerPoint, click a component check box in the Options scroll box.

- Clicking a component check box disables the entire component, and Setup won't install it.

■ Selecting an option and clicking the Change Option button allows you to select certain parts of the component you don't want to install.

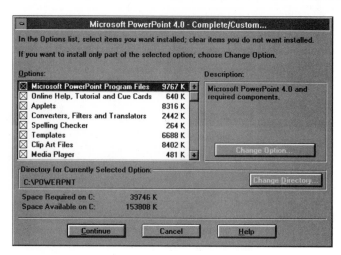

10 Click the Continue button.

The Choose Program Group dialog box appears.

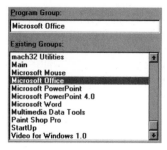

11 Click the Continue button to accept the default Program Group "Microsoft Office."

-or-

You can type a new group name in the Program Group box or select an existing group from the Existing Group list.

12 Click the Continue button.

Setup begins installing PowerPoint. Insert PowerPoint setup disks as requested to complete the installation. The PowerPoint and associated application icons are created and placed into the Program Group you selected.

13 Click the Continue button to restart Windows.

After you have installed PowerPoint, you can run PowerPoint Setup from the Program Group at any time to add or modify any PowerPoint component.

Administrator Installation

Installing PowerPoint on a network file server lets network users share the PowerPoint program and documents created in PowerPoint. The following Setup procedure covers the basics of installing PowerPoint on a network file server.

For a detailed explanation of how to use a network file server and network software, see your network documentation.

Before you install PowerPoint on a network file server, check the following:

- The network must be operational. You must have full access privileges to place PowerPoint in network directories.

- Microsoft Windows version 3.1 must be installed on the workstation you use to install PowerPoint on the network file server. All workstations that will run PowerPoint must have Windows installed.

- If any network users share the Windows operating system or other applications, they must be logged off from the network. Lock the network directories or shared volumes that contain shared components from user access—for example, W:\WINDOWS and W:\MSAPPS.

- Determine where the PowerPoint components should be installed. Setup suggests installing POWERPNT.EXE in the POWERPNT directory and installing shared components in the MSAPPS directory of the network file server or shared volume.

Set up PowerPoint on a network

1   If Windows is not currently running, type **win** at the MS-DOS prompt.

-or-

If Windows is running, close all open applications. Ask all users who are sharing Windows or Microsoft applications to disconnect from the network file server or the shared directory.

2   Insert the PowerPoint Setup disk (Disk 1) in drive A (or drive B if you are using the B drive).

3   From the Program Manager File menu, choose Run.

The Run dialog box appears.

4   Type **a:setup /a** (or **b:setup /a** if you are using the B drive) and click the OK button.

5   Follow the instructions on the screen that Setup displays. You'll need to do the following tasks to complete the network installation.

- Supply your company name.

- Supply the network directory in which you want to install PowerPoint (for example, W:\POWERPNT), and the directory for storing shared components (for example, W:\MSAPPS).

- Decide if the shared components will be installed automatically on individual workstations, if the components will be shared automatically from the network, or if the choice will be left to the user of each workstation.

6   Set the access privileges to read-only for the server directories in which you installed PowerPoint components, and ensure that all users who may need to install PowerPoint on their workstations from the network have read privileges for those directories.

Workstation or Shared Installation

For more information on workstation setup, see your network administrator.

In a network environment, you can run PowerPoint entirely off the network, without installing it on your local computer, or you can install PowerPoint on your local computer.

Set up PowerPoint from a network to a workstation

1   From the Program Manager File menu, choose Run.

The Run dialog box appears.

2   Type **w:\powerpnt\setup** and click the OK button or press ENTER.

The W:\POWERPNT directory is the network location for PowerPoint.

3   Follow the instructions on the screen that Setup displays. The instructions are similar to those for the local single-user installation discussed earlier in this appendix.

Graphic Import Filters Installed with PowerPoint

PowerPoint installs 14 graphic import filters that allow you to import pictures from different applications. PowerPoint uses the import filters when you choose Picture from the Insert menu. The PowerPoint Setup program installs the import filters in a shared location so that they can be used by other Microsoft applications. The import filters include the following:

- AutoCAD (*.adi, *.pli) Import Filters
- Windows Bitmaps (*.bmp, *.dib) Import Filters
- Corel Draw Graphics (*.cdr) Import Filters
- Computer Graphic Metafile (*.cgm) Import Filter
- Micrografx Designer (*.drw) Import Filter
- AutoDesk Drawing Exchange (*.dxf) Import Filter
- Encapsulated PostScript (*.eps) Import Filter
- CompuServe GIF (*.gif) Import Filter
- HP Graphic Language (*.hgl) Import Filter
- Kodak Photo CD (*.pcd) Import Filter
- Macintosh PICT (*.pct) Import Filter
- Lotus 1-2-3 Graphics (*.pic) Import Filter
- Tagged Image File Format (*.tif) Import Filter
- DrawPerfect Graphics (*.wpg) Import Filter

Installing and Selecting a Printer

This appendix provides information on installing and setting up a printer for use with Microsoft PowerPoint. In order to print a PowerPoint presentation, the target printer must be properly installed and configured in your Windows 3.1 Control Panel. After the target printer is installed, you can set PowerPoint print and slide options that allow you to print your presentation in the format of your choice.

Installing a New Printer

If your printer was not installed when you installed Microsoft Windows 3.1 or if you purchased a new printer, you can install a printer using one of two methods:

Setup Program   The Setup program you used to install Microsoft Windows 3.1 includes a printer setup section. You can run Windows Setup at any time to install a new printer. Refer to your Windows 3.1 Setup documentation for further information on setting up a printer.

Control Panel   The Control Panel is a Windows utility application that can run simultaneously with PowerPoint. Using the Control Panel is the recommended way to install a new printer, because printer changes can be made without closing your PowerPoint application.

The following basic procedures explain how to access the Control Panel, open the Printers dialog box to make changes, and open the Connect dialog box.

Open the Control Panel from PowerPoint

1   Hold down the ALT key and press the TAB key repeatedly until the Program Manager icon appears, and then release the ALT key.

    -or-

    Hold down the CTRL key and press the ESC key to get the Task List dialog box. Select Program Manager and click the Switch To button.

Control Panel

2   From the Main program group, double-click the Control Panel icon.

    The Control Panel window appears, showing various Windows environment settings that can be changed or modified (for example, date and time, screen colors, fonts, mouse actions, and desktop operations).

Your Control Panel window might look similar to the following illustration:

Install a new printer

Use the Printers dialog box in the Control Panel to install and configure a new printer.

Printers

1   From the Control Panel, double-click the Printers icon.

The Printers dialog box appears.

The Printers dialog box lists the printers installed on your system and the one that is currently the default printer.

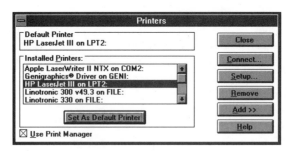

2   Click the Add button to expand the dialog box.

3   To install a printer, select the printer from the List of Printers box and click the Install button.

Note   If the Install Driver dialog box appears, insert the appropriate Microsoft Windows 3.1 disk to install the appropriate printer driver file.

The new printer appears in the Installed Printers area. To delete a printer from the Installed Printers area, select the printer and click the Remove button.

Configure a printer

Whenever you install a new printer and its appropriate printer driver file, you need to configure the printer by assigning it to a printer port in the Connect dialog box.

1   In the Installed Printers area, select a printer.

2   From the Printers dialog box, click the Connect button.

The Connect dialog box appears. The Ports box lists the printer ports available to connect your computer with your printer.

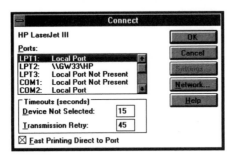

3   Select the appropriate port.

Printer port changes made in Control Panel's Connect dialog box change the settings in PowerPoint's Print Setup dialog box.

A port can have more than one printer assigned to it. You can set up this configuration by selecting the printer and assigning the same port for each printer (click the OK button and repeat the first three steps in this section). To determine which port is active for which printer, check the Print Setup dialog box in the PowerPoint File menu.

Close the dialog boxes and exit the Control Panel

Use the following procedure to close the dialog boxes and return to your PowerPoint presentation window. For a complete explanation of printer installation, port selection, and making printers active, see your Windows documentation.

1   To apply the changes you've made in the Connect dialog box, click the OK button.

-or-

To cancel the changes, click the Cancel button.

2   Click the Close button to close the Printers dialog box.

3   Double-click the Control-menu box to close the Control Panel.

Changing Print Setup Options

With certain printers you can change the settings for paper orientation, paper size, and paper source. If these options are available with your printer, the default settings can be set independently for each PowerPoint presentation. Use the Print Setup command to change these options.

Change printer settings

In PowerPoint, you can set the page orientation, paper size, and paper source for all your presentations using the following procedure:

1   From the File menu, choose Print.

2   Click the Printer button.

    The Print Setup dialog box appears with a list of printers.

3   In the Printers area, select the printer whose settings you want to change.

4   Click the Options button.

5   Click the drop-down arrow next to Paper Size and select a size.

6   Click the drop-down arrow next to Paper Source and select a source.

7   Click the drop-down arrow next to Resolution and select a dpi (dots per inch) setting, if available.

8   Change any other desired setting.

9   Click the OK button to close the Options dialog box.

10 Click the OK button to close the Printer Setup dialog box.

11 Click the Cancel button to close the Print dialog box.

PowerPoint Features at a Glance

Microsoft PowerPoint 4 for Windows has many new features, as well as improved ones, that make it easier for you to get great results. PowerPoint 4 for Windows is designed specifically for first-time users who want to get started quickly, and advanced users who need powerful, easy-to-use features. In PowerPoint 4 for Windows there are improvements in the following areas: creating a presentation, OfficeLinks with other applications, text handling, outlining, drawing, graphing, working with masters and templates, producing on-screen slide shows, and converting Harvard Graphics DOS and Freelance DOS files into PowerPoint presentations. PowerPoint also features IntelliSense technology—built-in intelligence that senses what you want to do and helps you produce the results you want so routine tasks become automatic and complex jobs become easier.

The following tables list the major features in PowerPoint 4 for Windows, along with the lesson in this book where you can learn more about each feature.

IntelliSense Features

To learn how to	See
Start a presentation using the AutoContent Wizard	Lesson 1, "Using the AutoContent Wizard"
Start a presentation using the Pick a Look Wizard	Lesson 2, "Using the Pick a Look Wizard"
Apply a template	Lesson 6, "Understanding and Applying Templates"
Apply a color scheme	Lesson 7, "Choosing a Color Scheme"
Create a slide with AutoLayout	Lesson 2, "Creating a New Slide in Slide View"
Access the most recently used files	Lesson 2, "Opening an Existing Presentation"
Access the most recently used fonts	Lesson 3, "Editing and Rearranging Text in Outline View"
Smart cut and paste	Lesson 3, "Editing and Rearranging Text in Outline View"
Change case	Lesson 4, "Changing and Replacing Text"
Change punctuation	Lesson 4, "Changing and Replacing Text"

Ease-of-Use Features

To learn how to	See
Access commands with default and customizable toolbars	Getting Ready, "Getting to Know PowerPoint"
Get help with ToolTips and the status bar	Getting Ready, "Getting to Know PowerPoint"
Access shortcut menus	Getting Ready, "Using PowerPoint Commands and Menus"
Display a tip of the day	Getting Ready, "Getting to Know PowerPoint"
Access Quick Preview	Getting Ready, "Getting to Know PowerPoint"
Access context-sensitive help	Getting Ready, "Getting Help"
Access Cue Cards	Getting Ready, "Using Cue Cards"

Text, Drawing, and Outlining Features

To learn how to	See
Edit text objects	Lesson 1, "Changing Text in Outline view"
Outline and rearrange text	Lesson 2, "Entering Text in Outline View"
Drag and drop objects and text	Lesson 3, "Editing and Rearranging in Outline View"
Create a label or word processing box	Lesson 4, "Adding Text"
Format text	Lesson 4, "Formatting Text"
Change line spacing	Lesson 4, "Adjusting Text"
Format text and objects	Lesson 4, "Formatting Text"
Draw objects with AutoShapes	Lesson 5, "Working with Objects"
Edit objects	Lesson 5, "Working with Objects"
Group objects	Lesson 5, "Grouping and Ungrouping Objects"
Rotate or flip text and objects	Lesson 5, "Rotating and Flipping Objects"

Microsoft Office Integration Features

To learn how to	See
Insert a Microsoft Excel worksheet	Lesson 12, "Embedding a Microsoft Excel Worksheet"
Insert a Microsoft Word table	Lesson 12, "Embedding a Microsoft Word Table"
Report slides to Microsoft Word	Lesson 12, "Reporting Slides to Microsoft Word"
Send a presentation with Microsoft Mail	Lesson 12, "Sending a Presentation with Microsoft Mail"

Object Linking and Embedding Features

To learn how to	See
Insert clip art	Lesson 11, "Inserting Clip Art"
Insert a graph	Lesson 8, "Starting Microsoft Graph"
Insert an organizational chart	Lesson 10, "Starting Microsoft Organization Chart"
Insert a Microsoft Excel chart	Lesson 12, "Linking to a Microsoft Excel Chart"
Insert Microsoft WordArt	Lesson 11, "Inserting WordArt"
Insert a sound or movie	Lesson 11, "Inserting Sound and Movies"

Slide Show and PowerPoint Viewer Features

To learn how to	See
Draw freehand annotations in Slide Show	Lesson 15, "Drawing Freehand in Slide Show"
Show formatting in Slide Sorter view	Lesson 15, "Viewing Slides in Slide Sorter View"
Create and preview a transition in Slide Sorter view	Lesson 15, "Setting Slide Transitions and Timings"
Rehearse timings	Lesson 15, "Setting Rehearsed Slide Timings"
Create a build slide	Lesson 15, "Setting Build Slides for a Slide Show"
Hide a slide	Lesson 15, "Hiding a Slide During a Slide Show"

File and Conversion Features

To learn how to	See
Find a file in PowerPoint	Lesson 2, "Opening an Existing Presentation"
Open Macintosh PowerPoint 4 presentations	Appendix D, "Opening Presentations on Different Platforms"
Open Harvard Graphics DOS 2.3 and 3.0 files	Appendix D, "Opening Files from Other Presentation Programs"
Open Freelance DOS 4.0 files	Appendix D, "Opening Files from Other Presentation Programs"

Feature Changes from PowerPoint 3 for Windows

For PowerPoint 3 for Windows users, some features have changed. The following table lists the features in PowerPoint 3 that have changed in PowerPoint 4.

PowerPoint 3 Feature	PowerPoint 4 Equivalent
Edit a text object	Click the text box or placeholder.
Move from slide to slide with the Slide Changer	Click the Next Slide button, click the Previous Slide button, or drag the elevator.
Click the depressed view button to switch to master view	Hold down the SHIFT key and click the corresponding view button.
Follow Master for color and shading	From the Format menu, choose Slide Color Scheme or Slide Background and click the Follow Master button.
Follow Master for background items	From the Format menu, choose Slide Background, and click the Display Objects On This Slide option button.
Pick Up Style and Apply Styles tools	On the Standard Toolbar, click the Format Painter button, click an object to pick up its style, and click another object to apply the style.
Add a title object or add a body object	Click the Layout button, select a layout, and click the OK button.
Change default settings in PowerPoint	Select the object and choose Pick Up Object Style from the Format menu. Click the Selection Tool and then choose Apply To Object Defaults from the Format menu.

Presentations on the Go

With PowerPoint, you can open, change, or show electronic presentations on different Windows-based and Apple Macintosh computers. Whether you're traveling across the country or to the office, you can work on your presentation up to the very last minute.

Opening Presentations on Different Windows 3.1 Systems

PowerPoint presentations created on a computer with one set of fonts might look different when opened on another computer. With PowerPoint and Windows 3.1, you can embed a presentation's fonts into a presentation, so when you move from one computer to another, the embedded fonts are included in your presentation and are available when you work on or show your presentation.

Which fonts can be embedded?

PowerPoint lets you embed only those fonts electronically marked by the font manufacturer to be "embedded and copied without restriction." These include any of the 22 TrueType fonts supplied with PowerPoint. If a font can't be embedded, PowerPoint will let you know.

The TrueType fonts that are supplied with Windows 3.1 should be available on all computers running Windows 3.1, so these fonts aren't embedded by PowerPoint.

When to embed fonts

Embed a font only when you think that the font will not be available on the system you'll be using. Including embedded fonts in your presentation adds to the file size. For example, if you embed Times New Roman Bold, the file size of your presentation will increase by about 60 KB. Remember that the different font styles—plain, italic, bold, and bold italic—are all separate fonts. Each font style increases the file size.

How to embed fonts

1   Open the PowerPoint presentation in which you want to embed fonts.

2   Be sure the presentation includes embeddable fonts.

3   From the File menu, choose Save As.

    The Save As dialog box appears.

4   In the File Name box, type a *filename*

5   Click the Embed TrueType Fonts check box.

The Save As dialog box should look similar to the following illustration:

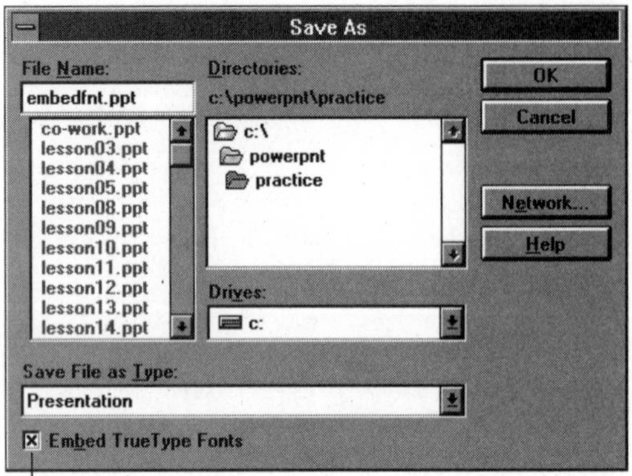

Click here to embed fonts

6   Click the OK button.

Opening Files from Other Presentation Programs

If you have presentation files from other presentation programs, such as Harvard Graphics DOS 2.3, Harvard Graphics DOS 3.0, or Lotus Freelance DOS 4.0, you can open them in PowerPoint 4 for Windows. PowerPoint converts all Harvard Graphics and Freelance objects to PowerPoint objects, which you can edit and modify.

Open other presentations in PowerPoint

1   From the File menu, choose Open.

The Open dialog box appears.

2   In the Drives box, click the drop-down arrow and select the disk or network drive with the presentation you want to open.

3   In the List Files Of Type box, click the drop-down arrow and select a presentation type from the translators listed below:

- Harvard Graphics 2.3 charts (*.cht)

- Harvard Graphics 2.3 shows (*.shw)

- Harvard Graphics 3.0 charts (*.ch3)

- Harvard Graphics 3.0 shows (*.sh3)

- Freelance DOS 4.0 shows (*.shw)

- Freelance DOS 4.0 (*.drw)

TROUBLESHOOTING: **If the presentation translators don't appear in the list of file types**   If the presentation file types don't appear, reinstall the presentation translators using PowerPoint Setup application.

4   In the File Name box, select a presentation file name.

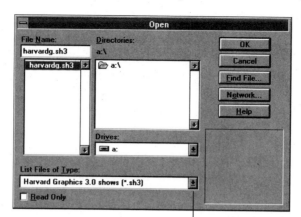

Click the drop-down arrow here and
select a presentation translation type

5   Click the OK button.

The presentation is translated and opened as an untitled presentation.

Opening Presentations on Different Platforms

You can open Macintosh PowerPoint 4 presentations in Windows. If you have a
Macintosh PowerPoint 3 presentation, you have to open the presentation in
Macintosh PowerPoint 4 before converting it to Windows or convert the presentation
to Windows PowerPoint 3 and then open it in PowerPoint 4 for Windows. Similarly,
you can open PowerPoint 4 for Windows presentations on the Apple Macintosh with
Macintosh PowerPoint 4. If you don't have the PowerPoint application available, you
can view presentations on either platform with the PowerPoint Viewer.

Exchange platforms

Opening presentations on either platform requires that you move the presentation to
the platform in which you want to open the file. Two simple ways to move a
presentation between platforms are to use a network to which Apple Macintosh
computers and Windows-based computers are connected or to use a file exchange
application. No special translators are needed to exchange a presentation between
platforms.

Open Macintosh presentations in Windows

1 From the File menu, choose Open.

The Open dialog box appears.

2 In the Drives box, click the drop-down arrow and select the disk or network drive with the Macintosh PowerPoint 4 presentation.

3 In the List Files Of Type box, click the drop-down arrow and select All Files (*.*).

Macintosh files do not have a *.PPT extension. Only the first eight characters of the Macintosh file name are used in Windows. For example, a Macintosh presentation with the name "Mac PowerPoint 4" appears as "!macpowe.rpo" in the Open dialog box.

4 In the File Name box, select the Macintosh file name.

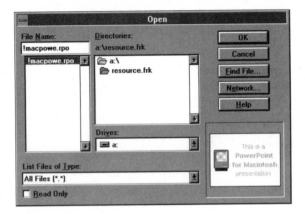

5 Click the OK button.

A dialog box appears.

6 Click the Continue button to translate the Macintosh file and open it as an untitled presentation.

Open Windows presentations on the Macintosh

Follow the same general steps in the previous section, "Opening Macintosh presentations in Windows," to open a PowerPoint 4 for Windows presentation on the Apple Macintosh.

List of Step by Step Practice Files

You'll find the Step by Step practice files on the Practice File disk included with this book. Be sure to use the installation program to copy the entire PRACTICE directory to your hard drive. The following files are in the PRACTICE directory:

CO-WORK.PPT	LESSON11.PPT	OUTLINE.DOC
LESSON03.PPT	LESSON12.PPT	SEAGUL.WAV
LESSON04.PPT	LESSON13.PPT	SHEET08.XLS
LESSON05.PPT	LESSON14.PPT	SHIP.WMF
LESSON06.PPT	LESSON15.PPT	SHOWLIST.LST
LESSON07.PPT	LINKCHRT.XLC	SLDSHOW1.PPT
LESSON08.PPT	LINKNEW.XLC	SLDSHOW2.PPT
LESSON09.PPT	LINK1.WMF	TEMPLT06.PPT
LESSON10.PPT	LOGO.WMF	

The following table lists the practice files used in each lesson. The name you used to rename the practice file appears in the last column.

In this lesson	Open this file	To create or review this presentation
Lesson 1, "Creating a Presentation"	New presentation	JJPROCES.PPT
Lesson 2, "Working with a Presentation"	New presentation CO-WORK.PPT	JJBASICS.PPT
Lesson 3, "Outlining Your Ideas"	LESSON03.PPT OUTLINE.DOC	JJOUTLN.PPT JJOUTRTF.RTF
Lesson 4, "Adding and Modifying Text"	LESSON04.PPT	JJTEXT.PPT
Lesson 5, "Drawing and Modifying Objects"	LESSON05.PPT	JJOBJECT.PPT
Lesson 6, "Changing Masters and Applying Templates"	LESSON06.PPT TEMPLT06.PPT	JJMASTER.PPT
Lesson 7, "Using a Color Scheme"	LESSON07.PPT	JJCOLOR.PPT

In this lesson	Open this file	To create or review this presentation
Lesson 8, "Creating and Editing a Graph"	LESSON08.PPT SHEET08.XLS	JJGRAPH.PPT
Lesson 9, "Formatting a Graph"	LESSON09.PPT	JJFMTGPH.PPT
Lesson 10, "Creating an Organizational Chart"	LESSON10.PPT	JJORGCHT.PPT
Lesson 11, "Inserting Information into PowerPoint"	LESSON11.PPT SHIP.WMF SEAGUL.WAV	JJINSERT.PPT
Lesson 12, "Linking Information with Other Applications"	LESSON12.PPT LINKCHRT.XLC LINKNEW.XLC LINK1.WMF	JJLINK.PPT JJLINK.DOC
Lesson 13, "Setting Up Your Slides and Printing"	LESSON13.PPT	JJPRNTNG.PPT
Lesson 14, "Producing 35mm Slides"	LESSON14.PPT	JJGENI.PPT JJ35MM.GNA
Lesson 15, "Producing an Electronic Presentation"	LESSON15.PPT SLDSHOW1.PPT SLDSHOW2.PPT SHOWLIST.LST	JJSLDSHO.PPT
Review & Practice	LOGO.WMF	

Glossary

Accent colors Three colors in the color scheme. These colors are designed to work as the colors for secondary features on the slide.

active cell The currently selected cell of a datasheet, indicated by a heavy border.

adjustment handle A diamond the size of a resize handle. Depending on the shape of the object, you can adjust its features by dragging this handle.

anchor point The point that remains stable as the text grows and shrinks during editing; for example, a top anchor point with a left text alignment allows the text to grow right and down as it normally would when you type. A top center anchor point would allow the text to grow left, right, and down.

application A piece of software, like Microsoft PowerPoint or Microsoft Excel.

application Control menu A menu that includes commands with which you can control the size and position of the PowerPoint window. If you want to display the application Control menu using the keyboard, press ALT+SPACEBAR.

attributes The features of an object, such as color, shadow, and pattern.

arrow keys The UP ARROW, DOWN ARROW, LEFT ARROW, and RIGHT ARROW keys, used to move the insertion point or select from a menu or list of options.

AutoLayout AutoLayouts contain ready-made placeholders for titles, text, and objects such as clip art, graphs, and charts.

AutoLayout object area Object placeholders for text, graphs, tables, organizational charts, and clip art. Click to add text in a placeholder, or double-click to add the specified object.

automatic link A link to information that is updated whenever the information is changed. With an automatic link, PowerPoint updates the information when the original has changed.

Automatic word selection This selection option makes it easier to select multiple words. Place the pointer anywhere in a word and drag to select the entire word.

AutoShapes Toolbar The tools on the AutoShapes Toolbar are used for drawing commonly used shapes such as stars, triangles, and diamonds.

axis A line that serves as a major reference for plotting data in a graph.

Background color   A color in the color scheme. The background color is the underlying color of a slide. All colors added to your presentation are added over the background color. To change the background color, change the first color of the color scheme.

background items   Objects you add to the master slide so they will appear on the slides in a presentation. Any object on the masters other than the title or main text objects is considered a background item.

build   A bullet point that has been given a build time setting for a slide show.

build slide   A progressive disclosure slide seen during a slide show. This is a slide that starts with the first major bullet point and then progressively shows the other major bullet points of that slide.

bullet   A mark, usually a round or square dot, used to emphasize or distinguish items in a list.

cell   One rectangle of the datasheet where you enter data.

chart window   The window within Graph that contains the sample graph in which your data appears in graph form as you enter it into the datasheet.

click   To press and release a mouse button in one nonstop motion.

Clipboard   A temporary storage area for cut or copied text or graphics. You can cut or copy contents from any application, such as PowerPoint or Word, to the Clipboard and then paste them into any application. The Clipboard holds only one cut or copied piece of information at a time.

Color Scheme   The basic set of eight colors provided for any slide. The color scheme consists of a Background color, a color for Lines and Text, and six Remaining colors balanced to provide a professional look to your presentation. Color schemes can be applied to slides and to notes pages.

column control box   The box to the left of the column heading. Click this box to select a column; double-click to exclude or include the data in the graph.

column heading   The left column of the datasheet where column labels are entered.

control handle   The square that appears at each vertex of arcs and freeform objects when you are editing them. Edit these forms by selecting and dragging the control handle.

Control Panel   The Microsoft Windows application that adjusts operations and formats, such as the date, time, screen color, fonts, and printer settings. The settings affect both Windows and PowerPoint.

Constrain keys   Holding down the constrain keys such as CTRL and SHIFT constrain how an object is drawn. Using these keys can constrain an object to draw from its center or draw regular shapes.

crop   To trim away the parts of a graphic or picture you don't want to display.

cut   To remove selected text or graphics from a slide so you can place it in another slide, presentation, or application. The information cut is placed on the Clipboard and stays there until another piece of information is cut or copied.

data marker   A bar, shape, dot, or symbol that marks a single data point or value. Related markers in a graph make up a data series. Data markers are the bars, columns, areas, pies, lines, and xy scatter points that make up a graph.

data point   A single cell item, representing a single item in a data series.

data series   A row or column of a datasheet used to draw one or more data markers on a graph.

datasheet window   The window within Graph that contains the sample datasheet in which you enter your data.

defaults   Predefined settings such as the slide size, slide orientation, color settings, and fonts. Use appropriate dialog boxes and master views to change defaults.

default presentation   The presentation PowerPoint uses as a template when you don't specify another. Any presentation can be chosen to be the default template.

dialog box   A box that displays available command options to review or change.

directories   Subdivisions of a disk that work like a filing system to help organize your files. You can create directories from the Windows File Manager.

double lines   Indicate separate data series between rows and columns.

drag   To hold down the mouse button while moving the mouse.

Drawing Toolbar   The Drawing Toolbar contains the tools to draw lines, circles, boxes, arcs, and freeforms and to rotate objects.

Drawing+ Toolbar   The Drawing+ Toolbar contains more tools to modify object attributes such as the fill color and line width.

edit   To add, delete, or change text, objects, and graphics.

embedded object   An object that is created with another application but is stored in PowerPoint. Any updating you do to an embedded object is done manually while you are working in PowerPoint.

embedding   Storing information inside your PowerPoint presentation that was created using an embedded application. The information that was not a part of your presentation before embedding now becomes a part of your presentation.

file   A presentation that has been created and saved under a unique file name. PowerPoint stores all presentations as files.

Fills color   A color in the color scheme. The Fills color is a good color to use to fill objects. This color contrasts with the Background and Lines and Text colors.

font   The general shapes for a set of characters. Each font has a name with which you can select the font and apply it to text.

Format Painter   The Format Painter picks up an object's format and applies that format to another object.

Formatting Toolbar   The Formatting Toolbar is available in Slide view, Outline view, and Notes Pages view and contains tools to modify text attributes.

frame   The line that forms the object. The four lines of a rectangle are its frame, the three lines of a triangle are its frame, etc. You can change the style of the frame by changing the line style.

four-headed arrow   The pointer you use to move text lines and paragraphs around in the main text.

graph text   The text that describes items or data in a graph.

Graph tool   The tool on the Standard Toolbar that allows you to access Microsoft Graph.

graph window   The window in which you work with Graph. It is similar to the PowerPoint window.

grid   An invisible network of lines that covers the slide. The grid automatically aligns objects to the nearest intersection of the grid.

grid lines   Optional lines that extend from the tick marks on an axis across the plot area to make it easier to view data values.

group   A multiple selection that is treated as a single object when you use the Group command in the Draw menu.

guides   Two straightedges, one horizontal and one vertical, used for visually aligning objects. Objects can be aligned at the corner or the center depending upon which is closer.

Hidden slide   A slide that isn't automatically displayed during a slide show or printed.

icon   A graphical representation of a file-level object (for example, a disk drive, a directory, an application, or another object that you can select and open).

landscape   A term used to refer to the horizontal page orientation; the opposite of portrait orientation.

legend   The key that identifies the patterns, colors, or symbols associated with the markers of a data series and shows the data series name that corresponds to each marker.

levels   The different paragraph indentations at which paragraphs appear in an outline.

Lines and Text color   A color in the color scheme, which contrasts with the background color for writing text and drawing lines on the slide. Together with the Background color, the Lines and Text color sets the tone for the presentation.

Linked object   A linked object is created in another application and maintains a connection to its source. A linked object itself is stored in its source document, where it was created. PowerPoint stores only a representation of the original document and information about its location.

linking   Using information within your presentation that is stored outside your presentation. The information remains "attached" to the original source while you work on it in your PowerPoint presentation. Linked information is automatically updated when the information in the source file and application changes.

main text object   The main text on a slide.

main text placeholder   The empty main text object that appears on a new slide.

manual link   A link to information that is updated only by the user.

master text   The formatted placeholder for the main slide text on the Slide Master. The master text controls the font, color, size, and alignment of the main text object as well as its placement on the slide.

master title   The formatted placeholder for slide titles on the Slide Master. The master title controls the font, color, size, and alignment of the title text as well as its object attributes (fill, line, and shadow), its shape, and its placement on the slide.

menu   A list of commands that drop down from the menu bar. The menu bar appears across the top of the application window and lists the menu names (for example, File and Edit).

Move Up/Move Down   To move a paragraph up is to exchange it with the paragraph above. To move a paragraph down is to exchange it with the paragraph below.

multiple selection   Selecting more than one object using the SHIFT+click method or by dragging the selection rectangle. When you flip, rotate, or resize a multiple selection, all objects in the multiple selection react independently.

object   A single component of your drawing. Objects can be drawn using tools from the Drawing Toolbar, which includes AutoShapes, ovals, rectangles, freeform shapes, and arcs.

Other colors   Non-scheme colors you can use for special purposes. Every color menu has an "Other Color" choice on it so you can choose a special color. Your "Other Colors" will not automatically change when you choose a different color scheme for a presentation.

outlining functions   Promoting and demoting paragraphs to different levels in the outline and moving them up and down within your presentation. These functions work in any PowerPoint view.

Outlining Toolbar   The Outlining Toolbar contains tools to rearrange outline title and paragraph text.

paragraph   Text that begins when you press ENTER and ends when you press ENTER again.

paste   To insert cut or copied text or graphics into a slide from the Clipboard.

paste special   To insert cut or copied text or graphics with a special format (for example, BMP and RTF for graphics and text, respectively).

picture   An image from another application. A picture has object properties. You can resize it, move it, and recolor it; and some pictures can be ungrouped into component objects. When ungrouping a picture, you separate it into PowerPoint objects that, when regrouped, become a PowerPoint object (not a picture).

placeholder   A reserved object to place information. Each placeholder is surrounded by a dotted line with a message telling you to click and type your text or to double-click to open an embedded application.

portrait   A term used to refer to the vertical page orientation; the opposite of landscape orientation.

PowerPoint Viewer   A special application that is designed to give electronic slide shows. The application is for those who are going to be running slide shows but who don't have PowerPoint. You can distribute the Viewer freely.

presentation Control menu   A menu with commands that control a document window's size and position. To display the slide Control menu-box using the keyboard, press ALT+HYPHEN.

promote/demote   To move lines of text or paragraphs out or in a level in the outline. Usually, when you promote text, it moves to the left; when you demote text, it moves to the right.

regular shape   A perfectly proportioned shape that can be inscribed within a square. You can draw regular shapes by using the SHIFT key. The following shapes can be made regular by using the SHIFT key: circle, square, diamond, cross, star, hexagon, equilateral triangle, and octagon.

Remaining colors   The six additional colors in the color scheme.

resize handle   The square at each corner of a selected object. Dragging a resize handle resizes an object.

row control box   The box above a row heading. Click this box to select a row; double-click to exclude or include the data in the graph.

row heading   The top row of the datasheet where row labels are entered.

ruler   A graphical bar displayed on the left and at the top of the PowerPoint window. From the ruler you can set tabs and indents to any text object.

scale   To change an object's size by reducing or enlarging it by a constant percentage.

scroll bar   A graphical device for moving vertically and horizontally through a presentation slide with the pointer. Scroll bars are located along the right and bottom edges of the presentation window.

selection box   The gray slanted-line or dotted outline around an object that indicates it is selected. Selecting and dragging the selection box moves the object.

series names   The names that identify each row or column of data.

Shadows color   The third color in the color scheme and the first Remaining color (*see* Remaining colors). PowerPoint applies the Shadows color to a shadowed object. The color is often a darker shade of the Background color.

shape   The form of an object, such as rectangle, circle, or square. The shape is also an attribute because you can change the object's shape without redrawing the object. Arcs, freeforms, and lines are not considered shapes.

slide icon   An icon that appears next to each slide title in the outline.

Smart cut and paste   The Smart cut and paste feature makes sure words are correctly spaced after using the Cut and Paste commands.

Smart quotes   The curly quotation marks used by typesetters ("like this").

source   The document that contains the original information; the document to which you are linking.

stacking   The placement of objects one on top of another.

template   A presentation whose format and color scheme you apply to another presentation. There are over 160 professionally designed templates (three categories) that come with PowerPoint, but *any* template can be used.

text attributes   Characteristics of text, including its font, type size, style, color, etc. You can change text attributes before or after you have typed the text.

text editing buttons   Buttons on the toolbars used to change the attributes of text, including the font size, bold, italic, underline, shadow, and bullet attributes.

tick-mark   A small line that intersects an axis and marks off a category, scale, or data series. The tick mark label identifies the tick mark.

tick-mark labels   The names that appear along the horizontal axis of an area, column, or line graph or along the vertical axis of a bar graph. When data series are in rows, the tick-mark labels are the column labels. When data series are in columns, the tick-mark labels are the row labels.

timing   The amount of time a slide stays on the screen during a slide show. Each slide can have a different timing.

title object   The title on the slide.

title placeholder   The title box that appears on a new slide.

Title Text color   A color in the color scheme. This color, like the Lines and Text color, contrasts with the Background color.

Toolbar   The graphical bar across the top of the presentation window with buttons that perform some of the common commands in PowerPoint. The toolbar changes in PowerPoint depending on the view, except for Slide and Notes Pages views, which uses the same toolbar.

transitions   The effects that move one slide off the screen and the next slide on during a slide show. Each slide can have its own transition effect.

vertex/vertices   The points where two straight lines meet.

view   A display that shows a presentation in a certain way. PowerPoint has four views—Slide, Outline, Notes Pages, and Handout.

window   A rectangular area on your screen in which you view and work on presentations.

Index

Train Yourself
With *Step by Step* books from Microsoft Press

The *Step by Step* books are the perfect self-paced training solution for Microsoft Office users. Each book comes with a disk that contains every example in the book. By using the practice files and following instructions in the book, you can "learn by doing," which means you can start applying what you've learned to business situations right away. If you're too busy to attend a class or if classroom training doesn't make sense for you or your office, you can build the computer skills you need with the *Step by Step* books from Microsoft Press.

Microsoft® Word 6 for Windows™ Step by Step
Catapult, Inc.
336 pages, softcover with one 3.5-inch disk
$29.95 ($39.95 Canada)   ISBN 1-55615-576-X

Microsoft® Excel 5 for Windows™ Step by Step
Catapult, Inc.
368 pages, softcover with one 3.5-inch disk
$29.95 ($39.95 Canada)   ISBN 1-55615-587-5

Microsoft Access® for Windows™ Step by Step
Catapult, Inc.
Covers latest version.
375 pages, softcover with one 3.5-inch disk
$29.95 ($39.95 Canada)   ISBN 1-55615-593-X
Available May 1994

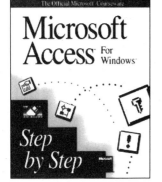

Microsoft® Mail for Windows™ Step by Step
Catapult, Inc.
Versions 3.0b and later.
224 pages, softcover with one 3.5-inch disk
$24.95 ($32.95 Canada)   ISBN 1-55615-571-9

Microsoft Press

Microsoft Press® books are available wherever quality books are sold and through CompuServe's Electronic Mall—GO MSP.
*Call 1-800-MSPRESS for direct ordering information or for placing credit card orders.**
Please refer to BBK when placing your order. Prices subject to change.
*In Canada, contact Macmillan Canada, Attn: Microsoft Press Dept., 164 Commander Blvd., Agincourt, Ontario, Canada M1S 3C7, or call (416) 293-8464, ext. 340.
Outside the U.S. and Canada, write to International Coordinator, Microsoft Press, One Microsoft Way, Redmond WA 98052-6399.

Boost Your Word Processing Skills

Word 6 for Windows™ Companion
The Cobb Group with M. David Stone & Alfred Poor and Mark Crane

"This book covers all the bases thoroughly." **PC Magazine**

This is the ultimate reference book, with more than 1000 pages of detailed information on Word 6 for Windows. Written with the clarity and easy-to-read style that is the Cobb Group hallmark, this book covers the essentials from the basics to advanced topics. Includes new two-color design with easy look-up features, lots of product tips, and an expanded, fully cross-referenced index.

1072 pages, softcover $29.95 ($39.95 Canada)   ISBN 1-55615-575-1

Running Word 6 for Windows™
Russell Borland

Master the power and features of Microsoft Word for Windows—version 6.0—with this newly updated edition of the bestselling guide for intermediate to advanced users. This example-rich guide contains scores of insights and power tips not found in the documentation and includes in-depth, accessible coverage on Word's powerful new features.

832 pages, softcover $29.95 ($39.95 Canada)   ISBN 1-55615-574-3

Microsoft® Word 6.0 for Windows™ Resource Kit
Microsoft Corporation

This is your one-stop guide to installing, customizing, and supporting Word 6.0 for Windows. It includes information on training new and migrating users, troubleshooting, preventing potential problems, and ensuring that users are taking full advantage of productivity-boosting features. The two accompanying disks include the *Microsoft Word 6.0 for Windows Converter*, customizable self-paced training exercises, 250 tips and tricks, and a helpful file to make custom installation easier.

672 pages, softcover with two 3.5-inch disks
$39.95 ($53.95 Canada)   ISBN 1-55615-720-7

MicrosoftPress

Microsoft Press books are available wherever quality books are sold and through CompuServe's Electronic Mall—GO MSP.
Call 1-800-MSPRESS for direct ordering information or for placing credit card orders.*
Please refer to BBK when placing your order. Prices subject to change.

*In Canada, contact Macmillan Canada, Attn: Microsoft Press Dept., 164 Commander Blvd., Agincourt, Ontario, Canada M1S 3C7, or call (416) 293-8464, ext. 340.
Outside the U.S. and Canada, write to International Coordinator, Microsoft Press, One Microsoft Way, Redmond WA 98052-6399.

The Step by Step Companion Disk

The enclosed 3.5-inch disk contains timesaving, ready-to-use practice files that complement the lessons in this book. To use the practice files, you'll need the Microsoft® Windows™ operating system version 3.1 or later, MS-DOS version 5.0 or later, and Microsoft PowerPoint® version 4 for Windows.

Each *Step by Step* lesson is closely integrated with the practice files on the disk. Before you begin the *Step by Step* lessons, we highly recommend that you read the "Getting Ready" section of the book and install the practice files on your hard disk. Remember, as you work through each lesson, be sure to follow the instructions for renaming the practice files so that you can go through a lesson more than once if you need to.

Please take a few moments to browse the License Agreement on the previous page. If your computer uses only 5.25-inch disks, we will gladly send you a replacement disk, free of charge. For ordering information, please see the bottom of the License Agreement page.